Men *of* Letters

IN THE EARLY REPUBLIC

Men *of* Letters

IN THE EARLY REPUBLIC

Cultivating Forums of Citizenship

CATHERINE O'DONNELL KAPLAN

Published *for the* OMOHUNDRO INSTITUTE
OF EARLY AMERICAN HISTORY AND
CULTURE, *Williamsburg, Virginia, by the*
UNIVERSITY OF NORTH CAROLINA PRESS,
Chapel Hill

The Omohundro Institute

of Early American History

and Culture is sponsored

jointly by the College of

William and Mary and the

Colonial Williamsburg

Foundation. On November

15, 1996, the Institute

adopted the present name

in honor of a bequest from

Malvern H. Omohundro, Jr.

Set in Sabon by Tseng Information Systems, Inc.
Manufactured in the United States of America
Library of Congress Cataloging-in-Publication Data
Kaplan, Catherine O'Donnell.
Men of letters in the early republic : cultivating forums of
citizenship / Catherine O'Donnell Kaplan.
   p. cm.
Includes bibliographical references and index.
ISBN 978-0-8078-3164-9 (cloth : alk. paper) —
ISBN 978-0-8078-5853-0 (pbk. : alk. paper)
1. United States—Intellectual life—1783–1865.
2. United States—Intellectual life—1783–1865—
Sources. 3. Citizenship—United States—History.
4. Forums (Discussion and debate)—United States—
History. 5. Social networks—United States—History.
6. Societies—United States—History. 7. Conversation—
Political aspects—United States—History. 8. Publishers
and publishing—United States—History. 9. United
States—Politics and government—1783–1865. 10. Political
culture—United States—History. I. Omohundro Institute
of Early American History & Culture. II. Title.
E164.K37 2008
973.3—dc22   2007031411

Parts of this book overlap with my previously published
articles: "'He Summons Genius . . . to His Aid': Letters,
Partisanship, and the Making of the *Farmer's Weekly
Museum*, 1795–1800," *Journal of the Early Republic*,
XXIII (2003), 545–571; "Elihu Hubbard Smith's 'The
Institutions of the Republic of Utopia,'" *Early American
Literature*, XXXV (2000), 294–336.

The paper in this book meets the guidelines for permanence
and durability of the Committee on Production Guidelines
for Book Longevity of the Council on Library Resources.

This volume received indirect support from an unrestricted
book publication grant awarded to the Institute by the
L. J. Skaggs and Mary C. Skaggs Foundation of Oakland,
California.

cloth   12 11 10 09 08   5 4 3 2 1
paper   12 11 10 09 08   5 4 3 2 1

For my parents,
Ed and Bobbie O'Donnell

ACKNOWLEDGMENTS

Like the Americans I study in this book, I have been nurtured by affectionate and demanding communities of readers, thinkers, and writers. Although I tend to shy from competition, I challenge anyone to produce a finer list of teachers than those I have had. At Amherst College, Daniel Barbezat, Francis G. Couvares, Robert A. Gross, Allen Guttman, and David Sofield introduced me to history, literature, and the hope of uniting vocation and avocation. At the University of Michigan, David A. Hollinger, Carol Karlsen, Bradford Perkins, John Shy, Carroll Smith-Rosenberg, James Turner, and Maris Vinovskis tried their best to make me a historian. The brilliance and kindness of Susan Juster saw me through the long semesters of writing a dissertation; she and Bob Gross provide models of mentorship both daunting and inspirational.

A great deal more research and writing was possible because of a postdoctoral fellowship at the Omohundro Institute of Early American History and Culture supported by the Colonial Williamsburg Foundation, the College of William and Mary, and the National Endowment for the Humanities. The people of the Omohundro Institute set standards of scholarship and collegiality that are to me the best the profession has to offer. Ronald Hoffman, Christopher Grasso, Philip Morgan, David Steinberg, Michael Jarvis, and the staff guided me in essential ways, as did wonderful scholars associated with the Institute, particularly David S. Shields and John L. Brooke. Virginia L. Montijo gracefully oversaw the copyediting of this manuscript and made it a better book. For Fredrika J. Teute, scholar and editor, I feel a gratitude that even she, with her insistence that I set aside timidity and indirection, cannot enable me to express. I'll keep trying, Fredrika.

Archivists and librarians are the keepers of the manuscripts, and I am grateful for the knowledge, efficiency, and patience of the staffs at the William L. Clements Library of the University of Michigan, the Houghton Library of Harvard University, the Cushing/Whitney Medical Library of Yale University, the Boston Athenaeum, the American Antiquarian Society, the Massachusetts Historical Society, the New-York Historical Society, and the Pennsylvania Historical Society.

A list of my helpful friends at Arizona State University would read like the department roster; I have been as absurdly fortunate in my colleagues as

I have been in my teachers. I thank in particular Brian Gratton and Rachel Koopmans for reviews of the manuscript.

Daniel Kaplan lived loyally with this book and its author through their formative years, and knows my love. The world's best boy and best girl, Thomas and Louisa Kaplan, learned recently that their mother has been writing a book. They have expressed a mild interest, and I value this considered opinion. Melody Smith and Phyllis Melcher helped me care for these children, making my book and career possible.

I dedicate this book to my parents, who taught me to read, write, and love.

CONTENTS

ILLUSTRATIONS

Men *of* Letters

IN THE EARLY REPUBLIC

INTRODUCTION

Does America need men of letters? Culturally ambitious Americans pondered the question during the first two decades of the early Republic. Political responsibilities seemed to subsume all other duties, political speech to drown out all other communication, and the American identity as citizen to supersede all other identities. Was there a need for poetry, for wit, for intimate conversation circles, and for transatlantic intellectual communities? The subjects of this study believed that there was. Elihu Hubbard Smith, Joseph Dennie, Joseph Stevens Buckminster, Arthur Maynard Walter, and William Smith Shaw founded conversation circles, periodicals, and cultural institutions in New York City, northern New England, Philadelphia, and Boston, and the fruits of their efforts reached readers throughout the United States and in Europe. They read books and circulated manuscripts. They conversed about poetry, art, and the nature of man. They pondered William Godwin and Edmund Burke more carefully than they did candidates for local elections and insisted other Americans should do so as well. They believed that neither the nation nor they themselves could achieve virtue and happiness through politics alone. They imagined a different kind of citizenship.

Conversation circles, belletristic clubs, and periodicals were traditional institutions of Anglo-American civil society. But those who participated in them in the new American nation faced unprecedented challenges. As it remade the political order, the American Revolution profoundly transformed civil society. Belletristic civil society had existed in England and the colonies as a kind of "utopia of sympathy" in opposition to the state. In coffeehouses and periodicals, people gathered to share ideas and bons mots, and in doing so opposed the voluntary, horizontal ties of shared taste and pleasure to the vertical, inescapable bonds of a monarchical state and hierarchical society. Such associations enacted a different kind of order from that on which the state relied, and their participants directly satirized political authorities. This realm of clubs, conversation, and manuscript exchange—influentially characterized by Jürgen Habermas as the public sphere—constituted, in England and in colonial America, "a public independent of state control and capable of criticizing state power." This public was capable of criticizing state power, but not, for the most part, of seizing it: the independence and pleasure of this realm were in no small measure functions of its distance from the levers of government.[1]

After Americans won their independence and founded a nation, the independent republic of civil society no longer existed in its traditional form. White propertied men possessed real political power. Most of those in the coffeehouse now had access to the statehouse. Thus, the American Revolution had in one sense institutionalized the public sphere by protecting liberties of speech and association but in another had destroyed it by rendering the people sovereign, obliterating any distinction between public and state. Gone was the distance that allowed for criticism and its pleasures. There was no tyrannical state—and yet neither was there an escape from the new tyranny of one's endless political relevance and responsibility. The egalitarian bonds of small voluntary societies, moreover, no longer differentiated them from the world outside: American men were now citizens, not subjects, and "the long intricate and oppressive chain of subordination" of monarchical society was no more. In fact, now that citizens in the polity were expected to feel a horizontal kinship with one another and to engage in unrestricted debate and conversation on political subjects, the exercise of American citizenship had come to bear remarkable similarities to the kind of fellowship and activities once confined to the realm outside the state.[2]

These transformations posed acute questions for those who participated in face-to-face and print belletrism in the new United States. Was participants' belief that the development of good men and good societies required intellectual labor, a belief that had seemed egalitarian when set against the hereditary hierarchies of Britain, now unacceptably elitist? Worse, were

1. David S. Shields, *Civil Tongues and Polite Letters in British America* (Chapel Hill, N.C., 1997), xiii–xix (quotation on xv); Jürgen Habermas, *The Structural Transformation of the Public Sphere: An Inquiry into a Category of Bourgeois Society*, trans. Thomas Burger with the assistance of Frederick Lawrence (Cambridge, Mass., 1989). The primary eighteenth-century theorist of these associations, Anthony Ashley Cooper, third earl of Shaftesbury, "wished to see the power of both Church and Monarch reduced" in favor of "a vision of eighteenth-century politics and culture that replaced godly and courtly understandings with a public gentlemanly one." See Lawrence E. Klein, *Shaftesbury and the Culture of Politeness: Moral Discourse and Cultural Politics in Early Eighteenth-Century England* (Cambridge, 1994), 21.

2. James Kent, *An Introductory Lecture to a Course of Law Lectures* . . . (New York, 1794), 22. Gordon S. Wood discusses the destruction of traditional ties and the hope of creating "new social bonds of love, respect, and consent" in *The Radicalism of the American Revolution* (New York, 1992), 229–243 (quotation on 229).

intellectual labor and the critiques of government and society it produced not simply inappropriate but also useless? Because citizens had increasing access to political power, that is, should they not vote, run for office, or form clubs devoted, not to conversing and communing, but rather to winning others' votes? Traditional civil society, moreover, had existed in a state of permanent opposition to the powers that be, but such unending dissent violated Americans' expectation that a republican people would achieve harmony. The development of the first party system troubled those who believed that the new nation had no need for the "factions" that characterized a monarchical polity, and the very intensity of partisan conflict reflected a point of agreement: the Federalist and the Republican Party each insisted it and it alone truly spoke for the nation. Participants in a critically engaged belletrism, however, rejected the goal that united those who disagreed on all else: the goal of converting the nation to their views. Rather than seeing the existence of dissent in a republic as a temporary imperfection or necessary evil, they conceived of it as an essential part of a healthy society. To demand respect for their kind of citizenship, therefore, was to demand that other Americans give up their dreams of perfect union.[3]

Not least among the challenges faced by men who engaged in belletrism was that conversation and manuscript exchange often involved women. In post-Revolutionary America, the categories of white manhood and of enfranchised citizen became congruent in a way they had never been in England or the colonies. Increasingly, to be a political actor was to be a white male, and to be a white male was to be a political actor. Seeking civic relevance through practices tied to conversation and writing departed from ideals of manhood, not once, but twice: it meant grounding one's identity and public usefulness in something other than formal politics, and it meant devoting one's energies to doing something that women could also do—indeed, to doing something that their own experience suggested women did well and men could not do without women's help. Ultimately, all of these issues pointed toward three questions: Could men of letters create a vantage point from which they could usefully think about, criticize, and affect

3. David Waldstreicher, *In the Midst of Perpetual Fetes: The Making of American Nationalism, 1776–1820* (Chapel Hill, N.C., 1995), 5–14; Richard Hofstadter, *The Idea of a Party System: The Rise of Legitimate Opposition in the United States, 1780–1840* (Berkeley, Calif., 1969), 8–10. Stanley Elkins and Eric McKitrick note that even James Madison did not entirely accept that order would emerge from competing interests; see *The Age of Federalism* (New York, 1993), 264–270.

the new Republic? Could they do so in a way they and others believed was manly? And did America need them to do these things?

The new nation's political order itself suggested that the answer to the last question might be yes. Republican ideology put forth political action as the essential duty of men, but the emergence of the first party system proved that political action alone would not be sufficient to create a virtuous, happy nation. Whereas republican citizens were supposed to work toward the public good through politics, the rhetorical, ideological, and physical battles between Republicans and Federalists demonstrated that, when citizens acted through politics, they often, indeed usually, did so to pursue interests that conflicted. In the new nation's contentious political arena, individuals seemed to pursue the good of some, not the good of all, and their protestations to the contrary only fueled the intensity of their disagreements with one another. And, even as republican theory maintained that the people, once freed from tyranny, would speak with one voice, the cacophony of argument and accusation grew louder. Perhaps, some Americans thought, the world of conversation, wit, literature, and fellowship—a world in which people listened as well as talked, in which they disagreed without rancor, in which they undermined pretension and false assumptions without destroying order—did have something to offer this strange new world. Perhaps it could allow for the exchange of ideas and the creation of bonds of affection and trust that the American polity demanded but failed to create.

Explored in the following pages are three models of the post-Revolutionary man of letters who aspired to be a different kind of citizen. The first is that developed by the physician and amateur cultural impresario Elihu Hubbard Smith while he lived and worked in New York City in the late 1790s. The second is that developed by Joseph Dennie during his editorship of two prominent early national literary and political periodicals: Walpole, New Hampshire's *Farmer's Weekly Museum* and Philadelphia's *Port Folio*. The third model is that developed by Joseph Stevens Buckminster, William Smith Shaw, and Arthur Maynard Walter in the first decade of the nineteenth century, as the three helped to found a private reading room, the Boston Athenaeum, and a periodical, the *Monthly Anthology, and Boston Review*. Smith, Dennie, and the Anthologists were writers and thinkers who developed cultural projects and nurtured networks of friends and associates, networks that created and circulated texts, ideas, and allegiances. These men also founded periodicals and cultural institutions that lasted well into the nineteenth century and, in the case of the Athenaeum, beyond; their more ephemeral associations inspired original writing and brought American and European works to press in the United States. They exposed to the light physical and moral ills of American society from yellow fever to racial slavery, and they created forums in which women and men read, thought, and argued together. Their combination of civic-mindedness and mistrust of politics, moreover, affected both partisanship and culture. Smith's scientific and literary projects drew together men of opposed political views during the superheated 1790s. Dennie's periodicals spread Federalist rhetoric in a way useful to the party's efforts to create community, but he also turned politics into performance art, sapping it of the power to reform. The Anthologists, envisioning a literature and literary life that transcended all conflict, worked to corral partisan disagreement and to create a bipartisan cultural elite whose shared goals would provide harmony and virtue to a nation they found lacking in both.

Elihu Hubbard Smith (1771–1798) grew up in Litchfield, Connecticut. He studied medicine with Benjamin Rush, then moved to New York City to begin practicing as a physician. During the 1790s, Smith slowly attracted patients and volunteered at New-York Hospital. It was not to medical practice, however, but rather to medical observation that Smith was truly suited. In addition to taking copious notes on his own reading and on the patients he saw and learned of, Smith urged others, in America and abroad, to collect information about the diseases and conditions they treated. This collection of medical information was part of Smith's broader plan to facilitate the collection and exchange of information on all possible subjects. Those subjects included himself: Smith kept a scrupulously detailed journal during the last three years of his life in which he recorded the books he read, borrowed, and lent, the visits he paid, and the letters he wrote. The diary offers a record of Smith's prodigious efforts to create, nurture, and continually enlarge a network of readers, writers, and exchangers of texts that reached up and down the East Coast.[4]

4. For discussion of Smith's life and projects, see James E. Cronin, "Introduction," in Cronin, ed., *The Diary of Elihu Hubbard Smith (1771–1798)* (Philadelphia, 1973), 1–16; and Cronin, "Elihu Hubbard Smith and the New York Friendly Club, 1795–1798," Modern Language Association of America, *Publications*, LXIV (1949), 471–479. Bryan Elliot Waterman, "The Friendly Club of New York City: Industries of Knowledge in the Early Republic" (Ph.D. diss., Boston University, 2000), offers extensive accounts of Smith and other members of the Friendly Club and attempts to determine the club's precise membership. See also Annie Russell Marble, *Heralds*

Smith participated in New York City's Friendly Club, a conversation circle that included the playwright William Dunlap, the legal scholar and Federalist politician James Kent, the lawyer and future legal reporter William Johnson, the Columbia professor and Republican politician Samuel Latham Mitchill, and Charles Adams, son of John Adams. He also enjoyed friendships with other prominent Americans, including Timothy Dwight, Noah Webster, and the Federalist senator Uriah Tracy, and he corresponded with the English scientists Thomas Beddoes and Robert John Thornton. During his twenty-seven years of life, Smith wrote fiction and nonfiction, poetry and prose, and published pieces in both American and British periodicals. He penned a libretto, a utopia, sonnets, essays, and satiric verse. He edited perhaps the first anthology of American poetry, *American Poems* (1793); founded, along with two other men, the nation's first long-lived scientific periodical, the *Medical Repository;* shepherded the works of his friend, the novelist Charles Brockden Brown, to press; helped to find both readers and content for Joseph Dennie's first successful enterprise, the *Farmer's Weekly Museum;* and in 1798 oversaw the first American edition of Erasmus Darwin's *Botanic Garden,* for which he wrote a preface in verse celebrating the spread of knowledge. Smith also developed relationships with printers that, in combination with his ability to marshal readerships, enabled him to influence what works were brought to press. Amid these many enterprises, Smith found time to lament that he was, as he put it, "the very slave and sport of indolence." Striving always for a self-mastery that would allow him to more efficiently pursue his goals, Smith restricted his dinners to "Milk and bread" and swore off the barber so that he could "save enough,

---

of American Literature: A Group of Patriot Writers of the Revolutionary and National Periods (1907; rpt. New York, 1967), 287–292; Robert Ferguson, "Yellow Fever and Charles Brockden Brown: The Context of the Emerging Novelist," *Early American Literature,* XIV (1979–1980), 295–297; Shields, *Civil Tongues and Polite Letters,* 324. Caleb Crain has recently offered a sympathetic portrayal of Smith's friendship with one Friendly Club participant, Charles Brockden Brown, in *American Sympathy: Men, Friendship, and Literature in the New Nation* (New Haven, Conn., 2001), chaps. 2, 3. Fredrika J. Teute examines the liveliness of Smith's cultural life outside his participation in the Friendly Club and his relationship with Brown; see "The Loves of the Plants; or, The Cross-Fertilization of Science and Desire at the End of the Eighteenth Century," *Huntington Library Quarterly,* LXIII (2000), 320–322, and "A 'Republic of Intellect': Conversation and Criticism among the Sexes in 1790s New York," in Philip Barnard et al., eds., *Revising Charles Brockden Brown: Culture, Politics, and Sexuality in the Early Republic* (Knoxville, Tenn., 2004), 149–181.

by the sacrifice of unnecessary, to provide for real [intellectual] wants!" A wry awareness of the loftiness of his ambitions and the imperfections of his efforts, however, saved him from the grim self-importance that might have driven off friends and collaborators. Although he began the third volume of his diary with a grand epigraph from Virgil's Fourth Eclogue, the opening phrase, "Jam nova progenies . . ." ("Now the new generation [is sent down from heaven on high]"), he began the fourth volume with "Ecce iterum Crispinus" (here, again, is Crispin), a line from Juvenal's Fourth Satire that served in Smith's day as a jaunty acknowledgment of the tedious persistence of human vice.[5]

Elihu Hubbard Smith believed he had a duty to improve America, and he believed he could do so, not through political action, but through continuing intellectual inquiry. In Smith's view, individuals created harmony and pursued justice through acquiring and circulating information. The information they gathered would reveal the truth of any problem and its best solution. Thus, in Smith's view, the world—and the American nation within it—would be improved, not through electoral politics and partisan debate, but through a kind of open-ended intellectual exertion that rendered political parties unnecessary.

One of the many young Americans with whom Smith corresponded on matters literary and logistical was Joseph Dennie (1768–1812). Dennie graduated from Harvard in 1790, and in the first years of the decade he ostensibly turned his attention to reading law in New Hampshire. As becomes clear in the apologetic letters Dennie sent to his parents explaining his lack of progress, his true desire was to be a man of letters. While still a college student, he began penning columns loosely modeled on those by the roving gentlemen of English periodicals such as the *Spectator*, and he also began to write essays under the name "The Lay Preacher" in which he combined Benjamin Franklin–style moral pronouncements with his own melancholic acerbity. In 1795, having gained confidence in his literary abilities and having become convinced that Boston's educated elite would become his eager patrons, Dennie founded an ambitious literary periodical he called the *Tablet*. Dennie was its editor and the writer of most of its content. The *Tablet* failed in less than six weeks.[6]

5. Cronin, ed., *Diary*, Sept. 17, Oct. 25, 1795, March, May 5, August 1796, 58, 81, 144, 163, 196.
6. A chronologically comprehensive account of Dennie's career can be found in

Dennie never forgave Boston its betrayal, but the bitter setback quickly propelled him to innovation and influence. Coming to terms with the reluctance of Boston to support the career of an ambitious litterateur, Dennie retreated far up the Connecticut River to Walpole, New Hampshire. There, in late 1795, he took over the editorship of the *Farmer's Weekly Museum*. The *Museum* was an uninspired four-page newspaper that Dennie transformed into a nationally circulated compendium of political opinion and original and collected literary matter. By 1797, Dennie was known as an editor and essayist of cantankerous, oddly inviting wit, and the *Museum* had close to two thousand paying subscribers, a number that rivaled the circulation of the most successful urban dailies of the period. As startling in the flesh as he was in his literary incarnations—one contemporary years later wrote a detailed description of the editor's frequent attire of "pea-green coat, white vest, nankin small-clothes, white silk stockings, and shoes, or *pumps*, fastened with silver buckles, which covered at least half the foot from the instep to the toe"—Dennie reveled in his success, and, in 1800, he returned south from Walpole in triumph. Moving to Philadelphia, he founded the *Port Folio*, a weekly magazine of literary and political content sold for the high price of eight dollars per annum. Dennie used his own writings for the magazine as well as contributions from readers around the nation and from members of the Tuesday Club, a group of educated men and women with whom he gathered in Philadelphia. He also brought British authors to American readers, including William Wordsworth, Samuel Taylor Coleridge, Thomas

---

Harold Milton Ellis, *Joseph Dennie and His Circle: A Study in American Literature from 1792 to 1812*, Bulletin of the University of Texas, no. 40 (Austin, Tex., 1915). For a brief account of Dennie's career before the *Port Folio*, see William Charvat, *The Profession of Authorship in America, 1800–1870* (Columbus, Ohio, 1968), 14–17. David Jaffee explores Dennie's editorship of the *Farmer's Weekly Museum* in *People of the Wachusett: Greater New England in History and Memory, 1630–1860* (Ithaca, N.Y., 1999), 227–237. Most analyses of Dennie focus on his work with the *Port Folio* (1801–1812). See William C. Dowling, *Literary Federalism in the Age of Jefferson: Joseph Dennie and the Port Folio, 1801–1812* (Columbia, S.C., 1999); Linda K. Kerber, *Federalists in Dissent: Imagery and Ideology in Jeffersonian America* (Ithaca, N.Y., 1970); Kerber and Walter John Morris, "Politics and Literature: The Adams Family and the *Port Folio*," *William and Mary Quarterly*, 3d Ser., XXIII (1966), 450–476; Ellis Paxson Oberholtzer, *The Literary History of Philadelphia* (Philadelphia, 1906), 176–177; Randolph C. Randall, "Authors of the *Port Folio* Revealed by the Hall Files," *American Literature*, XI (1940), 379–416; Michael Gilmore, "The Literature of the Revolution and Early National Periods," in Sacvan Bercovitch, ed., *The Cambridge History of American Literature*, I, 1590–1820 (New York, 1994), 567–571.

Moore, and Thomas Gray. The *Port Folio* did not bring Dennie riches, but it did allow him to live as a professional man of letters—one of the nation's very first such figures.[7]

The vision of the American man of letters that Elihu Hubbard Smith developed through his many projects sought to make politics irrelevant. Joseph Dennie instead determined to put political rhetoric and alliances to his own uses. In his periodicals, Dennie presented himself as a Federalist man of feeling, one who used the rhetoric of partisan animosity to express his own idiosyncratic social and cultural criticism. Entirely rejecting the idea that individuals could all work toward an inarguable, unitary public good, Dennie believed, with some satisfaction, that all human relationships and actions were grounded in self-interest. Rather than sharing Elihu Smith's belief in the usefulness of an endless, collective pursuit of empirical information, moreover, Dennie instead believed in the usefulness of ephemeral wit. Whereas Smith was, at root, a facilitator, Dennie was a performer. Smith made of the world an observatory; Dennie made of it a stage. Dennie shared with Smith a belief that the crucial civic act was, not voting, but, as an American man of letters, to puncture republican pretension: in his view, a republic needed a jester even more than a king needed one.

The third model of the American man of letters sprang from the collaboration of William Smith Shaw (1778–1826), Arthur Maynard Walter (1780–1807), and Joseph Stevens Buckminster (1784–1812) as they worked on behalf of the *Monthly Anthology* and the Boston Athenaeum. Shaw, Walter, and Buckminster's lives and projects were entwined, and they appear in this book as the trio that they were in life.[8]

7. Jeffrey L. Pasley, *"The Tyranny of Printers": Newspaper Politics in the Early American Republic* (Charlottesville, Va., 2001), 422 n. 2; Joseph T. Buckingham, *Specimens of Newspaper Literature: With Personal Memoirs, Anecdotes, and Reminiscences*, 2 vols. (Boston, 1850), II, 196.

8. For accounts of the Anthology Society, including Buckminster, Shaw, and Walter, and its projects, see Josiah Quincy, *The History of the Boston Athenaeum, with Biographical Notices of Its Deceased Founders* (Cambridge, Mass., 1851); Lewis Simpson, ed., *The Federalist Literary Mind: Selections from the Monthly Anthology and Boston Review, 1803–1811, Including Documents relating to the Boston Athenaeum* (Baton Rouge, La., 1962). See also Simpson, *The Brazen Face of History: Studies in Literary Consciousness in America* (Baton Rouge, La., 1980); and Simpson, "The Era of Joseph Stevens Buckminster: Life and Letters in the Boston-Cambridge Community, 1800–1815" (Ph.D. diss., University of Texas at Austin, 1948). For more recent discussions of the Anthologists, see Peter S. Field, "The Birth of Secular High Culture: *The Monthly Anthology and Boston Review* and Its Critics," *Journal of the Early Republic*,

The most prominent Anthologist then and since is Joseph Stevens Buckminster. After graduating from Harvard in 1800 at the age of sixteen, Buckminster followed his father into the ministry, but his increasingly anti-Trinitarian theology sharply divided the young man from his orthodox elder. Buckminster served as a minister at Cambridge's liberal Brattle Street Church and became known for eloquent sermons and appealing oratorical style. Buckminster also gained fame for his vehement rejection of the creedal Congregationalism then developing at Andover Seminary and his embrace of the German biblical criticism that disrupted traditional views of the origin and meaning of Scripture. Despite his sincere devotion to the ministry, Buckminster believed that his engagement in letters was as necessary to the cultivation of his and others' virtue as were his sermons. During the first decade of the nineteenth century, he contributed to the *Literary Miscellany* and the *General Repository*, two short-lived Cambridge periodicals, but it was to the Anthology Society that he devoted the greatest part of his talent and time. Along with Walter and Shaw, Buckminster drew up the society's formal constitution; he also helped to found the Boston Athenaeum and purchased books for it with his own funds, and he wrote many pieces published in the *Monthly Anthology.*[9]

Arthur Maynard Walter, four years younger than Buckminster, was also the son of a minister, and he was the great-grandson of the famous New England minister Increase Mather. Unlike Buckminster, Walter rejected his family's expectations that he become a clergyman; as a young man, he was

---

XVII (1997), 575-609; Field, *The Crisis of the Standing Order: Clerical Intellectuals and Cultural Authority in Massachusetts, 1780-1833* (Amherst, Mass., 1998), 83-84, 89-96; Timothy Patrick Duffy, "The Gender of Letters: The Man of Letters and Intellectual Authority in Nineteenth-Century Boston" (Ph.D. diss., University of Virginia, 1993), introduction, chap. 1; Lawrence Buell, *New England Literary Culture: From Revolution through Renaissance* (New York, 1986), 176-177, 201-203; Daniel Walker Howe, *The Unitarian Conscience: Harvard Moral Philosophy, 1805-1861*, Wesleyan ed. (Middletown, Conn., 1988), 201-203.

9. Eliza Buckminster Lee, *Memoirs of Rev. Joseph Buckminster, D.D., and of His Son, Joseph Stevens Buckminster*, 2d ed. (Boston, 1851), 228-231, 455-458; Simpson, "Era of Joseph Stevens Buckminster," 48, 70-72, 451-467. Johann Jakob Griesbach was among the pioneers of biblical textual criticism and the first to propose that the Gospel of Mark was a conflation of the Gospels of Matthew and Luke. Griesbach's New Testament was criticized even by some of those adopting a Unitarian faith, although the text became known as the "Unitarian new testament." See Earl Morse Wilbur, *A History of Unitarianism*, II, *In Transylvania, England, and America* (Cambridge, 1952), 338, 339.

delighted to be told that his long hair made him look like "a bard from Ossian," and he saw his role in the local community, in the nation, and in the world to lie in spreading good literature, not in spreading God's word. Walter studied law but devoted as much time as he could to the Anthology Society, for which he served as secretary. William Smith Shaw, the third of the trio of Anthologists, was a nephew of Abigail Adams. Impoverished owing to his father's early death, Shaw nonetheless managed to attend Harvard and graduated in 1798. He served his uncle, President John Adams, as a private secretary until Jefferson's election, when he began reading law in the Boston office of William Sullivan. From 1806 until 1818, he served as clerk of the District Court of Massachusetts, an undemanding but respectable post. Shaw was an impassioned friend to Buckminster and Walter and was the driving force behind the Anthology Society; in his later life, his devotion to the Boston Athenaeum—and to the preservation within it of the papers of his friends—earned him the nickname "Athenaeum" Shaw.[10]

Joseph Stevens Buckminster, William Smith Shaw, and Arthur Maynard Walter shared Smith's and Dennie's desire to be part of an international community of culturally enlightened individuals. When they turned their attention to the nation, the Anthologists agreed, moreover, that formal political action could not create a harmonious, virtuous republic. But they sought civic relevance for themselves and their cultural projects neither through Dennie's aggressive deployment of wit nor through Smith's quest to spur humanity toward a collective omniscience. Instead, these men created spaces—literal in the Athenaeum and rhetorical in the *Monthly Anthology*— that they conceived as refuges from the competing interests of the boisterous political and commercial world. They believed the American man of letters ought to transcend politics and reform the polity from the outside. But first, of course, they had to find a way to get outside it. The Anthology Society worked to create both the distance and the bridge: imagining a sphere of club life and literary production removed from the demands and opportunities of political engagement, the society then sought to demonstrate the relevance of that sphere to the polity it struggled to escape.

Elihu Hubbard Smith, Joseph Dennie, William Smith Shaw, Arthur Maynard Walter, and Joseph Stevens Buckminster participated in the late Enlightenment effort to improve mankind through the exercise of reason and the tutelage of feeling. They embarked on their projects during years

10. Arthur Maynard Walter Journals, Jan. 14, 1804, Boston Athenaeum; Lee, *Memoirs*, 302–316; Quincy, *Boston Athenaeum*, 13–44.

when the fractious American political system as well as the violent transformations of the French Revolution and its aftermath made it seem necessary to contemplate how societies were bound together and to propose—in
fact to embody—superior forms of community. They pursued their goals
and projects, moreover, in the United States during years when politics
threatened—or, in the eyes of some, promised—to supersede intellectual
and cultural activities and the forms of identity and manhood those activities offered. In the pages that follow, as I explore the models of intellectual
engagement developed by these men of letters, I ask the question that both
animated and haunted their projects: Was there a place and a use in the new
United States for these men and their different kind of citizenship?

CHAPTER ₁ *Sensibility and Sociability at Work in the World*

One September evening in 1795, Elihu Hubbard Smith sat up late writing in his diary. He had earlier in the day penned a rough accounting of his expenditures for the previous year, but he returned to his diary that evening because he thought it was important to write a detailed account of his visit to the home of a friend, Horace Johnson. "He was at home," Smith wrote: "His wife, and brother; and I found there Mr. and Mrs. Lovegrove. We drank tea. Amboy being mentioned, in the course of the conversation, gave occasion to Seth [Johnson] to relate his danger of being wrecked on South Amboy coast; and of the gratitude, or attachment, of a negro slave to his master. . . . This story introduced several others: instances of African attachment, fidelity and gratitude." As this conversation continued, Smith reported, he contributed information he had learned from a Connecticut physician who had spent time in the West Indies. Smith's account spurred the company on to still more conversation: "Some remarks on the nature and qualities of the Africans; on the iniquity of the Slave Trade; on the celebrated book of [the Dutch physician] Camper; on influence of climate, soil, food, and other physical and moral causes; and on the probable effects of education." This last subject prompted Mrs. Lovegrove to pass along a story she had heard from "an eye-witness" of "natives of New Holland" who, "instructed in the european method, in readg., writing, etc. . . . exhibited all the talents and ingenuity which European children usually do."[1]

It was quite a conversation. The six men and women gathered in the Johnson home offered to one another knowledge gained through reading, through conversation with others, and through reflection. In an atmosphere of open exchange and affection, they pondered specific subjects of humanitarian reform such as the slave trade, asserted the efficacy of education in

1. James E. Cronin, ed., *The Diary of Elihu Hubbard Smith (1771-1798)* (Philadelphia, 1973), Sept. 6, 1795, 47.

forming all humans, and implicitly agreed that it was their own "european" standard to which all people should aspire.

This conversation was in essence an oral gazette, a thing that would normally live on only in the memory of its participants. But that September night, Smith wrote down what he remembered of the conversation (excluding those parts he deemed "too imperfect to admit of narration") in the diary that he hoped would be "interesting . . . to the Historian and Philosopher." It would be of interest, in Smith's view, not despite such detailed descriptions of ephemeral exchanges, but because of them. Such conversations, Smith believed, brought their participants important facts about their physical and social surroundings and made it possible collectively to imagine ways of improving those surroundings. Such conversations, and the relationships that made them possible, were not only enjoyable but necessary to the development of good individuals and a good world. Such conversations mattered.[2]

Throughout England and America lived men and women who could have walked into the Johnsons' house, taken part in the discussion, and felt the same kind of satisfaction in the evening that Smith did. Among them were the subjects of this study: Joseph Dennie, William Smith Shaw, Arthur Maynard Walter, and Joseph Stevens Buckminster. They were exemplars of a much broader phenomenon. Over the course of the long eighteenth century, educated men and women on both sides of the Atlantic came to believe that the world and everyone within it could be transformed through reading, writing, and conversations such as the one that Smith and his friends enjoyed. These activities would produce the knowledge necessary to free individuals and societies from superstition, ignorance, and moral and physical ills. They would create the personal and market networks that would disseminate such information. And they would inspire the affectionate bonds that would spur further collaboration and inquiry.

This optimistic belief had roots in the late seventeenth century, when Anthony Ashley Cooper, third earl of Shaftesbury, proposed that the affectionate environment of small gatherings made possible the honest exchange of ideas. Free to analyze and criticize one another and the world outside, participants in such gatherings would be free as well to pursue and discover useful truth. Shaftesbury argued further that society itself, and not simply voluntary gatherings, was held together by human beings' natural interest in one another. Cultivating this capacity for sympathy would create a

2. Ibid., Sept. 6, 1795, March 1796, 47, 144.

more just and humane world. Shaftesbury's inquiry into the relationship between social bonds and the possibility of human improvement was part of a broader philosophical movement that had begun with latitudinarian divines and that would be continued by the philosophers of the eighteenth-century Scottish Enlightenment. Latitudinarians argued that individuals possessed an innate capacity for sympathy that drove them to alleviate the sufferings of others. Scottish philosophers such as David Hume and Francis Hutcheson argued that individuals possessed a "moral sense," or an ability immediately to apprehend right and wrong. There was considerable disagreement over the relative emphasis to be placed on the components of moral sense: Hutcheson portrayed it as akin to aesthetic judgment; Shaftesbury wrote that the moral sense impelled virtuous action "because the gratification of our natural benevolent urges is pleasurable"; and the philosophers Richard Price and Thomas Reid, whose works became important to the curricula of late-eighteenth-century American colleges, depicted moral sense as predominantly a rational and active power. All agreed, however, that moral sense was a matter of both intellect and emotion, that it served as the basis of sympathetic social bonds, and that those bonds, in turn, should serve as the basis of a just and virtuous society.[3]

3. Anthony Ashley Cooper, third earl of Shaftesbury, *Sensus Communis: An Essay on the Freedom of Wit and Humour* . . . (London 1709). For discussions of Shaftesbury, see Lawrence E. Klein, *Shaftesbury and the Culture of Politeness: Moral Discourse and Culture Politics in Early Eighteenth-Century England* (Cambridge, 1994); John Mullan, *Sentiment and Sociability: The Language of Feeling in the Eighteenth Century* (Oxford, 1988), chap. 1; David S. Shields, *Civil Tongues and Polite Letters in British America* (Chapel Hill, N.C., 1997), xiii–xviii. Early Americanists have explored club life through the prism of Jürgen Habermas's analysis of the "public sphere"; see Habermas, *The Structural Transformation of the Public Sphere: An Inquiry into a Category of Bourgeois Society,* trans. Thomas Burger with the assistance of Frederick Lawrence (Cambridge, Mass., 1989); and Habermas, *Between Facts and Norms: Contributions to a Discourse Theory of Law and Democracy,* trans. William Rehg (Cambridge, Mass., 1996). These accounts, which attend to the social and political purposes and effects of discursive practices, inform my study, although in most instances I have chosen to adopt the language and lens of eighteenth-century social analysis rather than those of Habermas or his many followers and critics. For examples of the productive ways in which early Americanists have adapted the concept of the public sphere, see John L. Brooke, "Ancient Lodges and Self-Created Societies: Voluntary Association and the Public Sphere in the Early Republic," in Ronald Hoffman and Peter J. Albert, eds., *Launching the "Extended Republic": The Federalist Era* (Charlottesville, Va., 1996), 273–377; Albrecht Koschnik, "The Democratic Societies of Philadelphia and the Limits of the American Public Sphere, circa 1793–1795," *William and Mary Quar-*

Such thinking hovered between the descriptive and the prescriptive. Human beings were naturally bound together by sympathy. But human beings should ideally form societies in which sympathy becomes a stronger force. That mixture of prescription and description was linked to another oscillation. Sympathetic identification was portrayed both as a universal human capacity and as a skill or ability possessed more by some than by others. Those who pursued Shaftesburian fellowship through institutions of civil society such as clubs, conversation circles, and periodical communities understood themselves as modeling the kinds of association that others should (but perhaps could not) emulate. Their sense of difference from the world outside was one of the delights of fellowship, even though obliterating that difference was one of the purposes of fellowship.[4]

Over the course of the eighteenth century, the ideal of sensibility emerged from the prescriptive and hierarchical tendencies embedded in the concept of moral sense. Like such other eighteenth-century ideals as virtue and republicanism, sensibility was vaguely defined, malleable, and ubiquitous. The correct sensibility was a kind of "virtuous responsiveness," a "psychoperceptual scheme" in which body, mind, and heart reacted simultaneously to environmental stimuli, be those stimuli physical, social, or even textual. Sensibility straddled the line between an innate trait and an acquired one: although it was an expression of an individual's true nature, the correct sensibility was also fully achievable only through proper education and immersion in sociable practices. And, although the correct sensibility was not the exclusive or natural property of aristocrats and kings, it created its own pecking order: those most sensible would be more wounded by vice and ugliness and also more likely to appreciate beauty and goodness. "In some,"

terly, 3d Ser., LVIII (2001), 615–636; Bryan Waterman, "The Bavarian Illuminati, the Early American Novel, and Histories of the Public Sphere," WMQ, LXII (2005), 9–30; Frans de Bruyn, "Latitudinarianism as a Precursor of Sensibility," Journal of English and Germanic Philology, LXXX (1981), 349–368; Karen Halttunen, "Humanitarianism and the Pornography of Pain," American Historical Review, C (1995), 304; Daniel Walker Howe, The Unitarian Conscience: Harvard Moral Philosophy, 1805–1861, Wesleyan ed. (Middletown, Conn., 1988), 45–50 (quotation on 46). For discussions of the Scottish Enlightenment, see Gladys Bryson, Man and Society: The Scottish Inquiry of the Eighteenth Century (Princeton, N.J., 1945); Norbert Waszek, Man's Social Nature: A Topic of the Scottish Enlightenment in Its Historical Setting (Frankfurt am Main, 1986).

4. G. J. Barker-Benfield, The Culture of Sensibility: Sex and Society in Eighteenth-Century Britain (Chicago, 1992), chap. 5.

wrote Robert Whytt in 1768, "the feelings, perceptions, and passions, are naturally dull, slow, and difficult to be roused; in others, they are very quick and easily excited, on account of a greater delicacy and sensibility of brain and nerves." Medical texts such as the influential work of George Cheyne set out an intricate hierarchy. Cheyne wrote: "There are as many and as different Degrees of *Sensibility* or of *Feeling*, as there are Degrees of *Intelligence* and Perception in *human* Creatures; and the *Principle* of both may be perhaps one and the same. One shall suffer more from the Prick of a *Pin*, or *Needle*, from their extreme *Sensibility*, than others from being run thro' the Body; and the *first* Sort seem to be of the *Class* of these *Quick-Thinkers* I have formerly mentioned."[5]

As Cheyne's description suggests, sensibility could lead to suffering. But suffering proved virtue. During the second half of the eighteenth century, authors and artists sought to elicit intense responses to scenes of pathos, and a self-conscious but sincere pain at others' distress was the goal of much of the literature enjoyed by those who gathered in conversation circles and clubs. Works such as the poetry of Arthur Young, Robert Southey, and Thomas Gray and the novels of Laurence Sterne and Henry MacKenzie depicted scenes of misery—"High in the air expos'd the Slave is hung / To all the birds of Heaven, their living food!" read lines from Southey's Sonnet 6 on the slave trade—in order that readers and viewers might exert and refine their own capacity for sympathy. The sympathetic identification felt by good readers of such texts was understood to be the essence of humans' ability to know—and even to feel the reality of—other people. "By the imagination," Adam Smith wrote of the suffering individual, "we place ourselves in his situation, we conceive ourselves enduring all the same torments, we enter as it were into his body, and become in some measure the same person with him, and thence form some idea of his sensations, and even feel something which, though weaker in degree, is not altogether unlike them."

5. Barker-Benfield, *The Culture of Sensibility*, xvii, 67; Ann Jessie Van Sant, *Eighteenth-Century Sensibility and the Novel: The Senses in Social Context* (Cambridge, 1993), chap. 6; Robert Whytt, *Observations on the Nature, Causes, and Cure of Those Disorders Which Have Been Commonly Called Nervous, Hypochondriac, or Hysteric, to Which Are Prefixed Some Remarks on the Sympathy of the Nerves*, in *The Works of Robert Whytt, M.D. . . . Published by His Son* (Edinburgh, 1768), 112; George Cheyne, *The English Malady; or, A Treatise of Nervous Diseases of All Kinds; as Spleen, Vapours, Lowness of Spirits, Hypochondriacal, and Hysterical Distempers, etc. . . .* , 3d ed. (London, 1734), 366.

Such identification provided the root of social justice and harmony: not reason alone but rather the ability to put oneself in another's place enabled an individual to understand, for example, that a farmer had a right to the fruits of his labor. Correctly cultivated sympathy was also thought likely to inspire people to reform the world by provoking them to wish to alleviate the conditions that caused others—and therefore themselves—pain. "No cold exemption from [sensibility's] pain," the British author Helen Maria Williams wrote in 1786, "I ever wish'd to know." The correct sensibility, in short, was a necessary attribute of the good individual. And that, together with the sociable practices that helped to produce it, was to form the basis of a world in which people were bound together, not through power or self-interest, but rather through shared feeling for each other and a collective pursuit of truth, beauty, and justice.[6]

Throughout the eighteenth century, educated men and women participated eagerly in private societies modeled on Shaftesburian ideals. They did so in order to enjoy fellowship, to sharpen their wits, and to cultivate, perform, and feel the correct sensibility. These societies took many forms in Great Britain and in the colonies. In England, coffeehouses such as the Carolina, the New England, and the Rainbow became sites of animated conversation. Inspired by both news and literature, coffeehouse denizens strove for the Shaftesburian delights of fellowship through unfettered communication and friendly intellectual rivalry. Such coffeehouse society was all male, but men and women participated together in conversation circles held in private homes. During the sixteenth century, salons in England and France were often directed by a "patroness" who encouraged genteel conversation—and admiration of her own charms—among the writers and wits she attracted to her circle. By the eighteenth century, gatherings were grounded more in friendship between men and women than in the adoration of a resident muse. At her home in Lichfield, England, during the 1780s, Anna Seward met and exchanged manuscripts with visitors including Erasmus Darwin, Robert Southey, Hester Piozzi, and Samuel Johnson, and during that decade and the next the publisher Joseph Johnson held lively dinners whose

6. Barker-Benfield, *Culture of Sensibility*, chap. 3; Janet Todd, *Sensibility: An Introduction* (London, 1986), 6–9; Mullan, *Sentiment and Sociability*; Robert Southey, Sonnet 6, *Poems by Robert Southey* (Boston, 1799), 28; Adam Smith, *The Theory of Moral Sentiments*, ed. D. D. Raphael and A. L. Macfie (Oxford, 1976), 9; Halttunen, "Humanitarianism and the Pornography of Pain," *AHR*, C (1995), 305–307 (Halttunen describes this phenomenon as "spectatorial sympathy," and I adopt her term); Helen Maria Williams, "To Sensibility," *Poems*, I (1786; rpt. New York, 1994), 21.

attendees included William Godwin, Mary Wollstonecraft, Anna Aikin, and Anna Barbauld.[7]

Both same-gender and mixed-gender sociability developed in colonial America as well. Coffeehouses existed throughout the colonies: Charleston had the French and the Exchange, Boston the Tontine, Philadelphia the London. All-male clubs included Annapolis's Tuesday Club, whose members celebrated and mocked their own sociable proceedings in oral salvos and witty writings, and Philadelphia's fishing clubs, where men enjoyed rural pastimes and celebrated wit and the pursuit of pleasure. During the same decades, students founded societies at America's colleges. At Harvard, the Tell-Tale Club and the Philomusarian Club were founded in the 1720s. Yale saw the Linonian Society and the Brothers in Unity created in the 1750s, and the American Whig and Cliosophic Societies were founded at the College of New Jersey in the 1760s. Some college circles modeled themselves on coffeehouse conversation, whereas others more earnestly sought the moral improvement of their members; all, however, were inspired by collegians' belief that the stagnant state of the curriculum and professoriate meant that they would have to educate themselves and that they could best do so through the fellowship and shared inquiry of club life.[8]

Shaftesburian fellowships presented themselves as models of association that were of value even when participants' purposes were restricted to sharing delight in beauty and wit. In the late colonial period, Benjamin Franklin and the circle he dubbed the Junto helped to create groups such as the American Philosophical Society and the Library Company in order to harness Shaftesburian fellowship to the intellectual and practical improve-

7. Elizabeth Eger et al., eds., *Women, Writing, and the Public Sphere, 1700–1830* (New York, 2001); Shields, *Civil Tongues and Polite Letters*, 15, 60–61; John Brewer, *The Pleasures of the Imagination: English Culture in the Eighteenth Century* (London, 1997), 573; Anne Janowitz, "Amiable and Radical Sensibility: Anna Barbauld's 'Free Familiar Conversation,'" in Gillian Russell and Clara Tuite, eds., *Romantic Sociability: Social Networks and Literary Culture in Britain, 1770–1840* (Cambridge, 2002), 62–81.

8. Shields, *Civil Tongues and Polite Letters*, 52, 62, 177–178, 188–189, 209–274; Dr. Alexander Hamilton, *The History of the Ancient and Honorable Tuesday Club*, ed. Robert Micklus, 3 vols. (Chapel Hill, N.C., 1990); Carl J. Richard, *The Founders and the Classics: Greece, Rome, and the American Enlightenment* (Cambridge, Mass., 1994), 23. David W. Conroy describes tavern sociability, which was characterized by an assertive egalitarianism and challenges to local social and political authorities; see *In Public Houses: Drink and the Revolution of Authority in Colonial Massachusetts* (Chapel Hill, N.C., 1995), 2.

ment of the local area. This last development urged Shaftesburian civil society in America toward a direct engagement with the world without severing it from its roots in communities differentiated by conduct and purpose from the hurly-burly of self-interest outside their doors.[9]

American women also created clubs and circles. During the 1770s, a group of young sisters and cousins living in Connecticut and New York formed the Union Club. Members exchanged ideas and shared feelings while also conversing and corresponding with male friends and relatives, including such prominent cultural figures as John Trumbull and Timothy Dwight. Earlier in the colonial period, Annis Boudinot Stockton had written and circulated neoclassical poetry, often on the theme of friendship, while Milcah Martha Moore copied the writings of Delaware Valley women friends into what she labeled "Martha Moore's Book." Perhaps the most famous female participant in the world of American sociability was one of those whose writings Moore transcribed, Elizabeth Graeme. Born into genteel society in the Delaware Valley, Graeme, like the women of the Union Club, circulated letters and manuscripts through a circle of women friends while also engaging in sociable gatherings and literary correspondence with men. Graeme celebrated friendship as superior to romantic love and wrote as well about the pleasing pains of sensibility: in one poem, which she explained "took its rise from a dispute, pasing one Evening in Company," she took up the question of "whether the feeling or insinsible Minds were the happiest this Life" and extolled the virtue of "a kind and Sympathizing Breast."[10]

9. Benjamin Franklin, *The Autobiography of Benjamin Franklin* (Mineola, N.Y., 1996), 45–53, 86. For the possibilities of viewing Shaftesburian societies as having practical or projecting effects as well as serving as aesthetic fields of play, see John D. Schaeffer, *Sensus Communis: Vico, Rhetoric, and the Limits of Relativism* (Durham, N.C., 1990); Shields, *Civil Tongues and Polite Letters,* 97–98.

10. Christopher Grasso, *A Speaking Aristocracy: Transforming Public Discourse in Eighteenth-Century Connecticut* (Chapel Hill, N.C., 1999), 294; Victor E. Gimmestad, *John Trumbull* (New York, 1974), 70–72; Carol F. Karlsen and Laurie Crumpacker, eds., *The Journal of Esther Edwards Burr, 1754–1777* (New Haven, Conn., 1984); Mary Kelley, "'A More Glorious Revolution': Women's Antebellum Reading Circles and the Pursuit of Public Influence," *New England Quarterly,* LXXVI (2003), 165; Kelley, *Learning to Stand and Speak: Women, Education, and Public Life in America's Republic* (Chapel Hill, N.C., 2006), 112–190; Carla Mulford, ed., *"Only for the Eye of a Friend": The Poems of Annis Boudinot Stockton* (Charlottesville, Va., 1995), 7–11; Elizabeth Graeme, "On the Preference of Friendship to Love," and Graeme, "A Pastoral Dialogue between Damon and Alexis," quoted in Shields, *Civil Tongues and Polite Letters,* 131, 132.

Disagreements such as the one that inspired Graeme's poem were integral to the practices and delights of sociability. "Disputes" were carried on not only through earnest discussion but also through raillery and banter. Pennsylvania's Henry Brooke wrote "A Discourse upon Je'sting Attempted in the Way of Horace," in which he poked fun at the conversation of his own conversation circle; Brooke's manuscript, which was circulated through more than one colony, no doubt inspired conversations and "je'sting" of its own. Clubs and salons allowed for a kind of refined playfulness thought impossible outside them—whether "outside" was understood to be the rigidly hierarchical and cautious court or the boisterously unreflective crowd. The exercise of wit also allowed for social and personal criticism to be expressed in a way that promoted intimate fellowship. In mixed-gender gatherings, moreover, women's wit allowed them to escape becoming simply the objects of men's romantic desire—or simply the audience of men's competition with each other. But, although wit made friendship possible, it also risked making enemies of friends. Witty salvos expressed and provoked competition among speakers and writers, and they posed a challenge to listeners and readers: Who would get the joke? Who would extend the metaphor? Who, through being either slow-witted or thin-skinned, would be left behind? Each moment of witty personal, political, or social commentary posed a test for all involved.[11]

Over the course of the eighteenth century, this sociable, witty world of conversation and manuscript exchange became increasingly entwined with print culture. In the first decades of the century, British periodicals such as Addison's *Spectator* and Addison and Richard Steele's *Tatler* offered descriptions in print of the convivial, witty gatherings belletrists cultivated in person. These periodicals, which portrayed the experience of the club to readers who might live far from a coffeehouse or salon, found eager readers. The young Benjamin Franklin came to consider himself a British citizen entitled to the full rights of an Englishman in no small measure by assiduously

11. Shields discusses Brooke's manuscript in *Civil Tongues and Polite Letters*, 70–75. On the social and literary uses of wit, see Elaine G. Breslaw, "Wit, Whimsy, and Politics: The Uses of Satire by the Tuesday Club of Annapolis, 1744 to 1756," *WMQ*, 3d Ser., XXXII (1975), 295–306; Joanne Dobson, "Sex, Wit, and Sentiment: Frances Osgood and the Poetry of Love," *American Literature*, LXV (1993), 631–650; Chris Holcomb, *Mirth Making: The Rhetorical Discourse on Jesting in Early Modern England* (Columbia, S.C., 2001); David S. Shields, "Anglo-American Clubs: Their Wit, Their Heterodoxy, Their Sedition," *WMQ*, 3d Ser., LI (1994), 293–304; Shields, *Civil Tongues and Polite Letters*, xvii, 45.

copying the *Spectator*'s prose, cultivating its sensibility and entering into its imagined club.[12]

During the second half of the eighteenth century, the number of newspapers in America grew from eighteen to more than one hundred. America was transformed from a society of information scarcity to one of abundance, and American belletrists began publishing satires and polite verse in these venues. Colonial newspapers such as the *South-Carolina Gazette*, the *Virginia Gazette*, and Boston's *Weekly Rehearsal* portrayed imaginary clubs like that of the *Spectator*. Publishing one's verse or essays in a newspaper was a way to gain status within one's circle and outside it, and the practice bore fruit for the editors of the newspapers as well. Provocative offerings attracted responses useful for filling pages and for gaining readers: when a woman named Elizabeth Magawley wrote an essay for the *American Weekly Mercury* tweaking men's unwillingness to engage in polite conversation with women, male would-be wits sent in responses that were published the very next week.[13]

As expressed both through face-to-face gatherings and in manuscript and print, sociable practices and the sensibility they nurtured were inspired by conflicting but coexisting desires. Participants delighted in the sense that their bonds of affection and their evenings of inquiry and wit differentiated them from the world outside. As a result, clubs and societies could become arch and self-referential; the intimate self-satisfaction of club life, moreover, could easily merge with a more general sense of cultural superiority, as in Smith and his friends' discussion of whether New Hollanders could ever be raised to the level of Europeans. But, as that same September evening discussion indicates, participants in these gatherings also believed that their clubs had the potential—through modeling good relationships and through discovering and circulating what they believed to be moral and scientific truths—to remake the world outside. As a result, reformist sentiment and reformist work often vied, in the lives and hearts of club participants, with escapism and elitism.

12. Edward A. Bloom and Lillian D. Bloom, *Educating the Audience: Addison, Steele, and Eighteenth-Century Culture: Papers Presented at a Clark Library Seminar, 15 November 1980* (Los Angeles, 1984); Michael Ketcham, *Transparent Designs: Reading, Performance, and Form in the "Spectator" Papers* (Athens, Ga., 1985); Franklin, *Autobiography*, 11.

13. Shields, *Civil Tongues and Polite Letters*, 92, 267; Richard D. Brown, *Knowledge Is Power: The Diffusion of Information in Early America, 1700–1865* (New York, 1989), 3–15, 111, 268–296.

The ideal of sensibility shared this potential of sociable practices to draw the gaze both inward and outward. The correct sensibility was a form of responsiveness to the world, but its cultivation required continual monitoring of one's mind, body, and heart—required, that is, a self-witnessing that competed with vigorous engagement in the very things to which one responded. By the 1780s and 1790s, some writers expressed the view that the literature of sensibility promoted the display of feeling as an end in itself, thereby cultivating the tendency toward self-satisfaction and quiescence that had always lurked within the ideal of sensibility. The "pleasing anguish" that the Scottish writer David Fordyce described was, to critics such as Oliver Goldsmith, Anna Letitia Barbauld, and William Hazlitt, a delight in others' misery. Such delight was not likely to spur a desire to change the circumstance that had elicited the "pleasing anguish," particularly when the wealth that bought the reader time to read also bought luxuries made possible by the very economic, social, and political circumstances that sparked empathetic reaction: in a lecture on the slave trade, Samuel Taylor Coleridge memorably excoriated the reader who "sips a beverage sweetened with human blood, even while she is weeping over the refined sorrows of Werther." Nurturing one's distress at others' suffering, furthermore, encouraged an emphasis on the performance of feeling as an end in itself and threatened to complete sensibility's inward turn. In the "sensible" individual as in the Shaftesburian society, connectedness found a rival in solipsism.[14]

Revolutions

Ideals of sensibility and sociability emerged from the effort to understand how human beings were and should be bound together in society; they were at their core, that is, not only aesthetic and social but also political. As such, institutions of civil society, including conversation circles, clubs, and periodical communities, were intricately bound up with the eighteenth century's revolutions.

14. David Fordyce, *The Elements of Moral Philosophy* . . . (1754), quoted in Haltunen, "Humanitarianism and the Pornography of Pain," *AHR*, C (1995), 308 (Haltunen discusses contemporary mistrust of the literature of sensibility's tendency to portray suffering [308–309]); Samuel Taylor Coleridge, "On the Slave Trade," in Peter J. Kitson, ed., *The Abolition Debate*, vol. II of Kitson and Debbie Lee, gen. eds., *Slavery, Abolition, and Emancipation: Writings in the British Romantic Period* (London, 1999), 218–219.

In the 1770s, 1780s, and 1790s, Americans pondered the nature of society as they won their independence from Great Britain and created a nation. Institutions of civil society were important to both processes, and both processes dramatically affected the practices of—and the meaning to participants of—civil society. Between the end of the Seven Years' War and the Declaration of Independence, colonists gathered in taverns and clubs and critiqued Britain's imperial policies. The purpose of these societies divorced them from the Shaftesburian sociability that had been enjoyed in the colonies before the imperial crisis. There was no tension between refuge and reform in these Revolutionary conclaves: their purpose was to gain entry for colonists into Britain's formal politics and, when that failed, to develop a way to sever the colonies from Britain through violence. Yet the influence of educated Americans' exposure to clubs and to print representations of clubs such as the *Spectator* is evident. From tavern gatherings grew not only arguments for resistance and independence but also the intense fellowship that made possible a shared worldview and the personal relationships that helped to circulate strategic information during the war itself. Participants in the Revolutionary era's correspondence societies, moreover, deftly used newspapers and pamphlets to spread the arguments and the sense of fellowship cultivated in face-to-face gatherings and in doing so applied the techniques of print-inflected sociability to the cause of direct political transformation. Even the use of pen names, although adopted primarily to avoid political persecution, provided to readers and writers the belletristic thrill of a publicly visible secrecy, an emotional charge that was useful to Revolutionary organizers seeking to create an intense brotherhood. Indeed, so powerful was the sense of participation in the Revolutionary cause instilled by this network of taverns, societies, and newspapers that soldiers who fought the war complained more than once that those who merely sat and read valued too highly their virtual service to the nation.[15]

When independence was won and the Constitution ratified—the latter achievement gained through, among other things, adroit use of print-inflected sociability—Americans had not only created a new polity but had also transformed the relationship between that polity and civil society. By

15. Conroy, *In Public Houses*, chap. 6; Simon P. Newman, *Parades and the Politics of the Street: Festive Culture in the Early American Republic* (Philadelphia, 1997), chap. 1; Charles Royster, *A Revolutionary People at War: The Continental Army and American Character, 1775–1783* (Chapel Hill, N.C., 1979), 104–107; David Waldstreicher, *In the Midst of Perpetual Fetes: The Making of American Nationalism, 1776–1820* (Chapel Hill, N.C., 1997), 34–35.

enfranchising white men of property and regularizing the creation of legis-lative districts, American political leaders provided access to political power to a broad range of citizens. Even if the realities of political influence and deference meant that this access was not equal, this development was still enormously important. Within the polity itself, men were now linked by the kind of horizontal bonds once imagined achievable only in civil society. But did those bonds have any emotional reality? And once freed from the chains of monarchy, would Americans create an orderly society or a chaotic one? In response to such challenges, Americans such as Benjamin Rush in-sisted on the need to educate citizens so that they might have the wisdom necessary for a stable republic. In an effort to create a shared "federal feel-ing," other Americans developed celebratory rites that they enacted in local gatherings and spread through print. These Americans believed that the nation could not be created solely through its founding documents and its elections but must also come to life through sociability and the cultivation of sympathy.[16]

Americans such as Rush not only put the ideals of sociability to political use but also hoped that America itself could become, like a Shaftesburian club, a forum for the honest exchange of opinions and a realm of affec-tionate harmony. Harmony was also the hope and expectation of Thomas Jefferson, who imagined that republican liberty would reveal a natural con-sensus among the people. Neither clubs nor elections, however, produced a united population. Americans were divided by circumstance and opportu-nity far more than were members of any small voluntary society, and liberty created, not unity, but a proliferation of competing interests. Even as they worked to develop a shared "federal feeling," citizens of the new nation came to dramatically different conclusions about what policies their state and federal governments should pursue.[17]

16. Albrecht Koschnik, "Political Conflict and Public Contest: Rituals of National Celebration in Philadelphia, 1788–1815," *Pennsylvania Magazine of History and Biog-raphy*, CXVIII (1994), 209–248; Newman, *Parades and the Politics of the Street*, chaps. 2, 3; Len Travers, *Celebrating the Fourth: Independence Day and the Rites of National-ism in the Early Republic* (Amherst, Mass., 1997); Waldstreicher, *In the Midst of Per-petual Fetes*, chap. 2.

17. On the Jeffersonian hope for a "straightforward and easily comprehended common good that citizens could collectively move toward and in which they could all mutually share," see Andrew Shankman, *Crucible of American Democracy: The Struggle to Fuse Egalitarianism and Capitalism in Jeffersonian Pennsylvania* (Lawrence, Kans., 2004), introduction (quotation on 1).

The competing strategic alliances that politically engaged Americans developed during the early 1790s quickly became America's rudimentary first parties, the Federalists and the Democratic-Republicans. Far from rendering irrelevant the old practices and pleasures of Shaftesburian fellowship, the parties used the practices of sociability to pursue their conflicting claims to political power and legitimacy. Federalists and Republicans gathered to discuss issues and to nurture fellow feeling through dinners and toasts, and they used newspapers to bring accounts of their meetings to other Americans who could then model their own practices and fellowships on those they saw represented in text. They argued, moreover, not only within their associations but also over the forms those associations took. Democrats mocked Federalist literary circles and periodicals as Anglophile and elitist. Federalists lambasted Republican clubs and street gatherings as unruly and mindlessly boisterous, and they organized competing, decorous celebrations of dates such as the Fourth of July and Washington's Birthday. Federalist leaders, moreover, portrayed their political allegiance as a correct responsiveness to events, as, in essence, a sensibility, and one strongly inflected by the sorrow that so much eighteenth-century literature advocated: the iconic moment in the career of the Federalist congressman Fisher Ames was his 1795 speech on the proposed Jay Treaty between America and England, in which Ames offered dire warnings while referring pointedly to his physical and mental suffering. In doing so, Ames converted his sensitivity into an indication of civic grace—and not only his own but that of his properly responsive Federalist audience as well. "Tears enough were shed," John Adams wrote home to his wife, Abigail, about the reaction of listeners to Ames's Jay Treaty speech. "Not a dry eye, I believe in the house, except some of the jackasses who had occasioned the necessity of the oratory." Three years later, the Federalists were still agonized, and the "jackasses" still unmoved. "To us," Ames lamented in a letter to the Federalist politician Timothy Pickering, "the wrongs of France are whips and scorpions"; to the "southern Congress men" with their "thick skins," they are "the strokes of a feather." A favorite theme of eighteenth-century belletrists, the difference between the sensible and the insensible, had been resurrected in the United States Congress as the difference between Federalists and Republicans.[18]

18. Fisher Ames, "Letter to Timothy Pickering," July 10, 1798, in W. B. Allen, ed., *Works of Fisher Ames as Published by Seth Ames*, 2 vols. (Indianapolis, Ind., 1983), 1287; Warren Choate Shaw, *History of American Oratory* (1928; rpt. Folcroft, Pa., 1979), 54; James Spear Loring, *The Hundred Boston Orators Appointed by the Municipal Authorities and Other Public Bodies, from 1770–1852; Comprising Historical Glean-*

During the 1790s, Americans did more than use the rhetoric and practices of sensibility and sociability to gain adherents and criticize opponents;
they also participated in debates over how and whether sensibility and sociability could be used to create a better society, debates rendered urgent by the
unfolding events of the French Revolution. Whereas the American Revolution had seemed to many to support the belief that order could be created
through the egalitarian social bonds proposed by theories of sociability, the
French Revolution affected the experience and the political resonances of
sensibility and sociability in a more complex way: sociability and sensibility
became sites in which battles were waged over what constituted the good
man and the good society. Two visions widely and passionately discussed on
both sides of the Atlantic informed the political arguments brewing in the
United States, that of William Godwin and that of Edmund Burke.

William Godwin, in his *Enquiry concerning Political Justice*, which was
published in 1793 and revised in 1798, attacked aristocracy, monarchy, and,
indeed, all institutions, including the family, which he believed limited the
scope of man's sympathy and so confined his intellectual freedom. Men
should act from a principle of "universal benevolence," Godwin argued.
The general ideal of sensibility had long entwined reason and feeling; Godwin argued that reason should tutor the feelings so that individuals would
pursue truth and justice without regard to private affections and prefer-
ences. If—as in his famous example—that meant saving a renowned author
from a fire rather than one's own family member, so be it. The pursuit of
justice, however, had itself to be impassioned, and not cold: "Virtue, sincerity, justice and all those principles which are begotten and cherished
in us by a due exercise of the reason," Godwin wrote, "will never be very
strenuously espoused till they are ardently loved."[19]

Despite Godwin's disdain for aristocracy and monarchy, *Political Justice*
was not an endorsement of the French Revolution. Godwin extolled the
potential of mankind, but he doubted the capacities of most men. Britain
and the world as a whole were not ready, Godwin believed, for the revo-

ings Illustrating the Principles and Progress of Our Republican Institutions, 3d ed. (Boston, 1854), 238. For a discussion of New England oratory, including Fisher Ames's
speech, see Lawrence Buell, *New England Literary Culture: From Revolution through
Renaissance* (New York, 1986), chap. 6.

19. William Godwin, *Enquiry concerning Political Justice, and Its Influence on Mod-
ern Morals and Happiness*, ed. Isaac Kramnick (Harmondsworth, 1976), 136–137, 170.
For a discussion of American interest in Godwin and his circle, see Henry F. May, *The
Enlightenment in America* (New York, 1976), 225–226.

lutionary destruction of social institutions; the vast majority of individuals had not yet achieved the correct sensibility and so were not yet capable of universal benevolence. "The time may come," he wrote, "when men shall exercise the piercing search of truth upon the mysteries of government," and at that time "it will be the duty of such as shall see these subjects in the pure light of truth to exert themselves for the effectual demolition" of unjust political structures. "But effectual demolition is not the offspring," he cautioned, "of crude projects and precipitate measures," and the truly rational man "will cherish no wild schemes of uproar and confusion." Godwin's belief that education and the practices of sociability could eventually render all people capable of true inquiry and affection cut his elitism with optimism. But he argued for the need for social transformation while expressing profound distrust for any immediate efforts to achieve it.[20]

The French Revolution prompted a very different response, but one also rooted in ideals of sensibility and authentic social bonds, from Edmund Burke. Unlike Godwin, Burke emphasized the importance of feeling over reason. In his *Reflections on the Revolution in France* (1790), Burke argued that all men of true feeling must deplore not only the conduct but also the principles of the French Revolution. Burke sought to elicit in his readers pain at the sufferings of the Revolution's victims, to evoke their pleasure in the beauty of monarchical societies' traditions and pageantry, and to applaud and nurture what Burke had characterized in earlier writings as their "awe, reverence, and respect" for those in power. Like Godwin's, Burke's vision partook of the hierarchy embedded in the ideal of sensibility. Although he implied that responsiveness to the horror of anarchy and the beauty of monarchical order were on one level natural human capabilities, the varying intensity of individuals' reactions in his view indicated their differing capacities for public virtue and refinement and so gave evidence of their differing suitability to positions of power. Burke, moreover, believed that, even among those possessed of a correct sensibility, the accumulated wisdom of the generations was necessary to prevent error. The social sympathies even of the "natural aristocracy" were in Burke's view necessarily limited. "*Universal Benevolence* toward all Men," the Scottish philosopher Francis Hutcheson had argued, "we may compare to that principle of *gravitation* which perhaps extends to all bodies in the universe; but increases as the distance is diminished, and is strongest when bodies come to touch each other." In Burke's Hutcheson-inflected thought, the institutions and tradi-

20. Godwin, *Enquiry*, ed. Kramnick, 256–257.

tions of monarchy and aristocracy not only served as repositories of generational wisdom; they were also necessary because sympathy and benevolence were far too weak to unite individuals across the vast physical and social differences of an eighteenth-century nation. Without the beautiful chains of monarchical hierarchies, Burke believed, society would fly apart; the destruction of institutions and traditions meant the destruction of community and of order.[21]

The American political argument was in important ways less total than the disagreement between Edmund Burke and William Godwin: Federalists and Republicans agreed that the new, republican government should be preserved, and they agreed to compete through elections. They agreed, that is, to act as if their differences were expressible and containable through formal politics. But partisanship was an imperfect way of grappling with more profound disagreements about how individuals should be bound together in societies and about what the effects of the Republic's theoretical and actual expansion of politics itself should be, and American partisan disagreements overlapped with and sometimes crossed the philosophical arguments of Burke and Godwin. When Democratic-Republican clubs, which were inspired both by French Jacobin societies and by Americans' own Revolutionary-era associations, formed to protest government policies, they presented themselves, not as one of a number of competing interests, but as the true voice of the people and as the state itself, an argument that gestured toward the possibility of a national benevolence, untroubled by private loyalties and competing interests, that was reminiscent of Godwin's proposed universal benevolence. But it was Federalists who found both Burke and Godwin most useful in conjuring ideal and nightmarish visions

21. Edmund Burke, *A Philosophical Enquiry into the Origin of Our Ideas of the Sublime and Beautiful*, ed. Adam Phillips (New York, 1990), 123; Burke, *Reflections on the Revolution in France*, ed. J. G. A. Pocock (Indianapolis, Ind., 1987), 60–67; Francis Hutcheson, "An Inquiry concerning the Original of Our Ideas of Virtue or Moral Good," in R. S. Downie, ed., *Francis Hutcheson: Philosophical Writings* (London, 1994), 101. For a discussion of Hutcheson and benevolence in the American context, see Garry Wills, *Inventing America: Jefferson's Declaration of Independence* (Garden City, N.J., 1978), 287–288. For useful discussions of Burke's views, see Marilyn Butler, *Romantics, Rebels, and Reactionaries: English Literature and Its Backgrounds, 1760–1830* (New York, 1982), 103–104; Frans De Bruyn, *The Literary Genres of Edmund Burke: The Political Uses of Literary Form* (Oxford, 1996); Claudia L. Johnson, *Equivocal Beings: Politics, Gender, and Sentimentality in the 1790s: Wollstonecraft, Radcliffe, Burney, Austen* (Chicago, 1995), 1–22; Chris B. Jones, *Radical Sensibility: Literature and Ideas in the 1790s* (London, 1993), 48–49, 85–86.

of society. The dominant Federalist model of the way to create a national community explicitly advocated the maintenance of the traditions and hierarchies Americans could be said to possess and asserted that humans were—and should be—capable only of bounded sympathies. "Love, to be anything, must be select and exclusive," Fisher Ames explained, in a Burkean reflection on the difficulties of creating a true American community among individuals united only by the abstract notion of citizenship. Like Burke, moreover, many Federalists saw revolutionary France as a society ransacked of beauty, order, and true sympathy, and they feared that Republicans would drag America into the same abyss. Arthur Maynard Walter deplored radical change in France and America in Burkean terms: "This world and this complex society is governed by forms and by ceremonies," he wrote firmly; "I will not excuse the person, who . . . tramples on authority for he or she breaks the bands, which hold society together." For some Federalists, including Walter, Godwin's philosophy provoked the fear that reason unhinged from love and respect for hierarchy would lead to bloodshed and chaos. But, for other educated young Federalists, including Elihu Smith, Godwin's mixture of demand for reform with rejection of immediate upheaval offered an enticing form of intellectually elitist radicalism.[22]

Americans turned to political philosophy such as that of Burke and Godwin and to partisan identification and rhetoric as they thought about social bonds and the way those bonds could be created and destroyed through both political and extrapolitical means. For Smith, Dennie, and the Anthologists, Federalism came closer than Republicanism to capturing their shared sense that a republic required the guidance of a cadre of enlightened leaders,

22. Explorations of the Democratic-Republican clubs that discuss their mechanics, transatlantic dimension, and claims to legitimacy include Brooke, "Ancient Lodges and Self-Created Societies," in Hoffman and Albert, eds., Launching the "Extended Republic," 273-377; Koschnik, "The Democratic Societies of Philadelphia," WMQ, 3d Ser., LVIII (2001), 615-636; Alfred F. Young, The Democratic Republicans of New York: The Origins, 1763-1797 (Chapel Hill, N.C., 1967). Andrew Shankman discusses the tendency of "Jeffersonian thinkers" to "generalize about the homogeneous category 'the people' while actual people's pursuit of capitalism was rendering the conditions that citizens experienced ever more heterogeneous" in Crucible of American Democracy, 1-15 (quotation on 4). See Fisher Ames, "The Dangers of American Liberty, Written in the Beginning of the Year 1805," in Allen, ed., Works of Fisher Ames, 138; Arthur Maynard Walter to William Smith Shaw, Sept. 28, 1799, William Smith Shaw Papers, Boston Athenaeum; Chandos Michael Brown, "Mary Wollstonecraft; or, The Female Illuminati: The Campaign against Women and 'Modern Philosophy' in the Early Republic," Journal of the Early Republic, XV (1995), 389-424.

and that ethos, along with familial and social ties to Federalist leaders, led all to consider themselves Federalists. But partisan rhetoric and allegiance also seemed to require a lack of intellectual openness and fluidity. In their writing and projects, Smith, Dennie, and the Anthologists often attempted to slip the surly bonds of partisan orthodoxy in order to criticize and to reform the new American nation. Nor did any European philosopher entirely satisfy them. Instead, they developed visions of the good society and good life that, although influenced by Burke, Godwin, or both, were coterminous with neither. Smith was a Federalist who, along with many of his close companions, found in Godwin's mixture of impatience with traditional social institutions, his belief in the perfectibility of man, and his dubious view of men's current moral and intellectual state a philosophical grounding for his own belief that an intellectual vanguard could and must lead America toward enlightenment. But Smith rejected Godwin's disdain for personal relationships such as friendship and felt sure that Godwin underestimated the potential for a government based in reason rather than corruption and oppression. Dennie took the more expected Federalist tack of deploring Godwin and admiring Burke, but Dennie's delight in exposing and undermining the weaknesses of the American Republic—such as its reliance on race-based slavery and the fuzziness of whether voters guide statesmen or statesmen guide voters—was anything but Burkean in its mocking approach to authority and (fledgling) American traditions. The Anthologists, for their part, strove to create a realm of pure literary beauty whose freedom from arguments over political and social organization marked a rejection of both Burke and Godwin's intensely politicized aesthetics. In the first decades of the new Republic, in short, finding a role for the American man of letters meant grappling with questions of what partisanship, philosophy, and art could and could not do and with questions of how individuals should be bound together in society.

Circles and Networks

The differing models of sensibility, sociability, and the American man of letters that Smith, Dennie, and the Anthologists developed had roots in the college literary societies and conversation circles that were even more popular in America after the Revolution than they had been before it. During the late 1780s and the 1790s, colleges such as Yale, which was Elihu Smith's alma mater, and Harvard, which graduated Joseph Dennie at the beginning of the period and William Smith Shaw and Joseph Stevens Buckminster at the end, were institutions whose intellectual liveliness continued to lie largely outside, and even in opposition to, their official curricula. John Quincy Adams, whose writings would appear both in the *Port Folio* and in the *Monthly Anthology,* indignantly described a typical recitation on John Locke at Harvard. "When the tutor inquires what is contained in . . . a section," Adams wrote, "many of the scholars repeat the first two lines in it, which are very frequently nothing to the purpose; and leave the rest for the tutor to explain, which he commonly does by saying over again the words of the author." Throughout the period, Harvard College's disciplinary records reveal numerous "rustications," or temporary banishments, allotted to students to punish them for their endless acts of disrespect toward the institution's rules and faculty. Joseph Dennie's own career as a student at Harvard College was interrupted by such a banishment, one which came with two striking elements. First, it had been prompted by the young man's performance of a declamation, in apparently admirable Latin, which the startled college administration realized days later had been a sarcastic attack upon itself. Second, Harvard's disciplinary records indicate that the administration, once cognizant of this assault on its dignity, took the unusual step of requiring Dennie to leave town by the following afternoon. As he emerged from his rustication, Dennie vowed vengeance with what would prove to be a characteristic lack of restraint. "So far from forgiving or forgetting their conduct," he declared of Harvard's administration, "those miserable wretches who are most obnoxious to my resentment shall one day be made sensible that my anger does not sleep." Years after his graduation, Dennie still inveighed against Harvard's curriculum as a "mortifying instance of dronish life and of 'thoughtless meditation'" that produced "nothing."[23]

Student societies offered forums in which disaffected young men such as Dennie could make their own intellectual choices among beloved peers rather than disdained authorities. By the mid-1780s, Yale's Brothers of Unity

23. Dennie to Roger Vose, Feb. 24, 1790, Dennie-Vose Papers, Massachusetts Historical Society, Boston; *Farmer's Museum; or, Lay Preacher's Gazette,* Aug. 5, 1799; Henry Adams, "Harvard College, 1786–87," *North American Review,* CXIX (January 1872), 124–125. The incident is described in a letter written by Joseph Willard, then president of Harvard College, to Dennie's parents (Dec. 21, 1789, Joseph Dennie Papers, Houghton Library, Harvard College Library, Harvard University, Cambridge, Mass.) as well as in the college's disciplinary records from that year, records that indicate the immediacy of his banishment was unusual. For descriptions of rustication practices, see Thomas Jay Siegel, "Governance and Curriculum at Harvard College in the Eighteenth Century" (Ph.D. diss., Harvard University, 1990).

had their own library of several hundred books, including works of travel, novels, and poetry. They, like members of clubs at other colleges, read and discussed texts of their choosing. At Harvard as at Yale during these years, students sought out formal and informal circles as verdant refuges from the barrenness of the formal curriculum. "Lured by [Poesy's] charms," the Harvard student Robert Treate Paine, a future contributor to the *Monthly Anthology*, wrote in 1797, "I left, in passioned hope, / My Watt's Logick for the page of Pope." What has been deemed "the neoclassical didacticism of Addison, Pope, and Johnson" was adored by young Americans who found in its arch wit a stance of mastery they could adopt in their own young lives—and who found in its controlled cadences rules they could attempt to follow in their own immature writing.[24]

As had their colonial forebears, college students of the post-Revolutionary period continued to admire periodicals such as London's *Spectator;* Joseph Stevens Buckminster, like many of his peers, read the *Spectator* (or borrowed it from a library). Students partook of the fellowship these periodicals offered and also, with wildly varying degrees of success, wrote columns modeled on those of Addison and Steele. The "Loungers" and "Spectators" of these decades-old British periodicals were roving, critical intelligences who achieved cultural status and authority through proffering and performing a confident, critical perspective on the world around them. Young Americans in the 1780s and 1790s still sought to achieve that kind of perspective, but reading the *Spectator* no longer asserted, as it had in Benjamin Franklin's day, one's identity as a British gentleman. Instead, it staked a claim to membership in a community of wit and learning that was intensely intimate, confidently supranational, and, in postcolonial America, defiantly rather than obediently Anglophile.[25]

Defiance runs through much of post-Revolutionary collegians' genteel love of literature and literary sociability. Neoclassicism's express "commitment to learned rather than popular modes of expression" offered in the American context precisely the kind of rebellion young men sought through the collegiate societies: one that rejected immediate authorities and conventional wisdom in favor of a voluntary enthrallment to genius or to truth. In

24. Grasso, *A Speaking Aristocracy*, 397; Richard, *The Founders and the Classics*, 23; Cronin, "Introduction," in Cronin, ed., *Diary*, 3; Robert Treate Paine, "The Ruling Passion," Phi Beta Kappa poem of 1797, quoted in Buell, *New England Literary Culture*, 94, 120.

25. Eliza Buckminster Lee, *Memoirs of Rev. Joseph Buckminster, D.D., and of His Son, Joseph Stevens Buckminster*, 2d ed. (Boston, 1851), 84.

Philadelphia, the future novelist Charles Brockden Brown led a young men's society called the Belles Lettres Club. In a speech to this society, Brown explained that he and his fellows sought to apprentice themselves, but only to their own vision of excellence. "We may justly be denominated pupils, since our design is to learn, or at least to improve what we have already learned," he declared, "but we are pupils to whom the pedantic character of a preceptor, and the servile forms of scholastic discipline are unknown." Like other participants in these youthful associations, Brown was advocating an education modeled on Shaftesburian ideals rather than on the pedagogical practices of American schools and universities. Young people were replacing the vertical ties that were to have bound them dutifully to professors with the horizontal, sympathetic bonds of belles lettres. But they also willingly created their own vertical ties to authors they admired. They took pride in their humility and decided whom to obey. In a poem commemorating the informal Harvard circle "ALS," Arthur Maynard Walter captured this air of defiant communion:

> When we sit around our social fires
> And tell the tales of learning's ancient sires,
> When we relate an anecdote of Young,
> Or tell when Alfred died, or Shakespeare sung;
> Or learn how Johnson penn'd a curious note,
> Why Priestley challenged, and why Gibbon wrote.
> We then receive a joy unknown before;
> Unknown to those, on whom we shut the door.

On whom did clubs such as ALS shut the door? On those who, by the poem's own assertion, did not know enough even to want to partake of the fellowship within. Such extracurricular circles engendered a habit of sociability and an oppositional stance toward constituted authority—and toward dullard peers—that would be integral to the models of intellectually engaged citizenship developed by Smith, Dennie, and the Anthologists.[26]

Participation in Shaftesburian fellowship was a way not only of asserting

26. Buell, *New England Literary Culture,* 88; Linda K. Kerber, *Federalists in Dissent: Imagery and Ideology in Jeffersonian America* (Ithaca, N.Y., 1970), chap. 4; Charles Brockden Brown, quoted in Paul Allen, *The Late Charles Brockden Brown,* ed. Robert E. Hemenway and Joseph Katz (Columbia, S.C., 1976), 24. See also Peter Kafer, "Charles Brockden Brown and the Pleasures of 'Unsanctified Imagination,' 1787–1793," *WMQ,* 3d Ser., LVII (2000), 546–547; Poem by Arthur Maynard Walter, Arthur Maynard Walter Journals, Boston Athenaeum.

one's distinctive aesthetic and intellectual judgment but also a way of asserting that such aesthetic and intellectual judgment mattered. The circles' express devotion to literature and to fellowship answered with an emphatic yes the post-Revolutionary question whether pursuits outside the political arena were still relevant. The clubs' claims on students' time constituted a continuing protest against expectations that young men devote themselves to practical, moneymaking pursuits. Far from being merely pre-professional societies, these circles promoted a devotion to literature that could compete with attention to one's future career. Young participants celebrated their imperviousness to the calls of money and success, but elders, even those who themselves valued cultural activities and ambition, often worried. Joseph Stevens Buckminster received a letter from his father cautioning, "I fear the advantages of your societies will not pay the expense of meeting." John Adams fretted over his son John Quincy's fondness for poetry: the young man "must not indulge it, but devote himself wholly to the Law." For their devoted participants, however, any risks to finances and professional advancement that the circles posed were outweighed by the pleasures of cultural investigation, friendly community, and intellectual self-governance that they offered.[27]

27. Joseph Stevens Buckminster, Sr., to Joseph Stevens Buckminster, June 16, 1800, quoted in Lee, *Memoirs*, 106; John Adams, quoted in Robert A. Ferguson, *Law and Letters in American Culture* (Cambridge, Mass., 1984), 4. For additional discussions of youthful circles, see Shields, *Civil Tongues and Polite Letters*, 165–168; James McLachlan, "The Choice of *Hercules:* American Student Societies in the early Nineteenth Century," in Lawrence Stone, ed., *The University in Society,* 2 vols. (Princeton, N.J., 1974), II, 449–494. Thomas S. Harding discusses slightly later societies in *College Literary Societies: Their Contribution to Higher Education in the United States, 1815–1876* (New York, 1971). Peter Kafer discusses the Belles Lettres Club, the Philomathian Society, which he finds to be "a coterminus liberal arts society with overlapping membership," and the "Society for the Attainment of Useful Knowledge," into which the Belles Lettres Club evolved, in "Charles Brockden Brown," *WMQ*, 3d Ser., LVII (2000), 546–547. David Lee Clark describes the Belles Lettres Club in *Charles Brockden Brown: Pioneer Voice of America* (Durham, N.C., 1952), 42–43. Albrecht Koschnik discusses a wide range of young men's voluntary societies, including but not limited to literary pursuits, in "Voluntary Associations, Political Culture, and the Public Sphere in Philadelphia, 1780–1830" (Ph.D. diss., University of Virginia, 2001), and "Fashioning a Federalist Self: Young Men and Voluntary Association in Early Nineteenth-Century Philadelphia," *Explorations in American Culture*, IV (2000), 220–257. Joseph Dennie and Charles Brockden Brown both became dissatisfied with law after it failed to meet their vision of a life devoted to thought and elegant prose; many of their peers continued to practice law but also wrote for periodicals and participated in belles lettres

As they began their professional lives, many young men continued the sociable practices they had begun in college. William Smith Shaw, Joseph Stevens Buckminster, and Arthur Maynard Walter helped to create the Anthology Society in Cambridge from the alumni of the college circle ALS. They, like others of their peers, were inspired not only by their own experience but also by their knowledge of English precedents. "One of the most pleasing thoughts of my future life," Walter wrote to Shaw in 1799, before the establishment of the Anthology Society, "is the happiness I might enjoy from an establishment of a Literary Club," such as those enjoyed by Dr. Samuel Johnson and Sir Joshua Reynolds. Elihu Smith, a Brother of Unity while at Yale, later numbered other former Brothers among his most faithful friends and correspondents, and he became a diligent member of New York City's Friendly Club. As a young editor in Walpole, New Hampshire, Joseph Dennie associated with a group of Harvard graduates who traveled up the Connecticut River to share stories and wine, and after his move to Philadelphia at the turn of the century he formed a circle, dubbed the Tuesday Club, to help write contributions for the *Port Folio*.[28]

As they developed their cultural networks and print communities, Dennie, Smith, and the Anthologists all relied for emotional and practical support—as well as for an ideal vision of human relationships—on a practice that was, like their club activities, both a product of their collegiate lives and an aspect of a much broader transatlantic trend: intense friendship. In the late eighteenth century, the ideal of friendship was entwined with the ideals of sensibility and sociability. Understood to emerge from and to nurture intellectual and emotional honesty, friendship was frequently portrayed as perhaps the most beautiful expression of the bonds of sympathy that sustained human society. Friendship loomed large in sentimental novels and in neoclassical poetry, and eighteenth-century men delightedly located friendship in the biblical relationship of Jonathan and David and in the stories of ancient Rome. During the trying days of the American Revolution, Alexander Hamilton and John Laurens passionately proclaimed their devotion to each other. "Cold in my professions, warm in my friendships," Hamilton wrote to Laurens in 1779, "I wish, my Dear Laurens, it might be in my

---

societies. See Ferguson, *Law and Letters*, 5; Frank Luther Mott, *A History of American Magazines, 1741–1850*, 5 vols. (New York, 1930), 154–156; Randolph C. Randall, "Authors of the *Port Folio* Revealed by the Hall Files," *American Literature*, XI (1940), 379–416.

28. Walter to Shaw, Mar. 29, 1799, Shaw Papers; Cronin, "Introduction," in Cronin, ed., *Diary*, 3.

power, by action rather than words, to convince you that I love you. I shall only tell you that 'till you bade us Adieu, I hardly knew the value you had taught my heart to set upon you." After the war, veterans of the American Revolution continued to treasure their distinctive communion. The *Boston Gazette* described a meeting of the Society of the Cincinnati in language that celebrated friendship as an exclusive form of sympathetic identification: "The day was passed with that harmony, festivity and joy which the meeting of real friends can alone excite.—In friendship formed in dangers, and cemented by mutual misfortunes, there arises a sympathetic pleasure not to be described, and to be conceived only by those who feel it."[29]

For post-Revolutionary Americans, friendship's voluntariness and internal egalitarianism made it appear to some an ideal republican relationship. But, although friendship was understood as a relationship between equals, true friendship was not thought to be a relationship in which all were capable of participating—as the *Gazette* piece's reference to "those who feel it" demonstrates. Like the ideals of sensibility and sociability with which it was entangled, the ideal of friendship projected the existence of a hierarchy. True friendship was a relationship that had to be cultivated and earned. Thus, Arthur Maynard Walter mused on his affection for his friend Benjamin Welles. "He has," Walter wrote, "something of the tender, and something of the spirited in human life, which disposes me to be attracted towards him with something bordering on superior love." "I hope I have

29. Alexander Hamilton to John Laurens, April 1779, quoted in Caleb Crain, *American Sympathy: Men, Friendship, and Literature in the New Nation* (New Haven, Conn., 2001), 5, (quotation) (see also 16–52); *Boston Gazette*, July 11, 1785, quoted in Waldstreicher, *In the Midst of Perpetual Fetes*, 80; E. Anthony Rotundo, "Romantic Friendship: Male Intimacy and Middle-Class Youth in the Northern United States, 1800–1900," *Journal of Social History*, XXIII (1989–1990), 1–25; Timothy Patrick Duffy, "The Gender of Letters: The Man of Letters and Intellectual Authority in Nineteenth-Century Boston" (Ph.D. diss., University of Virginia, 1993), 45–48. Rotundo's and Duffy's accounts portray male friendships as a refuge from the world. For accounts of intense male friendships that structured civic identities, it is necessary to turn to works of nineteenth-century history; see Frederick J. Blue, "The Poet and the Reformer: Longfellow, Sumner, and the Bonds of Male Friendship, 1837–1874," *JER*, XV (1995), 273–297; Donald Yacavone, "Abolitionists and the 'Language of Fraternal Love,'" in Mark C. Carnes and Clyde Griffen, eds., *Meanings for Manhood: Constructions of Masculinity in Victorian America* (Chicago, 1990), 85–95. All accounts of passionate same-sex friendships are indebted to Carroll Smith-Rosenberg's treatment of "romantic friendships" among women in "The Female World of Love and Ritual: Relations between Women in Nineteenth-Century America," *Signs: Journal of Women in Culture and Society*, I (1975), 1–29.

feelings of this nature. I should be sorry to believe that I was not well con-
structed for the reception of the sublime and beautiful in minds. I have an
high opinion of the nature of friendship."[30]

Educated young men of the post-Revolutionary generation believed that
intense friendships should be nurtured by conversation and correspondence.
In Philadelphia, James Gibson and John Fishbourne Mifflin used the pen
names Leander and Lorenzo as they communed. Joseph Dennie's Harvard
classmate Roger Marrett wrote passionately of their attachment in 1790.
"That spark of friendship, which has long subsisted between us," he urged
Dennie, "will be fanned by the gentle breezes of mutual affection, till it be
kindled into a flame and melt us into an indissoluble union." Dennie's own
letters to another classmate, Roger Vose, reveal another intensely loving
bond. "The only wish I form," Dennie wrote during a separation, "that
fortune, contenting herself with keeping us so long asunder, would now
wheel about and suffer you to live and study with me at Groton." "Depend
upon it, Vose, so well acquainted am I with your disposition and my own,
that united, we should enjoy as much felicity as this sublunary state can
furnish. Would to God this scheme were practicable; and for years to come
one might be our table and one our bed. This topic can never be exhausted."
Elihu Smith formed passionate attachments while at Yale and throughout
his short life. "You must not . . . be surprised," Smith wrote to his close
friend Theodore Dwight, "if . . . I use rather the expressions of a lover than
a man; for I feel for you all that Jonathan felt for David."[31]

Such friendship, like the cultivation of sensibility and like Shaftesburian
societies, was understood to be useful as well as delightful. Writing in 1803,
William Smith Shaw expressed the widely held view that friendship brought
moral improvement as well as emotional satisfaction. "I consider the selection of my friends as one of the most fortunate occurrences of my life," he
wrote, "as one of the greatest sources of all the pleasure I have enjoyed,
and of much instruction which I have received." Friendship inspired essays,
poems, and plays. Friendships sustained conversation circles and periodi-

30. Jay Fliegelman, *Declaring Independence: Jefferson, Natural Language, and the
Culture of Performance* (Stanford, Calif., 1993), 125–126; Walter, London journal, Dec.
9, 1803, Walter Journals.

31. Crain, *American Sympathy,* chap. 1; Fliegelman, *Declaring Independence,* 125–
126; Roger Marrett to Dennie, Mar. 18, 1790, Dennie Papers; Dennie to Vose, n.d.,
Dennie-Vose Papers; Elihu Hubbard Smith to Theodore Dwight, Aug. 30, 1796, in
Cronin, ed., *Diary,* 209.

cal communities. Friends wrote together, edited one another's works, and made the practice of mutual creativity part of their bond. Contemporaries agreed that friendship spurred the improvement of selves and societies. "Friendship is indeed the wine of life," Joseph Stevens Buckminster wrote in a college essay steeped in the language of friendship, sociability, and sensibility: "Conversation with friends is unrestrained. Here we may securely repose our cares, hopes, sorrows, and the secrets of our whole hearts. Here, concealed from the censorious and partial eye of the world, we may learn our faults and be assisted in correcting them. Here, as in the person of our friend, we have a constant stimulus to the practice of virtue and our love of it will imperceptibly increase." In keeping with his belief in the importance of friendship, Buckminster portrayed the archbetrayer Judas as incapable of it: "No one can be so absurd as to imagine that Judas was in any part of his intercourse with our Saviour carried away by his attachment to our Saviour," he declared in an 1808 sermon. A capacity for intense friendship was essential to virtue, and its absence proof of vice.[32]

Women

Even as Smith, Dennie, and the Anthologists participated in all-male conversation circles and enjoyed impassioned male friendships, they lived in a cultural world profoundly reliant on women's intellect, companionship, and work. Throughout the early national era, women and men together circulated texts and manuscripts and met for stimulating conversation. In Philadelphia during George Washington's administrations, Martha Washington held weekly levees in which men and women participated. Outside such formal gatherings, mixed-gender sociability also flourished; Moreau de Saint-Méry wrote in 1796 of the "unlimited liberty" enjoyed by Philadelphia's young women. Elihu Hubbard Smith's diary bears proof of his conviction that women were worthy, perhaps even preferable, intellectual companions. Joseph Dennie's Tuesday Club relied on the wit and writing of women such as Sarah Ewing Hall and Gertrude Gouverneur Ogden Meredith. Arthur Maynard Walter and William Smith Shaw admired Shaw's aunt, Abigail Adams, and the Anthology Society as a whole pub-

32. Shaw to Walter, Feb. 4, 1803, Shaw Papers; Buckminster college book, Essay 1, n.d., Sermon text, Apr. 20, 1808, Joseph Stevens Buckminster Papers, Boston Athenaeum.

lished a series of letters by Mary Moody Emerson and Mary Wilder Van Schalkwyk.[33]

That men and women participated in the same cultural projects does not mean that such participation was uncontroversial or uncomplicated. Indeed, in the highly politicized and highly gendered societies of Britain and America, the manliness of both cultural pursuits and models of citizenship was bound to, and did, become the site of struggle. Federalists and Republicans accused each other of failing to achieve the independent manhood both parties valued. In England, Edmund Burke grounded his conservative vision of sensibility in a manhood both chivalric and tender. (Unmoved, Thomas Paine called Britain's ruling elites a "seraglio of males," thereby attacking Burke on his own ground.) The poet Samuel Taylor Coleridge's struggles to assert the manliness of his sensibility and his identity as an artist led him to transform his ideas about power as the political tumult of the 1790s rolled on: early in the decade, Coleridge proposed a model of "fraternal affection" as the proper base from which to assert legitimate power, and then, as gentle benevolence was increasingly portrayed as effeminate, adopted a more authoritarian masculinity.[34]

33. Fredrika J. Teute, "Roman Matron on the Banks of Tiber Creek: Margaret Bayard Smith and the Politicization of Spheres in the Nation's Capital," and Jan Lewis, "Politics and the Ambivalence of the Private Sphere: Women in Early Washington, D.C.," both in Donald R. Kennon, ed., *A Republic for the Ages: The United States Capitol and the Political Culture of the Early Republic* (Charlottesville, Va., 1999), 95–96, 125–126; Catherine Allgor, *Parlor Politics: In Which the Ladies of Washington Help Build a City and a Government* (Charlottesville, Va., 2000); David S. Shields and Teute, "The Republican Court and the Historiography of a Women's Domain in the Public Sphere" (paper presented at the sixteenth annual meeting of the Society of Historians of the Early American Republic, Boston, July 1994); Kenneth Roberts and Anna M. Roberts, eds. and trans., *Moreau de St. Méry's American Journey* (1793–1798) (Garden City, N.Y., 1947), 285. See also Susan Stabile, "'By a Female Hand': Letters, Belles Lettres, and the Philadelphia Culture of Performance, 1760–1820" (Ph.D. diss., University of Delaware, 1996). Emerson had long carried on an intellectually ambitious project of reading, writing, and corresponding with female friends about subjects ranging from Protestant theology to William Godwin while also participating in mixed-gender gatherings. See Phyllis Cole, *Mary Moody Emerson and the Origins of Transcendentalism: A Family History* (New York, 1998), 95–97. Cole makes clear that, despite the existence of institutions such as the Concord Charitable Library, it was the loose association of "literate friends" (96) that brought a wide range of challenging texts and ideas into women's hands.

34. Tim Fulford, *Romanticism and Masculinity: Gender, Politics, and Poetics in the Writings of Burke, Coleridge, Cobbett, Wordsworth, De Quincey, and Hazlitt* (London,

In the United States, culturally engaged individuals such as Smith, Dennie, and the Anthologists struggled to claim the mantle of manliness for their cultural pursuits, and that struggle colored their efforts to claim a place for letters, for their communities of sensibility, and for themselves. A refusal to devote themselves to either politics or commerce as conventionally under-stood lay at the heart of all of their critiques of America's developing mores and institutions. Yet these refusals threatened to sever the men from some-thing they all valued: culturally sanctioned manhood. To insist that one's productivity and worth lay in intellectual and cultural ambition rather than in commercial or political activity was to lose access to proofs of American manliness. To insist on the responsiveness of one's mind, body, and heart, moreover, was to run the risk of seeming less than independent and so poten-tially less than manly. These problems were compounded by the importance of women to cultural life. The result was often an effort to recast one's cul-tural activities in manly political and commercial garb and a denial that women helped to sustain early national cultural labors and lives. Thus, the same Elihu Smith who sought out women's opinions on texts and ideas also believed that women should not be allowed to participate in the Friendly Club. The same Joseph Dennie who delighted in the wit of female friends projected an exclusively male clubbishness in the *Port Folio* and used gen-dered rhetoric to structure the periodical's social and political critiques. And the same Anthologists who published the writings of Mary Moody Emer-son and Mary Van Schalkwyk banned women from the Boston Athenaeum and asserted the martial manliness of cultural activities. Competing ideals of manliness and the shared high-stakes claim of a civically respectable man-hood inspired each of these quests for a different kind of citizenship.

From the materials of eighteenth-century ideals of sociability and sensi-bility, Smith, Dennie, and the Anthologists strove to create models of fel-lowship, intellectual inquiry, and cultural engagement that would render them happy and useful in America's post-Revolutionary society. To one side lay the threat of alienated irrelevance, to the other, the threat of capitula-tion. The next conversation, the next moment of communion and burst of laughter, the next chance to ask a question, prick a pretension, or form an idiosyncratic judgment beckoned.

1999), 13, 36; Jones, *Radical Sensibility,* 17. Dror Wahrman argues that the responsive, emotional "man of feeling" came under attack in the 1780s in *The Making of the Modern Self: Identity and Culture in Eighteenth-Century England* (New Haven, Conn., 2004), 36–44.

CHAPTER 2

Projects Literary
and Moral

A World of Creation
and Exchange

In the spring of 1798, Elihu Hubbard Smith wrote a letter to John Aikin, the editor of England's *Monthly Magazine*. The *Monthly Magazine* had been founded in 1796 by Joseph Johnson, printer to William Godwin and his circle. Smith hoped Aikin would welcome Americans into its community. Europeans, Smith politely but firmly informed Aikin, had a false vision of the United States, a vision that arose from "the ridiculous fictions of pretended philosophers and historians" printed in European periodicals. Because European periodicals "have an extensive circulation in our country," Smith continued, "the misrepresentations respecting many things relative to the United States are received as truth, by our young people, and being uncontradicted, form a part of their belief, and influence their conduct when arrived to maturity." Smith did not want to declare independence from European print culture; rather, he wanted to gain fuller access to it so that he could tell both Europeans and Americans the true story of American cultural flowering. Doing so was not a matter of appealing to nationalist pride. It was a way of instilling in Americans the confidence they needed to do cultural and intellectual work that America and the world still required.[1]

Smith proposed to Aikin that he would counter fiction with fact and supply the *Monthly Magazine* with accounts of American poets. He also offered to Aikin the continuing services of New York City's Friendly Club, the association of young doctors, lawyers, and businessmen who met in one anothers' homes to discuss literature, science, and political theory. Smith conceded that, in recent years, Americans' obsession with politics had outstripped their interest in collecting and conveying cultural and scientific information. "The contentions of political parties," he wrote to Aikin, "have presented the principal obstacle" to the diffusion of "faithful intelligence." But the success of the Friendly Club suggested that the era of stultifying

1. Elihu Hubbard Smith to John Aikin, Apr. 14, 1798, in James Cronin, ed., *The Diary of Elihu Hubbard Smith (1771–1798)* (Philadelphia, 1973), 438.

partisan contention was coming to an end. In its place was arising a different and more productive model of association. "There exists in this city," Smith wrote of the club, "a small association of men, who are connected by mutual esteem, and habits of unrestricted communication." "They are of different professions and occupations; of various religious or moral opinions; and tho' they coincide in the great outlines of political faith, they estimate very variously many of the political transactions of the men who have, from time to time directed the councils of the nation."[2]

Smith portrayed the club as a Shaftesburian society, placing it in a tradition well known to Aikin, who, along with his father, Dr. John Aikin, and his sister, Anna Barbauld, participated in the sociable circles of English Dissent. But Smith also made clear that Americans were shaping that Anglo-American tradition to meet the needs and circumstances of the new nation. America's literate, dispersed population lacked any single cultural and political metropolis as powerful as London, and that fact had changed the geometry of cultural association. Rather than a self-sustaining circle, the Friendly Club was a node in a network of linked and interdependent groups. Club members, Smith wrote to Aikin, "are in habits of constant communication with the several States, and are well informed of the state of letters, science, and opinions in these States." Smith's plea that Aikin make use of the club emerged from his belief that the duty of the American man of letters lay not only in creating beauty and attaining knowledge but also in sharing them as widely as possible and in inspiring others to crave them.[3]

2. Ibid. During the middle and late 1790s, the club included, along with Smith, the playwright, painter, and shopowner-turned-theater-impresario William Dunlap, the lawyers James Kent and William Johnson, the brothers and shopkeepers William Walton Woolsey and George Muirson Woolsey, the physician Edward Miller, the storekeepers Seth and Horace Johnson, Charles Adams, son of John Adams, and the Columbia professor, physician, and New York state legislator Samuel Latham Mitchill. Bryan Elliot Waterman, in "The Friendly Club of New York City: Industries of Knowledge in the Early Republic" (Ph.D. diss., Boston University, 2000), 15–27, works to identify the members of the Friendly Club based on participants' later recollections as well as Smith's remarks in his diary. Waterman's identifications differ somewhat from those offered by James Cronin in his edited version of Smith's diary, and Smith himself does not provide a comprehensive discussion of official membership throughout the period of his diary, although his notes on attendance and "visitors" offer guidance. See Cronin, ed., *Diary*, Sept. 6, 1795, 45–46.

3. Daniel E. White, "'The Joineriana': Anna Barbauld, the Aikin Family Circle, and the Dissenting Public Sphere," *Eighteenth-Century Studies*, XXXII (1999), 511–533; Smith to Aikin, Apr. 14, 1798, in Cronin, ed., *Diary*, 438.

Smith and his collaborators in the club and the larger network were inspired by the tradition of Shaftesburian sociability to create small societies in which intellectual exertion and trusting emotional communion could flourish. They used print, letter writing, and their own travel to spread books and ideas outside these circles. And, although the Friendly Club was indeed a "knot of men," as Smith described it, the larger network included women who sought, read, and commented on literary, historical, philosophical, and scientific works and who were essential to the "constant communication" that Smith described. Both men and women worked to advance knowledge, improve the reputation of American culture, and contribute to an international community of writers and thinkers.[4]

The Friendly Club and the larger network were drawn from a narrow range of early national society. The men with whom Smith conversed and corresponded were almost all college educated and pursuing careers in ministry, law, medicine, or business; all possessed sufficient financial resources so that they could spend considerable time on cultural pursuits. His well-educated female collaborators divided their time between household responsibilities and the reading, writing, and conversing in which they confidently participated. Despite their similarities, however, participants in this network disagreed on important issues. Some were Federalist and some Republican, some deist and some orthodox Christians. Some believed electoral politics had little to offer the nation; others believed that politics could, if properly paired with intellectual inquiry, create a good society. Given such differences, cultural activities were not genteel adornments to affections already ensured by unity of belief and purpose; instead, these activities knit together educated Americans during years when intense partisan conflict seemed likely to tear them apart.

Smith and his friends and collaborators pondered the largest issues confronting American society, issues such as slavery and the rights of women, in ways unbound to partisan agendas and unconstrained by a belief that the majority view was correct. Despite their many disagreements, they con-

4. Mary Kelley observes that "women readers active after the Revolution began to immerse themselves in secular literature." With women reading not only traditional religious works but also "history, biography, and travel literature" as well as "novels, tales, and sketches," their "selection of reading matter," Kelley argues, "was not sharply gendered." See "Reading Women/Women Reading: The Making of Learned Women in Antebellum America," *Journal of American History*, LXXXIII (1996), 404. See also, Kelley, *Learning to Stand and Speak: Women, Education, and Public Life in America's Republic* (Chapel Hill, N.C., 2006), 21–23.

FIGURE 1. Elihu Hubbard Smith. *By James Sharples. 1797.*
By permission, Collection of The New-York Historical Society

curred that gaining knowledge made one capable of virtue and capable of creating a society in which others might also progress toward virtue. They were influenced by Godwin and fascinated as well by the marquis de Condorcet, whose posthumously published *Sketch for a Historical Picture of the Progress of the Human Mind* (1794) argued that it was possible for an enlightened people to alleviate even the ancient human problem of poverty. Seeking beauty as well as justice, they loved the German author Friedrich von Schiller, whose ideal of the "beautiful soul" posited individuals of perfectly integrated emotions and reason joyfully acting for the good of others and resonated with the ideal of sensibility's "Feast of Reason and the Flow of Soul." They searched accounts of scientific developments for information about how to improve the healthfulness of their often pestilential city. Cultural producers as well as consumers, they wrote fiction and nonfiction exploring the nature of ideal and dreadful communities and relationships. By creating a network of readers, they also influenced printers' decisions about which works to bring to press. Through their many activities, they hoped to create a cadre of enlightened and sensible individuals who would reform a world that could not, through politics alone, reform itself.[5]

Elihu Smith lay at the heart of the network. He spurred others' creative work, served as unpaid copy editor and marketer for printers, and continually embarked on new correspondences and friendships, thereby creating new paths through which texts, ideas, and ambition flowed. But all who participated in the network contributed to its ability to disseminate ideas, make connections between people, and spur cultural production. The lives of three men, James Kent, William Dunlap, and Charles Brockden Brown, and one woman, a daughter of Connecticut named Idea Strong, demonstrate the widely different ways in which individuals used participation in sociable cultural activities to shape their lives and claim a place for themselves in the world.

William Dunlap (1766–1839) placed cultural pursuits at the center of his life. Although he had inherited a store from his father and was in a business partnership with fellow Friendly Club members William and George Woolsey, he believed that being a storekeeper suited neither his talents nor his vision of properly sincere human relationships. "I have been myself a shopkeeper but I never was a thorough bred one," Dunlap wrote after read-

---

5. Quoted from Alexander Pope, *Imitations of Horace: With an Epistle to Dr Arbuthnot and the Epilogue to the Satires,* ed. John Butt (London, 1939), 17 (satire 1, book 2).

ing Godwin's essay on "Professions." "I never forgo the dignity of man. . . . The tone of my voice, my gesture and my attitude were regulated by those of the person who addressed me; to the polite, I was polite, not from an insidious motive, but from genuine sympathy; with the haughty, I was reserved, and to the insolent I was—I fear sometimes insolent—always repelling." Such a view was compatible with Dunlap's understanding of dignified independence but less compatible with success as a shopkeeper, and he sought instead to make a living from the theater. Dunlap had begun writing plays in the late 1780s and over the next ten years wrote works such as *The Father; or, American Shandyism* (1789), a comedy of manners that was produced by the American Company and greeted with critical acclaim; two gothic tragedies, *The Fatal Deception* (1794) and *Fontainville Abbey* (1795); an opera on the subject of William Tell, *The Archers* (1796); and *André: A Tragedy* (1798), which was a blank-verse treatment of the story of a British spy executed during the American Revolution. In 1796, Dunlap purchased a half ownership in the American Company in partnership with the British actor and troupe manager John Hodgkinson, and for the next two years he wrote plays, managed the fractious actors, and built the new Park Street theater—all with the steadfast assistance of Elihu Hubbard Smith and other Friendly Club members and collaborators.[6]

Dunlap believed that theater could improve the moral health of the Re-

6. Dorothy C. Barck, ed., *Diary of William Dunlap (1766–1839): The Memoirs of a Dramatist, Theatrical Manager, Painter, Critic, Novelist, and Historian*, 3 vols. (New York, 1930), Sept. 3, 1797, I, 142. Dunlap noted of Godwin's essay, "It has no novelty, to me, yet its congeniality to my own sentiments makes it delightfull." Joseph J. Ellis argues that the death of Dunlap's father "released his creative energies" and allowed him to move away from the store and toward the theater (*After the Revolution: Profiles of Early American Culture* [New York, 1979], 126). See also Oral Sumner Coad, *William Dunlap: A Study of His Life and Works and of His Place in Contemporary Culture* (1917; rpt. New York, 1962), 35–56; Robert H. Canary, *William Dunlap* (New York, 1970), 19–23. Dunlap attended many theater performances during his stay in London; see William Dunlap, *A History of the American Theatre from Its Origins to 1832*, ed. Tice L. Miller (Urbana, Ill., 2005), x. A forthright letter from Smith to Charles Brockden Brown made clear Smith's belief that Dunlap's professional endeavors relied on the aid of his friends. "Our friend," Smith wrote, "risks the impression of 750 copies [of the opera William Tell]; and depends on your aid, in the disposal in some part of them. It is, indeed, in part, the purpose of this letter, to request of you to let us know how many copies you can circulate among your friends, and obtain immediate payment for; and how many you suppose you could put in a favorable situation for sale, and for the ready collection of the avails, when sold." See Smith to Brown, Mar. 27, 1796, in Cronin, ed., *Diary,* 146.

public. In plays such as *André*, he explored republican citizens' obligations to one another, to authority, and to the demands of sympathy, and he expected other writers to devote themselves to civic improvement. "The poets of every nation," he wrote in a review for the *New-York Magazine*, "have been amongst the foremost to point out improprieties and immoralities, both in nations and in individuals; thus asserting their claim to the honorable title of lovers of justice and teachers of mankind." Dunlap sought to assert his own such claim by writing theater criticism, poetry, and plays that put creative work to the cause of moral education. "Shall we apologize to the reader for leading him into a consideration of the unalienable rights of man, and his duties in society, when he expected only to be amused?" Dunlap wrote in one essay. He quickly answered: "No. We are happy at all times to bring to view those principles on which human happiness depends—and truth needs no apology." Literature, not politics, was the way to effect change. "Whilst the poet," Dunlap wrote, "is asserting the rights of humanity, the legislator is racking his stupid brain, and the pretended oracles of his God, in order to sanctify the highest violation of justice." A playwright such as Thomas Holcroft should be emulated by others so that the theater might become "the school of national morality." Those who thought and expressed themselves only through politics, by contrast, suffered intellectual calcification and promoted discord; in an unfinished novel, "The Anti-Jacobin," Dunlap deplored a Federalist clergyman who found in "the seven letters J,a,c,o,b,i,n, . . . all the signs necessary to indicate, innovator, disorganizer, anarchist, antifederalist, heretic, sceptic, materialist, infidel, deist and Atheist," and he expressed impatience with his friends' own immersion in partisan affairs and animus. On a visit to Boston, Dunlap wearily reported in his diary that, after listening to the complaints of "high federalists" and to his friend Samuel Cooper's relation of "the party conflicts of the Town in which he was the Federal Champion, cutting down French flags and liberty poles at the risqué of his life, fighting mobs etc. etc.," he had come home "and read in Voltaire." Philosophy, not political rhetoric or political pageantry, inspired Dunlap's respect.[7]

7. Barck, ed., *Diary of William Dunlap*, Oct. 2, Nov. 27, 1797, I, 155, 175; William Dunlap, "Theatrical Register for 1796, No. 1," *New-York Magazine; or, Literary Repository*, n.s. (February 1796), 92–93, 95. Dunlap's own poetry had appeared in the *New-York Magazine* as early as 1791 and, in somewhat modified form, appeared in Elihu Hubbard Smith's *American Poems* in 1793. See also Lewis Leary, "Unrecorded Early Verse by William Dunlap," *American Literature*, XXXIX (1967), 87–88. Fred Moramarco analyzes Dunlap's didactic aesthetic in "The Early Drama Criticism of

In Dunlap's view, nationalism was no more useful a sentiment than partisan loyalty. "What shall we say," he demanded in a 1797 *New-York Magazine* essay "Love of Country," "of that moralist. . . . Who says not love this thing because it is worthy of love; but love it because it is your own? Yet such is the doctrine of every man who recommends an unqualified love of country." Dunlap imagined that ever increasing knowledge and ever expanding circles of sympathetic identification would render attachment to a mere nation obsolete: "So has the period come," he wrote enthusiastically, "when the mind of man is expanding to receive the whole light of truth, and enjoy the whole beauty of benevolence; when he is no longer to be confined within circles, when to state anything short of the *whole* truth, is known to aid the cause of falsehood; when to prefer anything but for its superior worth, is acknowledged for injustice." Cultural activities were not refuges; instead, they would transform the world into a giant Shaftesburian fellowship in which love, inquiry, and communication reigned.[8]

James Kent enjoyed many of the same books and conversations that Dunlap did, and he enjoyed Dunlap's companionship as well. But cultural activities, politics, and professional duties played different roles in Kent's life than they did in Dunlap's. Kent often wrote of his longing for a life of quiet, literary retirement, and, when the yellow fever season of 1795 briefly forced him from the city, he happily passed six weeks in "the perusal of history, voyages, and travels." When not forced into such retirement, however, Kent assiduously pursued a legal career and was a committed Federalist. After becoming a lawyer in 1785, he spent eight years in Poughkeepsie, New York. A supporter of the Constitution and of the developing Federalist Party—and a young friend of Alexander Hamilton, whom he met during New York's ratifying convention in 1788—Kent served during his Poughkeepsie years in the New York Assembly. In 1792, he ran unsuccessfully for

William Dunlap," *American Literature*, XL (1968), 9–14, and Lucy Rinehart explores the civic consciousness embedded in *André* in "'Manly Exercises': Post-Revolutionary Performances of Authority in the Theatrical Career of William Dunlap," *Early American Literature*, XXXVI (2001), 273–279; see also Jay Fliegelman, *Prodigals and Pilgrims: The American Revolution against Patriarchal Authority, 1750-1800* (New York, 1982), 220-221. For an analysis of Friendly Club members' impatience with formal politics, see Fredrika J. Teute, "Sensibility in the Forest: Elihu Hubbard Smith's and William Dunlap's Dramatic Visions in the New American Nation" (paper presented at the annual meeting of the American Historical Association, January 2002).

8. William Dunlap, "Remarks on the Love of Country," *New-York Magazine; or, Literary Repository*, n.s. (November 1797), 582.

a seat in the United States Congress, then moved with his wife and young daughter to New York City. There he continued his legal practice, successfully bought and sold land, and was, on the basis of his Federalist credentials and the approval of John Jay, appointed professor of law at Columbia College. Kent served again in the state Assembly in 1796 and 1797, became recorder of New York in 1797, and in 1798 was named a judge of the state supreme court. He also practiced law with his friend Alexander Hamilton. As well as holding public office during these years, Kent joined Noah Webster in writing essays in defense of the Jay Treaty for Webster's newspaper, the *Minerva*.[9]

Kent believed that politics and the law could effect useful change; both, in his view, were "sciences"—systematized ways of understanding and controlling the environment—and both also had the potential properly to mold men's natural sympathies and affections. "The Science of law," Kent wrote, "has expressly for its object the advancement of social happiness and security." "It reaches to every tie which is endearing to the affections." "The Science of Civil Government," he explained in the same lecture, "has been here [in America] stripped of its delusive refinements, and restored to the plain principles of Reason." Kent's optimistic pronouncements calmly melded a Shaftesburian focus on sympathetic ties with a Godwinian belief in the ruthlessly productive power of reason. Kent argued that the United States could be a model society, avoiding "the artificial distinctions, the oppressive establishments, or the wild innovations which at present distinguish the Trans-Atlantic World." Sharing the ideals and intellectual influences of friends such as Dunlap, Kent pursued them and put them to use not only through Shaftesburian fellowship but also through a devotion to career and politics many of his close friends did not share.[10]

A friend of both Dunlap and Kent, Charles Brockden Brown wrote the

9. William Kent, ed., *Memoirs and Letters of James Kent, LL.D.* . . . (Boston, 1898), 79; John Theodore Horton, *James Kent: A Study in Conservatism, 1763-1847* (New York, 1939), 52-122; David W. Raack, "'To Preserve the Best Fruits': The Legal Thought of Chancellor James Kent," *American Journal of Legal History*, XXXIII (1989), 320. Under the pen name Curtius, Webster and Kent wrote papers in defense of the treaty, later published as part of a 1795 volume, *Treaty of Amity, Commerce, and Navigation, between His Brittanic Majesty, and the United States of America, Conditionally Ratified by the Senate of the United States, at Philadelphia, June 24, 1795; to Which Is Annexed, a Copious Appendix* (Philadelphia, 1795).

10. James Kent, *An Introductory Lecture to a Course of Law Lectures, Delivered November 17, 1794* . . . (New York, 1794), 4, 8.

novels for which he is celebrated because of the atmosphere and resources the cultural network provided him. A native of Pennsylvania, Brown studied law but longed to make his living as a writer. He met Elihu Hubbard Smith while the latter was studying medicine in Philadelphia in the early 1790s, and his literary ambitions and confidence were fueled by the atmosphere of learning, order, and inquiry Smith unfailingly created. Visiting Smith in Connecticut in 1793, Brown was enchanted by the culture and conversation that he found among Smith's family and friends. "You have read Eloisa," Brown wrote in a letter to his friend Joseph Bringhurst. "You recollect the situation of St. Preux in Wolmar's family. Such, believe me, my friend, is mine in this." Brown valued not only the intellectual stimulation but also the potential readership Smith's network provided: "I was surprised to find," he wrote to Joseph Bringhurst when he first became aware of Smith's networking on his behalf, "that among [Smith's] friends you and myself were almost as well known as in our native city."[11]

Brown's finances did not allow him to stay in that heady atmosphere, and he returned to Philadelphia. From there, he continued his correspondence with Smith, eventually spending a great deal of time visiting Smith and other Friendly Club members in New York City. The association brought intellectual enrichment: Brown partook of both Godwin and gothic novels in this environment and found in them the influences that would shape his own novels. Smith's friendship also inspired Brown. The young doctor prodded Brown to industry; when he decided that Brown had "been idle" in Philadelphia—"a few pages in his journal . . . are all that he had to shew me," Smith fussed—he proposed Brown's "temporary settlement in New York." Arriving a few weeks later, Brown stayed in the city for months. Smith was never quite satisfied with Brown's efforts: "I wish he would turn his Aloas and Astoias, his Buttiscoes and Carlovingas, to some account," he wryly complained of Brown's tendency toward inventing, naming, and abandoning characters. But Smith loved his friend and deeply respected his creativity, seeing it correctly as a capacity for invention he himself lacked. And Brown, immersed in the atmosphere of inquiry, affection, and orderly striving that Smith created, thrived. He wrote side by side with Smith many

11. Charles Brockden Brown to Joseph Bringhurst, Jr., May 22, [July] 1793, Charles Brockden Brown Papers, Bowdoin College Library. Robert A. Ferguson explores Brown and Smith's relationship in "Yellow Fever and Charles Brockden Brown: The Context of the Emerging Novelist," *EAL,* XIV (1979), 296–297. Crain portrays Smith as less impatiently paternalistic toward Brown in *American Sympathy: Men, Friendship, and Literature in the New Nation* (New Haven, Conn., 2001), 79–85.

a morning, their parallel efforts nurtured by the "hour in conversation" that Smith noted the two friends usually passed. Brown also read to Smith and to other friends from his journal and from his continuing projects: "Brown finished the reading of what he had written on his new romance," Smith wrote one fall morning in 1796; "Finished readg Wieland at S[mith] and J[ohnson]'s," Dunlap wrote in his diary in late July of 1798; "We had some conversation in respect to proposed alterations suggested to B[rown]."[12]

Such concerted attention and criticism was not always easy for Brown to accept; in his letters he sometimes frustrated his friends by intentionally obscuring the details of his life. Brown also questioned the usefulness of the belletristic life to which he was drawn. "It is not a matter of serious concern," he once wrote of the Philadelphia Belles Lettres Society, "but a matter of rational amusement only, that we thus associate together." This combination of engagement and skepticism combined to make these years the most creatively productive of Charles Brockden Brown's life. Brown examined, memorialized, and protested the intense fellowship that provided him with intellectual fodder and brotherly encouragement. His dialogue on women's rights, *Alcuin*, investigates the limits of the willingness and ability of conversation circles to affect the world, and his novel fragment *Carwin the Bioloquist* should be read not only as a commentary on the era's fears of the Bavarian Illuminati but also as an anguished portrayal of the demands for continual communication and total intimacy among Brown's New York City set. In his novels, Brown also addressed the largest public challenges of his era: the socially disintegrating effects of yellow fever, the constrained role of women in American life, and the potentially horrific consequences of religious fanaticism. Smith believed that Brown's writing would open Americans' eyes to the problems the nation faced, and he thought Brown and his friends risked calumny as a result. "What different sentiments it will excite!" Smith wrote of Brown's novel on the fever, *Arthur Mervyn*.

12. Barck, ed., *Diary of William Dunlap*, July 26, 1798, I, 317; Pamela Clemit, *The Godwinian Novel: The Rational Fictions of Godwin, Brockden Brown, Mary Shelley* (New York, 1993); Warner Berthoff, "Brockden Brown: The Politics of the Man of Letters," *Serif*, III, no. 4 (December 1966), 3–11; Colin Jeffrey Morris, "To 'Shut out the World': Political Alienation and the Privatized Self in the Early Life and Works of Charles Brockden Brown, 1776–1794," *Journal of the Early Republic*, XXIV (2004), 635–636. "C. B. Brown was here much of the forenoon," reads one of Smith's many accounts of Brown's visits; "We talked—principally in reference to political morality and happiness of man." See Cronin, ed., *Diary*, Aug. 5, Sept. 31, Dec. 10, 1796 (quotation), 197, 240, 271, 272.

"Storms and tempests hover over our heads, ready to burst, or are gathering in slow and sullen vengeance, to break, and overwhelm us with destruction. But I trust that we shall put forth the conductors of virtue, and turn aside, or disarm the lightnings of superstitious fury." Thrilled rather than daunted by the dangers he believed lay ahead, Smith worked diligently to bring Brown's novels to press and into circulation: Brown's artistry promised to convey the critical sensibility of the fellowship that sustained him to the world outside its doors.[13]

The quest for Shaftesburian fellowship, for a sense of membership in a transatlantic intellectual community, and for a critically engaged citizenship unconfined by partisan piety held broad appeal to educated young Americans. The network Smith nurtured had room—and a need—for Charles Brockden Brown, James Kent, and William Dunlap. One woman who participated put the network's resources to use to find not only intellectual companionship but personal liberation. The young Litchfield, Connecticut, woman Idea Strong was one of Smith's most valued correspondents. Living in Litchfield with an alcoholic father, Idea began as a young woman to sneak from her home into the sociable gatherings of her peers. "For several years she was [her father's] slave," Smith wrote in his diary, "writing, reading, and visiting, almost altogether by stealth." "Her reason at length acquired sufficient energy to enable her to throw off his tyranny, which had now become insupportable. This was about a year ago: when she came to an open determination with him—since which she has enjoyed a considerable share of liberty. She now visits who she pleases—but makes choice of those times when he—thro' intoxication—is too insensible to be conscious of her departure and return."[14]

Smith's account of Idea's troubles had been prompted by the single visit she made to Smith's family when the young man visited Litchfield in November 1795. During his next sojourn in Connecticut, in February 1796, Idea seems to have made an effort to see Smith as much as possible. "Sally Pierce, Idea Strong, and Abby Lewis (of Farmington) spent the noon-tide here," Smith wrote of the day of his arrival, "and Idea the afternoon and

13. Paul Allen, *The Late Charles Brockden Brown*, ed. Robert E. Hemenway and Joseph Katz (Columbia, S.C., 1976), 25; Morris, "Charles Brockden Brown," *JER*, XXIV (2004), 622–623; Dorothy J. Hale, "Profits of Altruism: Caleb Williams and Arthur Mervyn," *Eighteenth-Century Studies*, XXII (1988), 47–48; Ferguson, "Yellow Fever and Charles Brockden Brown," *EAL*, XIV (1979), 293–294; Cronin, ed., *Diary*, Oct. 17, 1795, 74.

14. Cronin, ed., *Diary*, Nov. 10, 1795, 87.

evening." "Idea Strong spent the day here," he noted the next day, and "Idea spent the day with us," the day after that. Having already enfolded herself in Litchfield's local society of writing, visiting, and reading, Idea was working to make herself part of the larger cultural networks to which Smith could connect her once he returned to New York. She succeeded. "I must send her 'The Heiress,'" Smith noted in his diary before leaving Litchfield, and he added, on his return to New York, "I have seen more of Idea Strong—and we have agreed to correspond."[15]

Correspond they did. Smith's letters, transcribed into his diaries, make clear his respect for Idea Strong's intellect and his high hopes for their association. "If we can mutually assist each other, in the acquisition of knowlege and virtue," he wrote on March 29, 1796, "if we can strengthen the dispositions to advance human happiness, which we already possess; if we may be the better enabled to be useful to others; if such will be the consequences of our correspondence, we can not commence it too speedily." Idea shared these intellectual ambitions. She also nurtured a dream both more daring and more pragmatic than Smith's vision of advancing the cause of human happiness. On June 18, 1796, Smith recorded in his diary "some pleasing intelligence." "Idea Strong has fled her father's—where she was cruelly maltreated—and is protected by my father, at whose house she lives, and is supported." Strong's flight was part of a project of intellectual investigation as well as personal liberation; less than three weeks later, Smith received a letter from the young woman in which she proposed examining "The Rights of Human Nature."[16]

Cultural engagement and cultural networks had not granted Idea Strong her escape from a cruel home—it was she who willed her way from her father's house, and it was Smith's father who provided her first place of refuge. Nor did she find an escape from the restrictions of her gender. The careers of ministry, law, and medicine, the paths taken by her male friends, were no more available to Idea after she became a part of the cultural networks than they were before. Yet the conversations and ideas, the letters, friendships, and confidence that participation in cultural exchanges brought her way helped her to save and to claim her life.[17]

15. Ibid., Feb. 22, 23, 27, 1796, 133–134. Smith himself did not notice, or at least did not comment, on Idea's ubiquity.

16. Ibid., Mar. 29, June 18, July 22, 1796, 148, 178, 188.

17. Idea's friend, the aspiring doctor Timothy Pierce (friend of Elihu and brother of Sally) did, however, write out, at Idea's request, "a few simple directions" for treating patients, and he directed her to "find rules for simple cases very plainly laid down in

Smith's assertion to Aikin that his collaborators shared "the great outlines of political faith" might seem unlikely given the vitriolic, highly personal partisan politics of the late 1790s. But his claim accurately reflects the
concord among the educated Republicans and Federalists with whom he
collaborated. Smith, a Federalist, collaborated with the Jeffersonian politician and scientist Samuel Latham Mitchill in founding the *Medical Repository,* and he counted as friends not only two Federalist congressmen from
Connecticut, John Allen and Uriah Tracy, but also the radical Philadelphia
Republican Michael Leib. Smith was not alone in his catholic alliances.
James Kent and his fellow young New Yorker Tunis Wortman could hardly
have differed more in their partisan identifications; Kent was a successful
Federalist politician, and Wortman was the secretary of the Republican
Tammany Society. But they shared conversation, literary pursuits, and a
belief in the need for and possibility of human improvement. Wortman's
*Oration on the Influence of Social Institutions upon Human Morals and Hap-
piness,* delivered before the Tammany Society in May 1796, celebrated "the
progression of the human mind during the close of the present century."
"Unparalleled," the young man wrote, "has been the increase of science,
and the advancement of the arts." In his series of lectures on the law delivered at Columbia College, Kent spoke with similar optimism about the
progress of enlightenment. Federalism for him did not mean a conservative
abhorrence of change; it was the belief that progress must be achieved without violent social disorder. So Kent reveled, as did his friend Wortman, in
the century's advances: "The human mind," he wrote, "which has been so
long degraded by the fetters of feudal and Papal Tyranny, has *begun to free
herself from Bondage.*"[18]

Just as Kent's Federalism was not filiopietistic, neither was Wortman's

---

an old rusty book in the bookcase, called Buchans Family Physician." See Timothy
Pierce to James Pierce, Sept. 10, 1799, printed in Emily Noyes Vanderpoel, *Chronicles
of a Pioneer School from 1792 to 1833; Being the History of Miss Sarah Pierce and Her
Litchfield School,* ed. Elizabeth C. Barney Buel (Cambridge, Mass., 1903), 371.

18. Tunis Wortman, *An Oration on the Influence of Social Institutions upon Human
Morals and Happiness, Delivered before the Tammany Society, at Their Anniversary, on
the Twelfth of May, 1796* (New York, 1796), 3; Kent, *Introductory Lecture,* 4. David W.
Raack argues that Kent's conservatism has been overstated and draws attention to his
interest in modifying English common law to suit American circumstances in "'To
Preserve the Best Fruits,'" *American Journal of Legal History,* XXXIII (1989), 335–
346.

Republicanism resolutely egalitarian. Kent and Wortman were united by the belief that knowledge was liberating human minds and potential and by the conviction that the enlightened and talented should lead. Just as John Adams and Thomas Jefferson would years later find common ground in their belief in a "natural aristocracy" of "virtue and talents," this younger Federalist and Republican pair shared a belief that America and the world should be governed, neither by uninformed masses nor by hidebound elites, but rather by those whose innate capacities suited them to guiding the populace through salutary transformation. Kent's insistence that "those who are favored with nobler and superior parts, with a brighter portion of moral and intellectual accomplishments," should lead finds its mate in Wortman's assertion that "in a well organized society" there should exist "two means of acquiring superior influence and distinction—the possession of exemplary virtue, and the possession of extraordinary talents." Distinctions based on such factors, Wortman added, "will promote a generous emulation without degenerating into jealousy or envy." The Federalist Kent and the Republican Wortman both believed that, in America, the many should and would consent to be guided by the meritorious few.[19]

A shared belief in the need for enlightened leadership and a shared conviction that government alone could not perfect humanity drew participants in this cultural network toward practical work as well as toward intellectual investigations. Men such as Kent, Wortman, and Smith shared a Franklinian sense that sociable practices, inquiry, and information gathering should be put to direct civic use. Aware of sensibility's tendency to curl inward on itself, Smith warned against reveling in one's discomfiture at the world's imperfections: "We must not," he scolded Charles Brockden Brown, "banquet on the pleasures of despair." Dunlap was equally convinced that true virtue required not simply benevolent feelings and rejection of vice but also talent and activity: "There can be no virtue without ability," he wrote in a piece for the *New-York Magazine*. This ethos of muscular idealism inspired Friendly Club members to combine intellectual inquiry with work in local civic organizations: James Kent and William Johnson were trustees of the New-York Society Library; Samuel Latham Mitchill was secretary of the Society for the Promotion of Agriculture, Arts, and Manufactures; Smith tried

19. Kent, *Introductory Lecture*, 5; Wortman, *Oration*, 18, 24; John Adams to Thomas Jefferson, Oct. 28, 1813, in Lester J. Cappon, ed., *The Adams-Jefferson Letters: The Complete Correspondence between Thomas Jefferson and Abigail and John Adams*, 2 vols. (Chapel Hill, N.C., 1959), II, 387–392.

to start a state medical society in Connecticut and volunteered at New-York Hospital; and Smith, Mitchill, and Edward Miller founded the *Medical Repository*. Even the Friendly Club itself, which was a conversation circle, not a civic organization, bears the marks of this urge toward engagement. Club members did not spend evenings writing and reading poetic descriptions of the club and its foibles, as did colonial and English coteries. Nor do they appear to have drawn up a membership list or a constitution. The Friendly Club lacked the self-defining and often self-congratulatory accoutrements of many other American and English Shaftesburian societies for a reason: it was intended to be an association that looked out at the world, not in at itself.[20]

During the late 1790s, New York's Manumission Society became the site of concerted efforts to unite dreams of human perfectibility to the practical labor of effecting change. Smith, Kent, Dunlap—who had freed his own family's enslaved laborers immediately after his father's death—William Johnson, and the Woolseys all participated in the Manumission Society. These young people knew that elected officials would not end slavery in New York. They believed that the practices of their cultural network, specifically the collection and dissemination of information, were better suited to destroying that pernicious institution.[21]

20. Smith to Brown, May 27, 1796, in Cronin, ed., *Diary*, 171; Dunlap, "On Innocence and Generosity," *New-York Magazine; or, Literary Repository*, n.s. (October 1797), 518; Toby Appel, "Disease and Medicine in Connecticut around 1800" (paper presented at the Connecticut Academy of Arts and Sciences, January 1999; revised July 1999). Club memberships are listed in *The American Almanack, New-York Register, and City Directory, for the Twenty-First Year of American Independence . . .* (New York, 1796); *The New-York Directory, and Register, for the Year 1795* (New York, 1795), 296–312.

21. The Manumission Society was founded in 1785 by elite New Yorkers, including Alexander Hamilton, James Duane, and Robert Troup; it established the African Free School one year later. See Robert J. Swan, "John Teasman, African-American Educator and the Emergence of Community in Early Black New York City, 1787–1815," *JER*, XII (1992), 334–335; Shane White, *Somewhat More Independent: The End of Slavery in New York City, 1770–1810* (Athens, Ga., 1991), 81–83. George Muirson Woolsey, the Reverend Samuel Miller, William Dunlap, William Woolsey, William Johnson, and Smith's brother-in-law Thomas Mumford were members when Smith joined; James Kent was proposed for membership the next year, and others of Smith's friends were members of other manumission societies. See Minutes from the Society for the Manumission of Slaves, VI (January 1785–November 1797), New-York Historical Society; and Cronin, "Introduction," in Cronin, ed., *Diary*, 13.

Society members were determined to put reason and spectatorial sympathy to use to end the practice. "Our duty," Smith declared in a 1798 address before the society, "is obvious and simple—to preserve the vivid recollection of the enormities which mark the reign of oppression; of the efforts which have been made to shorten or destroy it; of the motives which should compel us to proceed in this exalted labour: to disseminate the knowledge of them far and wide, to the young as well as to the old, to the enslaved as well as to the free." Dunlap wrote a condemnation of the slave trade presented before Congress and gathered testimony against slavers. Smith and other society members also worked diligently on behalf of the society's African Free School. Such work testified to their belief in the power of education to reform individuals white and black; Smith was delighted to appoint an African American man as head of the school and to record the pupils' progress under the man's direction. Unthinking paternalism lurks near the surface in these reformers. "A subject has suggested itself for my Manumission Oration," Smith wrote in August 1797, "viz. on the best means of civilizing, or making good citizens, of, the Negroes." "I wish also to write an essay on the best means of civilizing the Indian—and on the true obstacles to their civilization." But, although the hierarchy of sensibility was far from egalitarian and assumed the superiority of European American society, it did not assume that all whites were superior to all blacks; members of the Manumission Society instead conceived of a world in which civilization could be achieved by almost everyone, and had been achieved by almost no one.[22]

Despite participants' hours of labor, the Manumission Society proved no more capable of destroying slavery in New York than was republican poli-

22. E[lihu] H[ubbard] Smith, *A Discourse, Delivered April 11, 1798, at the Request of and before the New-York Society for Promoting the Manumission of Slaves, and Protecting Such of Them as Have Been or May Be Liberated* (New York, 1798), 6; Coad, *William Dunlap,* 51. Smith notes that he, often in the company of other Friendly Club members, worked on behalf of the society or the school (see, for example, Cronin, ed., *Diary,* Dec. 3, 4, 1795, Mar. 2, Apr. 1, 7, 20, Aug. 2, 1796, Jan. 4, Feb. 7, 15, 1797, 95, 135, 152, 153, 158, 197, 280, 289, 290). Robert J. Swan identifies John Teasman as an African American appointed principal of the Free School in 1799; Smith's diary suggests the association might have begun earlier (Swan, "John Teasman," *JER*, XII [1993], 331; Cronin, ed., *Diary,* Aug. 4, 1797, 341). Gordon S. Wood discusses the complex nature of early national "equality" in *The Radicalism of the American Revolution* (New York, 1993), 239–243. On the competing ways in which Republicans and Federalists discussed and portrayed equality, see David Waldstreicher, *In the Midst of Perpetual Fetes: The Making of American Nationalism, 1776–1820* (Chapel Hill, N.C., 1997), chaps. 4, 8.

tics. On one level, the society simply encountered the limits of moral suasion, as would pacifist abolitionists of the nineteenth century. But Shaftesburian reform also contained its own, distinctive weaknesses. The same intellectual and cultural framework that helped to draw individuals into the Manumission Society tinged their efforts with self-regarding quiescence. Smith's speech to the 1798 Manumission Society had more to do with C.-F. Volney's *Ruins,* in which the French author deplored temporal and spiritual tyranny as relics of mankind's primitive past, than it did with the plight of individual Africans and African Americans. "The history of man," Smith asserted, "is the history of slavery," and the specific evils of the enslavement of Africans were no more pressing than the problems of clerical and monarchical tyranny. Smith's assertion that Manumission Society members would "disseminate" knowledge of the evils of slavery "to the enslaved as well as the free," moreover, is careless at best: the enslaved themselves certainly did not need to be reminded by earnest society members of the horrors they endured.[23]

Even the belief in the power of education was a doubled-edged sword. It led participants to devote hours to the African Free School, but it also led them to consider ignorance as pernicious as enslavement and thus reduced members' urgency to effect change. Because he considered chattel slavery to be simply one manifestation of the larger problem of human enslavement to ignorance, tradition, and superstition, Smith expressed a calm acceptance that progress toward abolition might well be slow. And, despite his sincere commitment to ending slavery, William Dunlap suggested that education might be a more pressing need for the enslaved than freedom. Immediately liberating those in bondage, he wrote to British author Thomas Holcroft, "without altering those peculiar circumstances with which they are now surrounded: which should give them liberty without knowledge suiting the society into which they have been forced," might "not be an act of justice." Living in freedom, Dunlap imagined that liberty of mind was as important as liberty from bondage. As Adam Smith suggested, sympathy meant imagining oneself in another's place, not imagining oneself as the other. It marked the boundaries between humans even as it constituted their hope of connection.[24]

23. Smith, *Discourse, Delivered April 11, 1798,* 6.
24. William Dunlap to Thomas Holcroft, July 29, 1797, in Barck, ed., *Diary of William Dunlap,* I, 120.

Habits of Constant Communication

The cultural activities and ambitions Elihu Smith described in his 1798 letter to the English editor John Aikin leaped over the bounds of the Friendly Club, the Manumission Society, and all formal associations. The "habits of unrestricted communication" were fostered in innumerable conversations and manuscript exchanges that linked New York City to places including Connecticut, Philadelphia, upstate New York, and Europe. Participants' intense engagement in ideas simply could not be confined by memberships and meeting times. "Drank tea at Kent's," Smith wrote in his diary one non–Friendly Club night, "—and spent the evening at Dunlap's. W. Johnson there—and the Woolsey's. We talked on the politics of the day—and afterward had a lengthy argument on the perfectibility of man—the effect of knowledge—the populousness of the world—etc. etc. in which [Senator Uriah] Tracy and W. W. Woolsey, were opposed to Dunlap, Johnson, and myself. It was near ten when we separated." William Dunlap noted similarly impromptu conversations in his diary. "I had yesterday some agreeable conversation on man, and society, with Saltenstall," Dunlap wrote of a talk with a young man he had met just the day before: "Has not the human race so far progressed towards wisdom, as to have become ashamed of ignorance?"[25]

Because cultural exchange was not confined to club meetings, texts and ideas traveled far and fast. A young doctor named Amasa Dingley, never part of the Friendly Club, eagerly shared with Smith "a letter of [Joel] Barlow's, which he had seen, in which Barlow explicitly condemned Christianity, and disavowed it," as well as a manuscript copy of Barlow's poem "Hasty Pudding." The Swiss John Roulet and the Swedish chemist Henry Gahn, also not members of the club, passed afternoons in reading and conversation with Smith and his friends and introduced them to recent European works including Condorcet's *Sketch for a Historical Picture of the Progress of the Human Mind*.[26]

Women, who were excluded from the Friendly Club, participated avidly in the larger lattice of cultural exchanges in which the club was suspended. The English expatriate Mrs. Lovegrove, like John Roulet and Henry Gahn,

25. Cronin, ed., *Diary*, Nov. 30, 1795, 92; Barck, ed., *Diary of William Dunlap*, June 18, 1797, I, 70–72.

26. Cronin, ed., *Diary*, Sept. 4, Oct. 14, 1795, 43–44, 73. Smith mentions reading the Condorcet volume on, for example, Sept. 8 and 12, 1795, and notes that he is translating the introduction on Sept. 19, 1795 (48, 49, 53, 55, 59).

contributed to the pool of texts and ideas on which Friendly Club members drew, using her transatlantic connections to provide intimate and timely information about English authors and new works. "She read me a most remarkable fine letter, from her [English] friend Mrs. Briggs," Smith wrote of Mrs. Lovegrove one August evening in 1796. "In this letter mention is made of a promising young genius, of Mrs. B's acquaintance, whose name is Coldridge; and who is soon to publish a volume of Poems." Mrs. Lovegrove's information resulted in the introduction of Coleridge's poetry to the members of the Friendly Club. The club excluded the woman, but reveled in the leads she could provide. Other women also helped to move texts and ideas across the distances of the new nation. Sarah ("Sally") Pierce, the founder of Litchfield Academy, one of the early Republic's best-known and most rigorous academies for girls, corresponded with Smith and urged him to send her recent European productions; Pierce's request for Walpole's *Castle of Otranto* brought that work to Smith's attention and so into wider circulation. Susan Bull Tracy, the wife of Senator Uriah Tracy, was a valued intellectual correspondent to Smith. "Your letters were my great encouragers," he wrote to her in 1796, trying to spur her to more frequent correspondence, "not less by those sentiments of virtue and virtuous action, which they contained, than by the ceaseless inquiries after more certain science and more blameless morals to which they incited me."[27]

Reading and conversation sustained marriages and mixed-gender friendships. Margaret Bayard, daughter of the prominent Whig John Bayard, and one otherwise unidentified Miss Templeton were full participants in this vibrant cultural milieu. "Visit to Miss Templeton," Smith wrote in his diary in August 1798, "for the purpose of explaining to her more fully the doctrine of Chemical Affinity—than she had comprehended it from the perusal of Lavoisier." "Red Hume with [my son] John," William Dunlap wrote in his journal one summer day in 1797, "Read Condorcet on the Human mind to my Wife." When Smith brought a copy of Godwin's *Inquirer* to Dunlap, Mrs. Dunlap started reading it before her husband did. James Kent's wife,

27. Ibid., Nov. 18, 1795, Jan. 17 (Smith to Sarah "Sally" Pierce), Aug. 7, 31 (Smith to Susan Tracy), 1796, 90, 121, 199, 210. Smith would read "specimens of Coleridge's poetry, in the [Monthly] Review," in October 1796 and more of his verses in the *Monthly Magazine* in February 1797. He finally came into possession of the volumes themselves in February 1798, when he obtained them from one "Mr. Garnet," and he read them aloud to the Friendly Club the next week (Oct. 12, 1796, Feb. 25, 1797, Feb. 16, 24, 1798, 229, 296, 426, 427). On Sarah Pierce, see Kelley, *Learning to Stand and Speak*, 39.

Elizabeth Bailey Kent, shared her husband's interest in British radicalism: "Spent the intire evening at Kent's, till near ten," Smith wrote one March evening in 1796. "Both he and his wife are charmed with Godwin and Holcroft's Works; and there is some hopes of their conversion." The English expatriate Mrs. Lovegrove interpreted her worth as a mother through the lens of British radicalism: she worried to her friend Smith that her alarm over a child's minor accident demonstrated she had not yet achieved the calm rationality called for by Thomas Holcroft in his novel *Anna St. Ives.* Pondering the relationship of reason to feeling was not an esoteric intellectual exercise; it was the stuff of life.[28]

Married and single women contributed to the cultural network by challenging the thinking of culturally ambitious men. Mrs. William Woolsey questioned William Dunlap's developing deism: "Mrs. Woolsey the younger made some indirect attacks on my *infidelity,* we had much pleasant conversation, Beattie on Truth gave rise to it," Dunlap noted in his diary. Margaretta Mason, daughter of a minister and the future wife of Kentucky Congressman John Brown, was an irresistible and assertive companion. When Smith and Dr. Edward Miller visited her, they found Miss Mason's desirability as a companion did not arise from her deference to male friends' judgment: Smith noted with some irritation after one visit that she preferred Cajetan Tschink's "Victim of Magical Delusion" to Schiller's "Ghost Seer"; the next month, when he and a friend visited and found Miss Mason "surrounded with a world of company," they patiently "waited till they withdrew; and then had an hour of social conversation." Smith's sister Mary, living in upstate New York, was an ambitious, independent-minded reader and correspondent as well. In just one letter written in June 1796, Smith responded to Mary's remarks on William Godwin's *Caleb Williams* and on two gothic romances, Cristiane Naubert's *Herman of Unna* and Ann Radcliffe's *Mysteries of Udolpho;* apologized for his delay in sending her "a brief statement of my sentiments, relative to the true principles of Educa-

28. Cronin, ed., *Diary,* Sept. 9, 1795, Mar. 29, 1796, Sept. 16, 1797 (Smith to Brown), Aug. 2, 1798, 49–50, 147, 364, 459. In 1800, Margaret Bayard Smith would publish an essay and poem, the latter celebrating her friendships with men and women of Smith's network, in Charles Brockden Brown's *Monthly Magazine* (Fredrika J. Teute, "The Loves of the Plants; or, The Cross-Fertilization of Science and Desire at the End of the Eighteenth Century," *Huntington Library Quarterly,* LXIII [2000], 339–340). Dunlap notes in his diary that his wife "reads in the Inquirer"; he himself first mentions reading it on Aug. 31, 1797; see Barck, ed., *Diary of William Dunlap,* July 21, Aug. 27, 31, 1797, I, 110, 138–141.

tion"; and opined on what he deemed "the force of passion and sentiment in Rousseau's *Julie.*" For her part, Mary was, like the young women of New York City, happy to engage in assertive disagreements over the worth and meaning of books. "You have entered into a most elaborate vindication of Mrs. Radcliffe, to which I do not feel myself able to reply," Smith, for once feeling overmatched, wrote to her in 1796.[29]

The Friendly Club, in short, was simply one part of a heterosocial set of interconnected and porous circles. This was not, moreover, a metropolitan cultural world surrounded by provinces. Smith and his friends in New York City were able to obtain certain books more quickly than their friends in more remote areas, but they sometimes learned of those books from just such a friend, and they were not satisfied until they had discussed the book with such friends through correspondence or during visits. In Connecticut towns such as Litchfield and Middletown lived men and women to whom reading and conversation were as important as they were to Smith and his New York friends. Visiting his hometown of Litchfield in November 1795, Smith read Godwin to Susan Bull Tracy, had "various and interesting" conversations with the Connecticut representative John Allen, and discussed with a local doctor and his wife the same subjects that engaged Smith and his friends in New York City: "theatres—the stage—it's effect, etc. etc." as well as "Novels. Medicine and Law" and "Moral Philosophy; to which Politics became attached." William Dunlap found his own Connecticut friends equally caught up in new texts and ideas. "The conversating," Dunlap noted in his journal, "turning on St. Pierre 'Etude etc' we sent to Mr. Russell's for it. . . . Look over reviews. What a sublime specimen of Coleridges poetry! Richd [Alsop] show'd me a literal translation of Ugolino's story from Dante, it is the best I have seen."[30]

Residents of Connecticut and other states corresponded with friends in New York, Philadelphia, and elsewhere, discussed books and ideas, and offered practical assistance in literary and scientific projects. A Connecticut physician and longtime friend of Smith's named Mason Cogswell wrote letters filled with information on subjects medical and literary. Thomas O'Hara Croswell, a son of Litchfield, Connecticut, who had settled as a doctor in the Catskills, in the late 1790s exchanged thoughts about patients and dis-

29. Barck, ed., *Diary of William Dunlap*, Oct. 1, 1797, I, 153-154; Cronin, ed., *Diary*, June 28, Oct. 4 (Smith to Mary Sheldon Mumford), 7, 1796, Oct. 21, Nov. 10, 1797, 182, 226, 228, 383, 391.

30. Cronin, ed., *Diary*, Nov. 9, 12, 1795, 87, 88; Barck, ed., *Diary of William Dunlap*, Nov. 19, 1797, I, 171.

eases with Smith and helped to find subscribers for two of Smith's projects, the *Medical Repository* and his libretto, *Edwin and Angelina*. Samuel Miles Hopkins, a young lawyer, exchanged long letters with Smith on subjects both scientific and literary as Hopkins traveled in the United States and in Europe, and the young Bostonian Josiah Quincy was a useful collaborator as well. A devoted Federalist hopeful of being tapped by party leaders for local or state office, Quincy found in Smith's network a meaningful way of creating intellectual fellowship and of improving the nation through diffusing information. After meeting Smith on a trip to New York, Quincy became a supporter of the *Medical Repository* and, it seems likely, a sponsor of Smith's honorary membership in the Massachusetts Historical Society.[31]

A letter Smith wrote to a Connecticut friend, the poet Richard Alsop, reveals the many purposes served by long-distance cultural exchange. ("There must be *some* labour," Smith dryly declared at the start of it, "or you would have no room for the display of your friendship.") "I have been hitherto unable to fulfill your wishes, in respect to 'Earl Walter's Chace,' and 'Fiesco,'" Smith wrote. "Neither of them have reached us. But in further return for your Translation from the Italian, I shall send you one of mine from the German—which perhaps you may have seen, as it has not been lately done. It will be new, however, to Mrs. Alsop; and possibly to some others of our friends." So began Smith's letter. "I am satisfied with your opinion of Dr. Mitchill's Imitation," he continued, "but you say nothing of the Extract from the *Columbiad*—a thing so precious that I expected a volume of

31. Smith to Samuel Hopkins, Mar. 16, 1798, in Cronin, ed., *Diary*, 430–432. In a 1794 letter to Mason Cogswell, Smith acknowledges that Cogswell had sent him a letter to be carried by Mr. Gahn, although Smith had not yet met Gahn (Nov. 5, 1794, Cogswell Family Papers, Yale University Library, New Haven, Conn.). Smith and Quincy's relationship can be traced through 1797 and 1798: Cronin, ed., *Diary*, May 11, 25, 27, Dec. 20, 1797, June 1, 1798, and Smith to Quincy, Dec. 20, 1797, 317, 318, 319, 405, 407, 417, 447; Barck, ed., *Diary of William Dunlap*, Nov. 27, 1797, I, 174. Quincy had known Joseph Dennie while the two were at Harvard, and, although they had not been close friends, they, too, became partners within the cultural economy. In early 1797, Quincy obtained or renewed a subscription to Dennie's *Farmer's Weekly Museum* (Joseph Nancrede to Joseph Dennie, February 1797, Joseph Dennie Papers, Houghton Library, Harvard College Library, Harvard University, Cambridge, Mass.), and, in the years that followed, Quincy would write a series of scabrous satirical pieces for the *Port Folio*, Dennie's successor to the *Farmer's Weekly Museum*. These activities of Quincy go against the grain of his biographer's declaration that "Josiah Quincy spent his life doing things in a corner of Massachusetts" (Robert A. McCaughey, *Josiah Quincy, 1772–1864: The Last Federalist* [Cambridge, Mass., 1974], vii).

comment on it, in your letter." "Do you wish the author's tragedy? He has published it here." Smith then provided what he deemed "a more serious piece of literary intelligence." "I am about publishing, by subscription, a performance of our friend Charles B. Brown," he informed Alsop. "Do you wish to subscribe?" Even after closing, Smith had one last request. "P.S.," he scrawled. "When you write next, be so kind as to inform me what you gave for a copy of Strutt's Dictionary of Engravers, which you bought, when you lived here, at an Auction, for Mr. Riley. I have purchased it of him, and am to have it at the exact price you gave." Alsop and Smith spurred each other to intellectual exertion in the translations, and those translations made texts available to Americans otherwise unable to read them. The friends' willingness to take subscriptions in one another's projects and to share information about the cost of books also made texts more accessible. Fellowship created knowledge and sent it on.[32]

Because this extended cultural network was not only a source of delight to its participants but also a means of transmitting information and opinion, it attracted the unlikely assistance of two prominent Americans. The famed minister Timothy Dwight was a philosophical opponent but cultural ally throughout Smith's time in New York City. Dwight deplored as "building air castles" the "modern Philosophic opinions, concerning government," that so interested Smith and his friends, and his fears that radical French and British philosophers were corrupting America's men of letters might have been inspired by the Friendly Club itself: the intellectual adventurousness that young men such as Dunlap and Smith believed fulfilled their duties as educated citizens Dwight considered to be a betrayal of those duties. But Dwight was also a believer in Shaftesburian fellowship; he loved manuscript exchange and cultured gatherings, and his poetic praise of the state of Connecticut overflowed with the love of inquiry and information that inspired Smith and his collaborators: "Every mind, inspir'd / With active inquisition, restless wings / Its flight to every flower, and, settling, drinks / Largely the sweets of knowledge," Dwight effused. In 1789, Dwight had even expressed his hope for a "new system of science and politics" in America. "It is to be ardently hoped," he wrote, in words that presaged those of Tunis Wortman and James Kent, "that so much independence of mind will be assumed by us, as to induce us to shake off these rusty shackles, examine things on the plane of nature and evidence, and laugh at the grey-bearded decisions of doting authority." A shared belief in mankind's potential for reform and

32. Smith to Richard Alsop, Dec. 18, 1797, in Cronin, ed., *Diary*, 406.

in the need for the educated to lead society toward virtue combined with affection for his former student and family ties—Dwight's sister had married Friendly Club member William Woolsey—overmatched Dwight's worries about the potential radicalism of Smith's cultural network and turned him into a collaborator. Dwight gave Smith an original poem to include in his 1793 anthology, *American Poems,* and allowed the young man to reprint eight others; his participation likely elevated the marketability of the volume. Dwight also expressed interest in Smith's plans for a second volume and helped the young man find subscribers for his libretto, *Edwin and Angelina.*[33]

Whereas Dwight and Smith were drawn together by sincerely if imperfectly shared visions of the spread of true knowledge, a different son of

33. Timothy Dwight, *Greenfield Hill: A Poem in Seven Parts . . .* (New York, 1794), 17, 170 (Dwight's footnote to line 225); Dwight, *The Triumph of Infidelity* (Hartford, Conn., 1788); Dwight, "The Nature and Danger of Infidel Philosophy; Preached to the Candidates for the Baccalaureate in 1797," in Dwight, *Sermons,* 2 vols. (New Haven, Conn., 1828), I, 310–342; Theodore Dwight, Jr., ed., *President Dwight's Decisions of Questions Discussed by the Senior Class in Yale College, in 1813 and 1814; from Stenographic Notes* (New York, 1833), 331–332. Dwight's belief in the explanatory and salutary power of science corresponded with that of members of the Friendly Club, continuing the compatibility between "natural religion," Lockean epistemology, and Newtonian science that had characterized the eighteenth century. For discussions of this compatibility, see A. Owen Aldridge, "Natural Religion and Deism in America before Ethan Allen and Thomas Paine," *WMQ,* 3d Ser., LIV (1997), 835–837; John C. Greene, *American Science in the Age of Jefferson* (Ames, Iowa, 1984), 16–19. Samuel Miller, Presbyterian minister and brother of *Medical Repository* coeditor Edward Miller, celebrated science in his *Brief Retrospect of the Eighteenth Century . . .* (New York, 1803), reconciling it with his belief in the truth of the Bible. See Timothy Dwight, "Tryal of Faith," "Address to the Convention," "Columbia," "Seasons Moralized," "Hymn," "Song," "The Critics," "Letter to Col. Humphries," in Elihu Hubbard Smith, ed., *American Poems* (1793), facs., ed. William K. Bottorff (Gainesville, Fla., 1966), 33–84. Smith reported Dwight's continued interest in Smith's *American Poems* in a letter to Cogswell, Jan. 27, 1794, Cogswell Family Papers, and he sent a letter requesting that Dwight circulate subscription papers for *Edwin and Angelina* on Feb. 13, 1797 (Cronin, ed., *Diary,* 290). Christopher Grasso explores Timothy Dwight's views of the proper role of the minister and man of letters in *A Speaking Aristocracy: Transforming Public Discourse in Eighteenth-Century Connecticut* (Chapel Hill, N.C., 1999), chap. 7. Colin Wells discusses Dwight's mistrust of what Wells deems "the optimistic vision of Thomas Paine, William Godwin, and Condorcet of a future in which the evils of human society would be eradicated and an earthly utopia of reason and virtue created" in *The Devil and Doctor Dwight: Satire and Theology in the Early American Republic* (Chapel Hill, N.C., 2002), 17–21 (quotation on 18).

Connecticut, the Federalist senator Uriah Tracy, cooperated with Smith so that each could pursue goals of little interest to the other. Tracy disagreed, as did Dwight, with the views of Smith and his collaborators and by the late 1790s even intervened to keep from his wife, Susan Bull Tracy, some of the radical British literature Smith wished her to read. Nonetheless, Senator Tracy and Smith had a continuing and mutually beneficial relationship: Tracy used Smith to pursue his desire to collect political information, and Smith used Tracy to pursue his desire to disseminate cultural information.

Tracy, Smith's diary reveals, habitually relied on Smith for news of the political climate in New York City. Smith's letters to the senator reveal that the senator tasked him with turning his habits of conversation and fellowship to the collection of public opinion. After passing along what information he had gleaned, Smith asked the senator's assistance in finding subscribers for cultural projects. "The importance of this [state legislature] election, as it respects the Federal Government," Smith wrote to Tracy in April 1796, "has given an extraordinary impulse to both parties—especially to the Anti-federal." "So much for politics," he concluded abruptly, after two paragraphs of such discussion. "Our friend Dunlap has written an Opera, on the story of William Tell. . . . I trust your recommendations will promote the sale." A few weeks later, Smith informed the senator that "the feelings of our citizens have undergone a rapid and pleasing change within the last few days" owing to the ratification of the Jay Treaty, then directed the senator to find copies of Dunlap's opera for sale at the printer Mathew Carey's shop. Tracy was well placed to find subscribers, perhaps ones whose names might themselves attract other subscribers, for the kinds of texts Smith thought would effect change. Tracy, for his part, must have recognized that Smith offered access to the opinions of New Yorkers who were likely to talk, correspond, and so shape others' opinions. Tracy and Smith had no interest in converting the other to his views; instead, each used the other to pursue his own model of influential citizenship.[34]

Smith and his collaborators conceived of that citizenship in broad terms—they were citizens not only of the nation but also of the larger republic of letters. The idea of *translatio studii*, or the gradual movement of learning from east to west, had informed educated Americans' thinking

34. "On general politics, or rather on those [of] our Country at large," Smith wrote the senator when he felt he had been remiss in the task, "I have had opportunity of talking but little, of late; and, consequently, of collecting but few opinions." See Smith to Tracy, Dec. 24, 1795, Apr. 10, May 3, 1796, in Cronin, ed., *Diary*, 112, 155, 162.

since the seventeenth century and formed another point of agreement between Timothy Dwight and the young people whose ideas he mistrusted
but whose ambitions he shared. By the 1790s, cultural strivers such as Elihu
Smith believed they had something to offer to Europe as well as much to
learn from it. Mason Cogswell arranged to send the poet William Cowper a
copy of Smith's anthology of American poetry. Smith wrote to the English
scientist Erasmus Darwin and enclosed not only the American edition of
Darwin's *Botanic Garden*, which Smith had overseen, but also a copy of his
own edited volume, *American Poems*. By writing a preface to Darwin's volume, moreover, Smith assertively joined the company of Cowper, William
Hayley, and Richard Polwhele, whose verse was included in the London
edition of the text. William Dunlap determined to put himself and friends in
direct contact with none other than William Godwin and Thomas Holcroft.
"Dunlap came in, and agreeably suprized me, by shewing me letters, which
he had recd. from Holcroft and Godwin—in reply to his," Smith wrote in
his diary in March 1796.[35]

Dunlap demonstrated confidence in the intellectual and logistical powers
of his cultural network by writing to two such prominent men of letters.
Holcroft's initial response showed that the author understood and approved
of the sociable and civic impulse that had inspired Dunlap's bold missive:
"The ardour, with which you desire the intercourse of men whose principles
you approve," Holcroft wrote to the young American, "demonstrates that
your own principles are not the buried talent; but are put into that activity
without which they would be of little worth." As the correspondence continued, however, Dunlap realized that his vision of the man of letters differed from that of the English author he so admired. When Dunlap tried to
weave Holcroft into the American network of unpaid manuscript and text

35. On *translatio studii*, see Lewis P. Simpson, ed., *The Federalist Literary Mind:
Selections from the "Monthly Anthology" and "Boston Review," 1803-1811, Including
Documents relating to the Boston Athenaeum* (Baton Rouge, La., 1962), 105-108;
Cronin, "Introduction," in Cronin, ed., *Diary*, 15. Whether Cowper received the letter
is unclear; Cronin charmingly muses that Cowper might have passed his last, deranged
days "gloomily leafing the pages of a minor Connecticut Wit." See Smith to Erasmus
Darwin, Aug. 10, 1798, in Cronin, ed., *Diary*, 461; Teute, "Loves of the Plants,"
HLQ, LXIII (2000), 331. "They are both fine letters—especially Godwin's," writes
Smith. "Johnson came in—and the Woolseys—to see the new Satire, in the Connecticut Courant, on certain members of Congress: they all read the letters, and with pleasure." "Johnson's night [to host the Friendly Club]," Smith continued; "Kent read the
above-mentioned letters, and those of D. which gave rise to them—with great marks
of satisfaction" (Cronin, ed., *Diary*, Mar. 25, 1796, 143).

exchange by sending him some of Dunlap's writing to critique, Holcroft refused, claiming he had no time for such activities. Dunlap's confidence held. Rather than feeling embarrassed, Dunlap wrote back with some asperity that as an American he had not realized there could be "a man whose time is so unremittingly employ'd in literary pursuits as that the reading a Tragedy, or attending to a request for a pamphlet, should be serious interruptions." His sarcasm is unmistakable: Dunlap disapproved of anyone who devoted himself to his individual muse at the expense of the cultural community. The cultural network he, Smith, Kent, and their many collaborators loved arose from the collaborative efforts of men and women who believed that the labor of recommending texts, critiquing others' writing, and circulating information made good friendships, good people, and a good world. "Tho' 'the progress of knowledge is gradual,'" Smith wrote to his friend Theodore Dwight, "yet knowledge does progress."[36]

Print

Smith and his collaborators formed a geographically extensive confederation whose exchanges of books, manuscripts, letters, and ideas connected city dweller to townsman, Republican to Federalist, and man to woman. Conversation, correspondence, and manuscript exchange created this confederation. So, too, did print and the market.

Neither the interstate cultural network that Smith and his friends pieced together nor the intimate evenings of conversation they loved could have existed without print technology. Print made it possible for them to read the English, French, and German authors they admired. Periodical editors fueled the fire of cultural ambition by soliciting and printing the works of their readers; the accounts of Connecticut Wits that Smith sent to John Aikin were published in the *Monthly Magazine,* and Smith, Dunlap, and Brown all wrote for American periodicals and newspapers. Authoring a book meant that one's ideas could pass through even more time and space

36. Holcroft to Dunlap, Mar. 25, 1796, William Godwin to Dunlap, n.d., both in Dreer Collection of English Poets, Historical Society of Pennsylvania, Philadelphia; Dunlap to Holcroft, July 29, 1797, in Barck, ed., *Diary of William Dunlap,* 118; Smith to Dwight, Nov. 22, 1796, in Cronin, ed., *Diary,* 263. Smith places the first phrase in quotation marks twice in this letter. I have been unable to identify the source, but Smith might simply have been repeating an oft-expressed eighteenth-century sentiment. Adrian Johns describes the transformative role of print in *The Nature of the Book: Print and Knowledge in the Making* (Chicago, 1998), 444–542.

than those in a newspaper or periodical. "Performances . . . falling from the pens of persons not intent on literary fame," Smith wrote in his preface to the anthology of American poems he edited in 1793, "or intent on reputation different from poetical reputation; or whose names have not yet been dignified by national applause notwithstanding their desert, are constantly liable to be forgotten and lost." "And the publishers have observed it to be a matter of much regret, among persons of reading and taste, that the frail security of an obscure newspaper, was the only one they had for some of the handsomest specimens of American Poetry. To afford a stronger, and more durable security, is one of the objects of this Publication."[37]

Physical robustness was not all a book had to offer. A book's higher price might result in fewer readers than newspapers or magazines had, but they would be of the right kind: "Many persons, acting with a proper regard to the worth of their own writings," Smith explained, "would readily give up that advantage, which newspapers bestow, of having them known to every body; if they could by means of a Work like the present one, secure them a certain conveyance to the attention of the scientific and refined." Books would find their way to people such as those who participated in Smith's cultural network and would spur writing as well as reading. Books such as Godwin's *Inquiry* and Volney's *Ruins* suggested that the destiny of the human race was to progress toward enlightenment. Since the efforts of all thinking and reflecting individuals were essential if that destiny was to be fulfilled, readers were to write and to publish as well as to read. Smith was determined that the works he brought to press should so function. Ameri-

---

37. Smith, "Preface," *American Poems*, ed. Bottorff, iii, iv. Smith's contributions to the *Monthly Magazine* were all signed "H." "Account of Dr. Timothy Dwight" was dated May 1798 and published in the August 1798 issue (1); "Account of Mr. Joel Barlow, an American Poet," was dated August 1798 and published in the October 1798 issue (250–251); "Account of Dr. Hopkins, an American Poet," was dated September 1798 and appeared in the November 1798 issue (343–344). That selection also includes discussion of "the Anarchiad," and the review continued the discussion, as a separate article, dated October 1798 (erroneously, since this date was after Smith's death) and published in December 1798 (418). Smith's biographies were reprinted in Joseph Dennie's *Farmer's Museum; or, Lay Preacher's Gazette*, Apr. 1, 8, 15, Sept. 2, 23, 1799. Brown's contributions to periodicals included "The Zephyrs, an Idyl (Translated from the German of Gesner, by W. Dunlap)," *New-York Magazine; or, Literary Repository*, VI (December 1795), 760; "First Idyl of Gesner (Translated from the German by Wm. Dunlap) Daphne-Chloe," ibid., n.s., I (January 1796), 49; "On Innocence and Generosity," ibid., n.s., II (October 1797), 518; "Remarks on the Love of Country," ibid., n.s., II (November 1797), 582.

cans, Smith noted in his preface, would be emboldened to write if they had the hope of finding their poetry displayed with that of authors such as those in his *American Poems* anthology. Smith's confidence that American authors would seek publication is the reason the stand-alone *American Poems* bears the optimistic label "Volume I."[38]

That a text was printed meant that it reached a larger audience than a manuscript could have. It did not mean that the text was in a completed and unalterable state qualitatively different from a manuscript shared among friends. On the contrary, these readers treated all texts as raw material from which to make new texts. William Coxe's *Russian Discoveries* made an appearance at the Friendly Club on September 24, 1796: "W[illiam]. W[oosley]. read us the Conquest of Siberia, from Coxe's 'Russian Discoveries,'" Smith noted in his diary that evening. One month after that Friendly Club meeting, Charles Brockden Brown appeared at Smith's home and, Smith wrote, "read me some notes towards his *great* plan, drawn from reading Coxe's 'Russian Discoveries.'" Smith, for his part, mused on the possibility of turning one of the tales from Helen Maria Williams's *Letters from France*—the story "of an old gentleman, in the neighborhood of Vaucluse, his niece and son—ruined by the horrible blood-hounds of Robespierre"—into "a good drama" in which he could substitute for the terror of the French Revolution the progress toward enlightenment he believed possible: rather than being "ruined" as was the man in Williams's account, Smith's protagonist escapes death, defeats the "cut-throats," and "proclaims the triumph of Humanity." Smith also wrote a libretto, *Edwin and Angelina*, in which he crossed Schiller's *Robbers*, a story of banditry in the forest, with a pastoral ballad by Oliver Goldsmith. Schiller's tale was a dark one ending in death, but in Smith's libretto the corrupt aristocrat who serves as the story's villain abandons vice and feudalism, and the banditti give up their alienation and their marauding. Offering plots of land to the bandits, the former villain exclaims, "O! we will form / A little world of love; all wrongs forgot." "Twas man's oppression made me what I am," one bandit responds; "Let it be due to man that I become such as I ought to be." In one text, Smith not only drew on Goldsmith and Schiller but also made

38. "It was likewise the wish of the Publishers," Smith wrote, "to excite the attention of those possessed of talents and leisure, to similar pursuits; by holding out to them a Work where, united with the like performances of the most celebrated among their Countrymen, their Poems may be equally secure of preservation and notice." See Smith, ed., *American Poems*, ed. Bottorff, iii–v.

Shaftesburian sympathy warm a soon-to-be-Lockean landscape of yeoman farmers.[39]

A Lockean belief in property rights was essential not just to the ending of Smith's opera but also to this network's theory and practice of cultural production. They continued traditional patterns of conversation, borrowing, and lending, treated printed texts much as they would manuscripts or conversations, and considered artistic expression a civic duty, not a personal indulgence. But Smith and his collaborators assertively believed that ideas were individual property protected by law. Smith registered his libretto's copyright with the secretary of state and along with two other Friendly Club members, James Kent and William Johnson, played a role in one of the nation's first copyright cases.[40]

The case arose when an Englishman named William Winterbotham had included in his history of America vast stretches of Jedediah Morse's *American Geography*. Morse wrote to attorneys Alexander Hamilton and James Kent in January 1796, wanting to know what his rights were under the Copyright Act of 1790. Hamilton was too busy to pursue the case, but Kent and Noah Webster attempted to press matters along. In April 1797, Kent succeeded in having Smith and his roommate, the lawyer and Friendly Club member William Johnson, appointed to compare Morse's and Winterbotham's books. The two not only concluded that Winterbotham had stolen "more than three hundred pages of the last mentioned Book" but also went on to state what the dangers would be of such unauthorized use. Their argument adopted that of the 1790 act itself, which was titled A Bill to Promote the Progress of Science and Useful Arts. Were Winterbotham's printer, New York bookseller John Reid, not found to have violated the Copyright Act of 1790, the report concluded, "there is no industrious author, who might not lose the fruits of his Labor, by the easy contrivance of an indolent Compiler." "If the uniting of separate original works, or large portions of them

39. Cronin, ed., *Diary*, Aug. 6, Sept. 24, Oct. 27, 1796, 197, 222, 238; William Coxe, *Account of the Russian Discoveries between Asia and America; to Which Are Added, the Conquest of Siberia, and the History of the Transactions and Commerce between Russia and China* . . . (London, 1780); Friedrich von Schiller, *Die Räuber* (The robbers) (1781) (an American edition was printed in New York by Samuel Campbell in 1793); Smith, *Edwin and Angelina; or, The Banditti* (New York, 1797), 69. Goldsmith's poem, "Edwin and Angelina," was first publicly published in 1766 in *The Vicar of Wakefield*; it had been "printed privately for the amusement of the Countess of Northumberland" the year before.

40. Cronin, ed., *Diary*, May 21, 1797, 318.

together with a few additions, and publishing the whole under a new title, should not be deemed an infringement of the Copyrights of the respective authors, the act would afford no Encouragement to Learning, because it would not secure to the learned, the effects and produce of their industry."[41]

The cultural world of Smith, Kent, and Johnson had roots in belles lettres and in a quest for sociability and sensibility. But it was also a Lockean world in which individuals and society benefited when laborers were entitled to the fruits of their toil. Friendly Club members and their collaborators contributed to a community organized around exchange and communication rather than profit, but they were determined to ensure that personal creativity and property rights were respected. Being paid meant that authors could continue to devote time to cultural labors without risking penury and a loss of independence. That was good for authors and for the cause of improvement. These inveterate borrowers and lenders of texts even asked payment of each other, when doing so seemed necessary for the continuation of the work. "I recd from [Elihu Smith] No. 1 Vol: 1 of the Medical Repository," William Dunlap wrote in his diary in the summer of 1797, "and paid as the proposals require." To serve the public good, writing sometimes had to be a good.[42]

41. Writing to his client to explain the plan, James Kent described Smith and Johnson as "two Gentlemen [who] lodge together and are very upright, conscientious and literary men" (Kent to Jedidiah Morse, Apr. 17, 1797, Morse Family Papers, Yale University Library). For a discussion of the case, see John D. Gordan III, "Morse v. Reid: The First Reported Federal Copyright Case," *Law and History Review*, XI (1993), 23–27, 30. The 1710 English Statute of Anne articulated a similar purpose of copyrighting, and Connecticut's 1783 copyright legislation, which was the first in the nation, stated that the security of receiving profits from the sale of literary texts "may encourage Men of Learning and Genius to publish their Writings; which may do Honor to their Country, and Service to Mankind" (quoted in Bruce Bugbee, *Genesis of American Patent and Copyright Law* [Washington, D.C., 1967], 108). Meredith L. McGill argues that American law "rejects both common-law copyright and the Lockean argument that undergirds it," but her exploration focuses on the 1834 case *Wheaton v Peters* and later nineteenth-century developments ("The Matter of the Text: Commerce, Print Culture, and the Authority of the State in American Copyright Law," *American Literary History*, IX [1997], 21–59 [quotation on 21]).

42. Barck, ed., *Diary of William Dunlap*, Aug. 8, 1797, 133. Christopher Grasso argues, "Traditional, republican, and liberal constructions of public writing—along with a conception of literary practice drawn from the sociable community of polite letters—should be considered less as successive stages or distinct epochs than as over-

Print and the market dramatically expanded the reach of sociability. Sociable practices, in turn, created valuable markets that professionals attempting to negotiate the early national transition from printing to publishing could exploit. During the colonial and Revolutionary periods, printers were usually craftsmen who also sold books from their shops. They had customarily been so unwilling to assume the risk of book and pamphlet publication that they charged for the paper or demanded that authors provide it themselves, passing along all costs other than labor and overhead to the customer who wanted the work done. To print a work meant simply "setting type and pulling the press." Between 1790 and 1840, however, printers in cities such as Philadelphia, Boston, New York, Charleston, and Baltimore became "entrepreneurs of the book trade"—no longer craftsmen who simply produced the printed sheets, but instead merchants who invested in authors and texts and assumed the risk of book publication. They then needed to piece together credit and distribution networks to finance and distribute works. The risks of failure—failure to recoup money, failure to find readers, failure to sustain useful relationships—were high, but the new system also held out the hope of greater profits.[43]

The relationships Smith developed with printers demonstrate that the work of unpaid "marketers" facilitated the shift from printer to publisher in the early Republic. Accounts of English and American book circulation in this era have focused on professional printers and paid itinerant sellers when accounting for the spread of texts, but the subscription gathering and market-oriented cooperation with booksellers that Smith recorded in his voluminous diaries reveals a new agent in this critical historical process. Labors of love and intellectual ambition anticipated those of the paid agents that printer-publishers would use to establish national markets.[44]

---

lapping and even concurrent possibilities" (*A Speaking Aristocracy,* 323–324). Cathy N. Davidson suggests that authors in the early Republic "vacillated between the older aristocratic notion of the gentleman author and the republican notion of the novelist as a professional wage earner" (*Revolution and the Word: The Rise of the Novel in America* [New York, 1986], 34).

43. Rosalind Remer, *Printers and Men of Capital: Philadelphia Book Publishers in the New Republic* (Philadelphia, 1996), 1–4.

44. James Gilreath, "American Book Distribution," American Antiquarian Society, *Proceedings,* XCV (1985), 501–583; William J. Gilmore, *Reading Becomes a Necessity of Life: Material and Cultural Life in Rural New England, 1780–1835* (Knoxville, Tenn., 1989), chap. 5; Remer, *Printers and Men of Capital,* 18–19, 46–48, 125–148. Michael Everton describes animosity and mistrust, rather than cooperation, between

During the 1790s, Elihu Hubbard Smith solicited subscriptions from his network when he wished to persuade printers to bring his own writing and that of friends such as Charles Brockden Brown to press. Smith nurtured long-term relationships with printers, providing them with information about what he and his friends would like to read. He offered printers ad hoc interstate distribution and marketing networks as well as pre-publication market research. In 1797, Smith and his friends persuaded a printer to assume the risk of importing books, most likely by assuring him that they themselves would purchase and publicize the works. And as early as 1791, Smith began to try to persuade printers to print works on the understanding that he would help to sell them. By 1793, he had established what would be a long association with the Connecticut printer Thomas Collier. Collier, along with his colleague David Buel, printed the *American Poems* anthology that Smith edited and advanced Smith funds necessary to the printing; Smith then found purchasers by enlisting the aid of friends to gather subscription money.[45]

Collier was evidently pleased with his association with Smith, because he continued it throughout the decade. By 1795, when Collier wished to act as American publisher for Schiller's gothic novel fragment, the *Ghost-Seer*, he asked Smith for help in obtaining a copy. The request is suggestive: if Collier did not have a copy of the text, it seems likely he had decided to publish it because Smith had told him that Schiller's works would sell. Smith did not disappoint Collier. From his friend Dunlap, he obtained a copy of the book, which was an unfinished exploration of the supernatural. Avocation

------

authors and printers in "'The Would-Be-Author and the Real Bookseller': Thomas Paine and Eighteenth-Century Printing Ethics," *EAL*, XL (2005), 90–92.

45. Smith to Cogswell, June 21, July 6, Oct. 10, 1793, Cogswell Family Papers. Smith dejectedly reported the result to his cousin in Connecticut: "We have been attempting, for some time, to force our booksellers into the practice of importing new books," he wrote, "when, at last, we had persuaded one of them to enter into the measure, with some spirit, the French have captured the ship" (Smith to Elnathan Smith, Jr., Jan. 14, 1798, in Cronin, ed., *Diary*, 419). When Collier declined to print texts, Smith directed Cogswell to enlist the help of other printers: "Go to Babcock with the 'Third' [one of the texts] and get him to print Six Hundred Copies for which you may promise him the pay—which I will make as soon as I return. When they are printed—let one hundred be sent under cover to Mr. Isaac Beers at New Haven, with this writing, 'Sir, I take liberty of sending you for your own disposal and profit the inclosed Poems.' . . . Let Babcock keep another 100, and sell—which if he pleases he may place in discharge of my account—but if he can not sell—let him give them away" (Smith to Cogswell, Jan. 26, 1791, Cogswell Family Papers).

and vocation were united: borrowing served the interest of the printer who wished to sell and, had Collier brought the text to press, it would have been available not just for purchase but also for further borrowing.[46]

Collier, as it turns out, did not bring the *Ghost-Seer* to press, but another printing house, one even more closely associated with Elihu Smith, did, T. and J. Swords of New York City. The relationship between T. and J. Swords and Elihu Hubbard Smith, even more than that between Smith and Collier, reveals the powerful symbiosis between those who used texts to make a world and those who used texts to make a living. The Swordses sold books and magazines, and it was at their store that Smith found John Aikin's *Monthly Magazine* as well as other valued periodicals. The Swordses also printed works, and, during Smith's years in New York, he developed with them the kind of relationship that Godwin's more renowned coterie enjoyed with the printer Joseph Johnson.[47] The Swordses printed or published a long list of publications linked to Smith's cultural network: Smith's libretto, *Edwin and Angelina*; his 1798 *Discourse* before the Manumission Society; the *Medical Repository*, which Smith, Samuel Latham Mitchill, and Edward Miller edited; the first American edition of Erasmus Darwin's *Botanic Garden*, which Smith championed and edited and for which he wrote a poetic preface; two of Charles Brockden Brown's works, *Alcuin* and *Wieland*; Brown's 1799–1800 periodical, the *Monthly Magazine, and American Review*; three of Dunlap's plays; Samuel Miller's 1803 *Brief Retrospect of the Eighteenth Century*; and the *New-York Magazine; or, Literary Repository*, a magazine dear to Friendly Club members because it published Godwin, Mary Wollstonecraft, and some of the members' own writing.[48]

46. Cronin, ed., *Diary*, Nov. 28, 1795, Jan. 21, Mar. 28, 1796, 92, 125, 134.

47. Friedrich von Schiller, *The Ghost-Seer; or, Apparitionist . . . from the German of Schiller* (New York, 1796). On Feb. 20, 1797, for example, Smith read numbers of the *Monthly Review* and the *Monthly Magazine* at the Swordses' shop (Cronin, ed., *Diary*, 294). See Leslie F. Chard II, "Joseph Johnson: Father of the Book Trade," *Bulletin of the New York Public Library*, LXXIX (1975), 65–66; Anne Janowitz, "Amiable and Radical Sociability: Anna Barbauld's 'Free Familiar Conversation,'" in Gillian Russell and Clara Tuite, eds., *Romantic Sociability: Social Networks and Literary Culture in Britain, 1770–1840* (New York, 2002), 70–71.

48. [Erasmus Darwin], *The Botanic Garden: A Poem, in Two Parts . . . with Philosophical Notes; the First American Edition* (New York, 1798); Charles Brockden Brown, *Alcuin: A Dialogue* (New York, 1798); Brown, *Wieland; or, The Transformation: An American Tale* (New York, 1798); William Dunlap, *The Archers; or, Mountaineers of Switzerland . . .* (New York, 1796); Dunlap, *Tell Truth and Shame the Devil: A Comedy, in Two Acts, as Performed by the Old American Company* (New York, 1797); Dunlap,

The relationship with Smith's cultural network allowed the Swordses' shop to move cautiously toward accepting the risks associated with publishing. Although they were publishers of the *Medical Repository*, they were only printers for several works by Brown and Dunlap and were listed on the title page of other Dunlap works just as a place at which the text could be purchased. In the case of Smith's libretto, *Edwin and Angelina,* the Swordses appear to have wanted to be more than printers but less than publishers. They began producing copies of *Edwin and Angelina* before Smith had filled any of the subscription papers; they were initially willing to assume the risk of publication. But, after Smith returned the first complete set of proofs to the printers and issued unspecified "directions," he received news that was, as he put it, "quite inconvenient, as well as unexpected": the Swordses wished Smith "to advance 55 dols. for the purchase of paper, when I have not five dollars in the world, of my own." Smith had likely asked the Swordses to print more copies than they believed he could sell. This awkward moment reveals the nature of the underlying relationship. T. and J. Swords knew that Smith would not only copyedit his own and his friends' work without charge but would also piece together, from across the eastern United States, a subscription list for his and his friends' projects. To find purchasers for *Edwin and Angelina,* for example, Smith sent subscription papers to friends and family throughout Connecticut, in Philadelphia, in Walpole, New Hampshire, upstate New York, and even England, where, owing to the efforts of the traveling Samuel Miles Hopkins, Smith's libretto and Dunlap's *Tell Truth and Shame the Devil* and *Archers* were briefly noted in the *Monthly Review.*[49]

André: A Tragedy, in Five Acts: As Performed by the Old American Company, New-York, March 30, 1798 . . . (New York, 1798). The Swordses, printers of the 1797 *Longworth's American Almanack, New-York Register, and City Directory for the Twenty-Second Year of American Independence* . . . (New York, 1797), also placed "A View of the New Theatre in New York"—Dunlap's Park Street Theater—as the frontispiece of that publication.

49. Cronin, ed., *Diary,* Feb. 8, 1787, 289. See *Pizarro in Peru; or, The Death of Rolla: A Play in Five Acts; from the German of Augustus von Kotzebue; with Notes Marking the Variations from the Original, The Virgin of the Sun: A Play, in Five Acts; from the German of Augustus von Kotzebue; with Notes Marking the Variations from the Original, The Wild-Goose Chase: A Play, in Four Acts, with Songs; from the German of Augustus von Kotzebue; with Notes Marking the Variations from the Original;* all three plays list the following publication information: "New-York: Printed by G. F. Hopkins for William Dunlap, and sold at the office of the printer . . . T. and J. Swords . . . Gaine and Tenbyck . . . John Black . . . Alex. Somerville . . . and most other booksellers

The relationship between Smith and the printers with whom he worked had the potential to lessen the risks involved in the printers' capital out-lays while furthering the creative and distributive powers of Smith and his friends. The mix of financial incentives, intellectual ambition, and personal relationships served both literati and printers well. In the summer of 1800,

<hr>

in the U. States, 1800." Smith does not explain in his diaries where he unearthed the cash—financial details, unlike details of pages read, were usually beneath his notice. Friction characterized Smith's relationship with Collier as well. As mentioned, Collier decided not to publish the *Ghost-Seer,* despite his asking Smith to find him a copy, and he was also reluctant to publish the second volume of Smith's *American Poems.* Smith finally wrote that, if Collier was unwilling to publish the book, "I design, at some future period, to publish it, at my own risk" (Smith to Theodore Dwight, Jan. 17, 1796, in Cronin, ed., *Diary,* 121). Cathy Davidson notes that "perhaps the largest obstacle" faced by authors in the early Republic "involved the distribution of the public work" (*Revolution and the Word,* 33). Smith worked diligently to solve this problem. In January 1797, Smith noted in his diary that he "wrote several snip-snap letters to inclose subscription-papers for my Opera." Later entries make clear that Smith turned to friends and acquaintances to find purchasers for his opera; these included Thomas O'Hara Croswell of Catskill, New York; the lawyers William Pitt Beers and James Kent in Albany, New York; John Williams, a fellow Yale graduate, in Wethersfield, Connecticut; Smith's cousin Elnathan in Berlin, Connecticut; and Thomas Mumford in Onondaga, New York (Cronin, ed., *Diary,* Jan. 9, Apr. 3, 18, 20, Dec. 20, 1797, 281, 305, 309, 313, 407). The Americans' works were noted in the "Monthly Catalogue" of the October 1797 *Monthly Review:* in "Art. 35" and "Art. 36," Dunlap's *Tell the Truth* was praised as the equal of "many of our minor [En-glish] dramas," and *The Archers* as a "liberty-play . . . well calculated for the soil into which it has been transplanted" (218). Of Smith's *Edwin and Angelina,* the reviewer wrote: "Although this production is highly romantic and unnatural, as most operas are, it has had the power of interesting us in the perusal; and we doubt not that it has been performed with good stage-effect in America" ("Art. 37," 219). Dunlap commented on these reviews on Feb. 8, 1798, when he first saw that edition of the periodical (Barck, ed., *Diary of William Dunlap,* 219). The next day, Smith wrote that the pieces were "all briefly noticed—and with as much commendation as was to be expected" (Cronin, ed., *Diary,* 423). At least one printed copy of *Edwin and Angelina* hints at Smith's unofficial assistance to his printers; its construction indicates that conjugate leaves were cut apart, an unusual procedure that likely arose because, S. W. Reid notes, copies of the libretto "left the shop either enclosed with Smith's letters to friends and subscribers or in odd lots," and often Smith "packed them and sent them off himself" ("An Anomalous Copy of Smith's *Edwin and Angelina,* 1797," *Library: The Transactions of the Bibliographical Society,* 5th Ser., XXXII [1977], 55). On the Swordses' shop, see "Antiquary: T. & J. Swords; Part One: Printers during the Federal Period . . . ," *Confessional Presbyterian,* II (2006), 211–236.

the New Yorker John Pintard wrote of T. and J. Swords: "They have risen to some degree of wealth by their industry, have two printing presses of six or eight hands, with more work to execute than they can perform." For Friendly Club members, the association with the Swordses offered a way to bring texts into more hands and minds than would otherwise have been possible. Nor was that all. Rather than weakening or replacing intimate relationships, the market nurtured them: gathering subscriptions knit together friends and acquaintances in a community of shared labor and purpose. The work of circulating Smith's *Edwin and Angelina* even strengthened friendships threatened by religious contention. Two friends troubled by Smith's rejection of orthodox Christianity, Theodore Dwight and William Woolsey, made known their continued affection for Smith by subscribing for the libretto and finding other subscribers for it. Dwight "asked about my Opera," Smith wrote one day in his diary, "but not about me." When Smith then learned that Dwight had arranged to purchase a copy of Smith's opera, Smith wrote to his old friend, urging, "Let not our friendship be lost or impaired!" William Woolsey, for his part, set aside his qualms over Smith's deism and sent Smith a subscription paper on which he had collected seventeen purchasers for the libretto. Smith instantly recognized this for the labor of love that it was. "I shall send twenty Copies," he responded warmly. "The one in blue you will please to accept, as a mark of friendship."[50]

Texts carried ideas and carried love. They were objects—proofs of membership in a friendship or a fellowship—and they were conduits of thought. Selling texts furthered the ideals of cultural improvement, fellowship, and information diffusion that Friendly Club members and their collaborators pursued. And sociable practices, born in private conversation and manuscript exchange, helped to develop an American print marketplace.

50. John Pintard, quoted in Austin Baxter Keep, *History of the New York Society Library; with an Introductory Chapter on Libraries in Colonial New York, 1698-1776* (1908; rpt. Boston, 1972), 241; Cronin, ed., *Diary*, Mar. 2, Apr. 15, Aug. 26 (Smith to Theodore Dwight), 1797, 298, 310, 350. In 1801, the English author and wit John Davis made the Swordses' shop his first stop on a trip to New York City, and he encountered there the famous scientist Joseph Priestley. See Davis, *Travels of Four Years and a Half in the United States of America during 1798, 1799, 1800, 1801, and 1802* (1803), ed. A. J. Morrison (New York, 1909), 217-218.

Alcuin

Charles Brockden Brown's provocative text *Alcuin* emerged from the social and intellectual resources of the cultural network. The salon it describes resembles the gatherings Brown knew in New York City. The book was published because of Smith's relationship with the printers T. and J. Swords. And by exploring themes such as the role of women in cultural life, the status of women in the nation, the risks of dramatic social change, and the practical effects of intellectual inquiry, Brown revealed tensions at the center of the vibrant milieu that sustained him.

By the summer of 1797, Elihu Smith knew that his friend Brown needed money. Smith was corresponding with the editor of the *Farmer's Weekly Museum*, Joseph Dennie, and he proposed that Dennie pay Brown to write for the *Museum*. Smith believed one should write for free for periodicals if that best served the advancement of knowledge. But a starved and discouraged Charles Brockden Brown would be of no use to anyone, and Smith suspected that Dennie could afford to hire a talented author. Dennie, however, never responded to Smith's suggestion. The cultural network itself thwarted Smith's plan: there were plenty of people, including Smith, whose writing Dennie could publish for free, so Dennie had no reason to pay Brown. Smith's suggestion to Brown that Dennie might pay for content, however, led Brown to give Smith the first sections of what would become the intriguing dialogue on women's rights, *Alcuin*.[51]

When it became clear Dennie would not pay Brown, Smith turned to a familiar set of practices. First, he circulated the manuscript through friends and family. Once Brown sent the first installment of the text to Smith in New York, *Alcuin* became the subject of myriad exchanges. "S[mith] shews me 2 dialogues called Alcouin sent on by [Brown] to be forwarded to Dennies paper," William Dunlap wrote in his diary in early August 1797, adding, "There is much truth philosophical accuracy and handsome writing

51. Smith to Brown, July 11, 1797, Smith to Dennie, July 24, 1797, in Cronin, ed., *Diary*, 332, 335–336. When Brown wrote *Alcuin* is not clear; it was, however, Smith's request for manuscripts for the *Museum* that led Brown to "publicize" the manuscript within the network, and that "publication" helped lead to its printing. The favorable and puzzled response of Smith and his friends, moreover, seems to have spurred Brown to add to the original text. Robert D. Ardner places *Alcuin*'s most likely beginnings during the fall and winter of 1796 but notes that it is impossible to date the piece with any certainty ("Historical Essay," in Charles Brockden Brown, *Alcuin: A Dialogue; Memoirs of Stephen Calvert*, bicentennial ed., ed. Sydney J. Krause et al. [Kent, Ohio, 1987], 274–276).

in the essay." Men and women read the manuscript alone and together and puzzled over its meaning. Smith and his associates essentially commissioned the final parts of *Alcuin,* since it was their demands for clarification and elaboration of this ambiguous text that prompted Brown to write parts 2 and 3. "I have a . . . desire to see your continuation of 'Alcuin,'" Smith wrote urgently a month after he received the first installment; "In this, at least," he added wryly, "I am not singular."[52]

Smith also shepherded the text to press. Charles Brockden Brown is conventionally thought of as a writer aloof from the demands of the literary marketplace; in reality, however, he quite astutely had faith that his loyal friend Smith would help him spin words into bread. He was not disappointed in his hopes. "I opened my subscription for 'Alcuin' to-day," Smith noted in his diary soon after Brown sent him a manuscript. The existence of eager readers and writers had stymied Brown's effort to be paid for periodical writing. But those same people helped to turn Brown into a published and paid author by subscribing to buy copies of *Alcuin* and Brown's other novels and by helping to circulate subscription sheets. (Brown also published *Alcuin,* in slightly changed form, in a Philadelphia periodical, the *Weekly Magazine,* until Smith learned of it and wrote to him "injoining his silence till the Dialogue should be published" by T. and J. Swords. As always, Smith balanced his desire for the widest possible circulation of texts with an understanding of the needs of the marketplace.) In late February, Smith returned to the Swordses' shop: "Put into his hands 'Alcuin,' for printing, and paid him towards it, twenty three dollars and fifty cents." By March, Smith was correcting *Alcuin*'s proofs.[53]

52. Barck, ed., *Diary of William Dunlap,* Aug. 8, 1797, 133; Cronin, ed., *Diary,* Aug. 7, 8, 25 (Smith to Brown), Sept. 16 (Smith to Brown), 1797, 342, 349, 364.

53. Michael Gilmore notes that Smith is named "proprietor" in the copyright notice for *Alcuin* and deems this a gesture of "patrician aloofness" on Brown's part ("The Literature of the Revolutionary and Early National Periods," in Sacvan Bercovitch, ed., *The Cambridge History of American Literature,* I, *1590–1820* [New York, 1994], 554). Brown, though, had hoped to earn money from the work, and it is likely that Smith's "proprietorship" simply reflects his willingness to attend to the logistics of the print marketplace, rather than his intention to keep any potential profits or Brown's lack of interest in such money. As always, the relationship between amateurs and printers was mutually dependent but strained; Smith later complained that "sordid doubts among our booksellers" meant that "Sky-Walk" could not yet be published (Cronin, ed., *Diary,* Apr. 20, 1798, 439). Sordid doubts or no, the Swordses had that spring not only printed *Alcuin* but also Smith's edition of Darwin's *Botanic Garden,* and they were publishing the *Medical Repository* as well (Cronin, ed., *Diary,* Feb. 21,

Alcuin's intended life as a magazine serial explains aspects of the text both small and large. That *Alcuin* focuses exclusively on "the rights of women" reflects the truncated nature of a would-be serial. The question of how women's roles should change, and whether they should change at all, was only one of a number of questions about the proper nature of society and the proper limits of social transformation that intrigued Brown and the friends who were his first readers. The male host of the "coterie" depicted in *Alcuin*, for example, is a figure of some interest: he is a doctor, "a man of letters, who, nevertheless, finds little leisure from the engagements of a toilsome profession," and he might have represented Brown's worries that his own physician friend, Elihu Hubbard Smith, was becoming too absorbed in his profession. This intriguing host disappears entirely from the dialogue, but, had *Alcuin* become a series in Dennie's *Farmer's Weekly Museum*, the doctor would undoubtedly have become a recurring character, perhaps one who discussed the conflicting claims of literary and professional ambition. The slightly disorienting nature of *Alcuin* also reflects its roots in Brown's intention to write a serial for Dennie. Reading *Alcuin* in book form, one cannot but expect resolution. Alcuin and his partner in dialogue, Mrs. Carter, are, however, evenly matched as they disagree over women's current and ideal roles, and at its end the book has to be laid down with a shake of the head. What is less than artful as a book, however, would have been entirely appropriate in a magazine serial. Brown was writing for an audience that sought questions and conversations rather than closure, and he was writing for a genre that demanded ever more writing, not climax and conclusion.

Shaped by genre and happenstance, Brown's *Alcuin* was also informed by the reading material and conversations flowing through his cultural milieu. Brown represented rather than resolved the tensions that characterized the world he knew, and he both placed a woman at the center of the salon he described and effaced her. Brown makes the guiding spirit of the salon a woman called Mrs. Carter—her name perhaps inspired by the famous English author and scholar, Elizabeth Carter. Yet Brown also writes that, although "the conversation of the lady [was] not destitute of attractions . . . an additional, and perhaps the strongest inducement, was the society of other visitants." "Mrs. Carter's coterie became the favourite resort of the

28, Apr. 4, 1798, 427, 436; S. W. Reid, "Textual Essay," in Brown, *Alcuin*, ed. Krause et al., 317). Four 1798 issues (Nos. 7–10) of the *Weekly Magazine* contained extracts from the first two sections of *Alcuin*. At fifty cents a copy, *Alcuin* had so far found forty-seven subscribers.

liberal and ingenious," Brown wrote, but "these things did not necessarily imply any uncommon merit in the lady." Brown cannot conceive of cultural life without a woman near its center, but he asserts that the woman is not necessary. He was not alone. By restricting their ranks to men, Friendly Club members made a similar claim that their intellectual life was not dependent on women—a claim as unconvincing, given the larger cultural network's heterosocial nature, as Brown's efforts to efface the importance of Mrs. Carter. In both cases, downplaying women's role emerged from a need to assert the manliness of cultural activities rather than from denigration of women's intellectual capacities: women's successful participation was what made their containment necessary.[54]

After introducing the salon, Brown crafts an argument over women's rights. Mrs. Carter deplores the ill effects of women's constrained education and rights on both men and women. She appears to be drawing on Wollstonecraft's *Vindication of the Rights of Woman*, and Brown might have modeled her on Susan Bull Tracy, who had read and agreed with that text, arguing that women should be able to pursue "scientific knowledge" and that current gender roles made the average man into a "cunning tyrant" and the average woman into "a simpleton, at least." The character of Alcuin opposes Mrs. Carter's Wollstonecraftian analysis with a Godwin-inflected quiescence: "Human beings, it is to be hoped," Alcuin declares, "are destined to a better condition on this stage, or some other, than is now allotted them," but to change the role of women now would be harmfully precipitous. In Brown's final section, Alcuin proposes a vision of transformation whose radicalism mitigates against change as effectively as his earlier defense of the status quo. In it, Alcuin tells Mrs. Carter that he has visited a "paradise of women," in which the sexes dress alike, marriage does not exist, and the differences between men and women are reduced to the anatomical; in modern terms, there is no gender, only sex. Mrs. Carter recoils. "When I demand an equality of conditions among beings that equally partake of the same divine reason," she reproves him, "would you rashly infer that I was an enemy to the institution of marriage itself?"[55]

54. Brown, *Alcuin*, ed. Krause et al., 3. Harriet Guest describes Elizabeth Carter's achievements and fame in *Small Change: Women, Learning, Patriotism, 1750–1810* (Chicago, 2000), chap. 4.

55. Susan Bull Tracy to Smith, Jan. 25, 1794, in Cronin, ed., *Diary*, 109; Brown, *Alcuin*, ed. Krause et al., 53. Fredrika J. Teute discusses the Smith set's admiration of Wollstonecraft's "promulgation of social intercourse based on equitable rights" in "The Loves of the Plants," *HLQ*, LXIII (2000), 320. Anita M. Vickers discusses

Mrs. Carter does not seek a revolution in private life but only its improvement so that women would have property rights within marriage and be no longer forced to make "a promise of implicit obedience and unalterable affection." The character's views accord with those of participants in the cultural network, who believed that an enlightened domesticity could serve as a model of sympathetic, rational attachment and provide a congenial setting for unfettered intellectual inquiry. Men and women such as the Dunlaps, the Kents, and the Woolseys balanced domesticity with cultural life, noting but accepting the moments of friction: "I have read [Wollstonecraft's] Work," Susan Tracy wrote wryly, "with as much attention as my domestic avocations would admit." Interested in the liberation of women's minds but not in the disruption of private life or the social order, Mrs. Tracy would have found a kindred spirit in Brown's character of Mrs. Carter, who argued for greater freedoms for women but bridled at any suggestion that she agreed with "that detestable philosophy which scoffs at the matrimonial institution."[56]

Brown's *Alcuin* contains arguments for and demonstrations of women's intellectual equality to man. But it does not argue that intellectual equality should result in legal and political equality, much less in the destruction of all gender conventions. Despite the power of Mrs. Carter's complaints, *Alcuin* was not a protofeminist text. Brown's first readers found in it no convincing argument for change. "Mrs. S. Johnson," Smith wrote in a letter to Brown, "has read the 1st and IInd parts, and is anxious to know how all this is to end. . . . From what she has seen, she infers his object to be to render women satisfied with their present civil condition. I can not pretend to enlighten her." Fascinatingly, Brown has the character of Mrs. Carter

---

Brown's treatment in *Alcuin* of Godwin's and Wollstonecraft's ideas in "Pray Madam, Are You a Federalist? Women's Rights and the Republican Utopia of *Alcuin*," *American Studies*, XXXIX, no. 3 (Fall 1998), 89–104.

56. Susan Bull Tracy to Smith, Jan. 25, 1794, in Cronin, ed., *Diary*, 109; Brown, *Alcuin*, ed. Krause et al., 54. When William Dunlap read Wollstonecraft's *Vindication of the Rights of Woman* in 1797, he became more impressed as he read. "There is much good sense in her volume," he wrote in his first diary entry, "but much error, a bad style and strong indications of vanity." "She assumes the character of a philosopher and teacher, as such she is not great." When he read chapter 8 and forward, however, in which Wollstonecraft set out her view of proper filial relationships and of the "pernicious effects" of "unnatural distinctions" in society, including those between men and women, and proposed a system of national education, Dunlap found "much excellent sense in them" and offered no criticism. See Barck, ed., *Diary of William Dunlap*, July 12, 18, 1797, 101, 108.

confront the frustrating limitations of the text in which she finds herself. She begins by repeatedly refusing to answer Alcuin's question, "Are you a federalist?"[57]

It would seem a sign of respect for the lady's intellect that Alcuin asks the question, and Mrs. Carter's first demurral—"that she had been often called upon to listen to discussions of this sort, but did not recollect when her opinion had been asked"—suggests she is merely startled by a welcome inquiry. The silence Brown has written for her, however, has a more profound cause. "What have I, as a woman, to do with politics?" she demands when Alcuin repeats his question, and then she finally asserts, "No, I am no federalist." Whatever her political views might be, Mrs. Carter goes on to explain, she refuses to identify herself as a Federalist or Antifederalist because as a woman she is "excluded from all political rights without the least ceremony." And she is infuriated that the framers did not even find it necessary to make her disenfranchisement explicit. "Law-makers," Mrs. Carter asserts, "thought as little of comprehending us in their code of liberty as if we were pigs, or sheep."[58]

Mrs. Carter's disdain for myopic "law-makers" seems moored in the impatience with formal politics that was widespread among cultural network participants. But Mrs. Carter is not only annoyed at politicians. She is also infuriated by Alcuin's assumption that she will be happy to discuss political matters over which she has no say. Mrs. Carter laments women's role in the American polity, but she also deplores the assumption of many of those in Brown's circle that it was sufficient to respect women's intellect without changing their social and political roles.

Mrs. Carter holds court in the realm of conversation but longs for the civic authority and identity that politics provided. By creating her character, Brown does more than reiterate the cultural critiques of his friends and acquaintances; he challenges the ethos of the cultural network itself. Mrs. Carter scoffs at Alcuin's Godwinian disdain for government. When Alcuin calmly assures her that "the chief purpose of the wise is to make men their own governors, to persuade them to practice the rules of equity

57. Brown, *Alcuin*, ed. Krause et al., 7; Smith to Brown, Sept. 16, 1797, in Cronin, ed., *Diary*, 364. The remark parallels the comment Daniel Lewis, a Connecticut participant in Smith's extended cultural network, had made about Godwin's writings: "Were it not the design of the author shewes itself," Lewis had mused to Smith, "it might be supposed written . . . to make people contented with whatever government they happened to live under" (Cronin, ed., *Diary*, Nov. 5, 1795, 85).

58. Brown, *Alcuin*, ed. Krause et al., 22, 23.

without legal constraint," Mrs. Carter informs him with some asperity that some form of government will always be necessary, and, as a result, "nothing interests me more nearly than a wise choice of master." Mrs. Carter counters Alcuin's Godwinian vision of mankind's transcendence of government with a hardheaded argument that governments matter, and therefore so does her disenfranchisement. Just as Dunlap took for granted his freedom when he opined that intellectual liberty was as important as liberty from slavery, so does the character of Alcuin downplay the importance of the suffrage he took as his due. In Mrs. Carter, Brown created a character who truly sees the importance of politics because she is denied its privileges. She has achieved, against her will, the critical distance from the polity that men such as Elihu Hubbard Smith wished to achieve. Ironically, that distance reveals to her the centrality of the political engagement Smith and so many of his collaborators mistrusted.[59]

Alcuin celebrates the world of intellectual sociability in which Brown participates. It also quietly poses the question whether that world mattered outside its own borders. We turn to the two projects through which Elihu Hubbard Smith attempted to prove that the answer to that question was yes: the *Medical Repository*, which he edited, and the utopian state he secretly imagined.

59. Ibid., 26–27.

3

Two Visions of Circulation

The Medical Repository *and "The Institutions of the Republic of Utopia"*

In September 1795, New York City was suffering through one of the terrible yellow fever epidemics that afflicted American seaports during the decade. Many residents fled to safer ground, and those who remained anxiously tried to avoid contracting a disease whose method of transmission was a terrifying mystery. Determined not to leave New York, Elihu Hubbard Smith sought to understand the epidemic in order to control it. He walked his city, ascending hills, surveying swamps and slums, and trying to determine why some areas saw so many deaths and others so few. Smith was appalled not only by the sickness around him but also by what he called "fever talk." "People collect in groups to talk [the epidemic] over," Smith wrote, "and to frighten each other into fever, or flight. . . . In one shape, or other, the fever is constantly brought into view; and the soul sickens with the ghastly and abhorred repetition." Discussions of the danger, he complained, "buz continually in my ears, and rattle incessantly in my head; so that I can think, consistently, on nothing." Aimless, anxious chatter was the opposite of the collaborative inquiry in which Smith believed; it was not communication but contagion. Smith loathed it as he loathed yellow fever itself. The war between disease and health was a war between ignorance and knowledge, and Smith considered the battle joined.[1]

The yellow fever epidemic spurred Smith to find a way to accelerate

1. James E. Cronin, ed., *The Diary of Elihu Hubbard Smith (1771–1798)* (Philadelphia, 1973), Sept. 18, 20, 1795, 58, 60; John Duffy, "An Account of the Epidemic Fevers that Prevailed in the City of New York from 1791 to 1822," *New-York Historical Society Quarterly*, L (1966), 333–364; "Facts, Relative to the Fever, I," in Cronin, ed., *Diary*, 75–76. Smith was influenced by the efforts of his former teacher Benjamin Rush to understand yellow fever's origin and spread. On Rush's theories of causation and treatment, see Paul E. Kopperman, "Venerate the Lancet: Benjamin Rush's Yellow Fever Therapy in Context," *Bulletin of the History of Medicine*, LXXVIII (2004), 539–554.

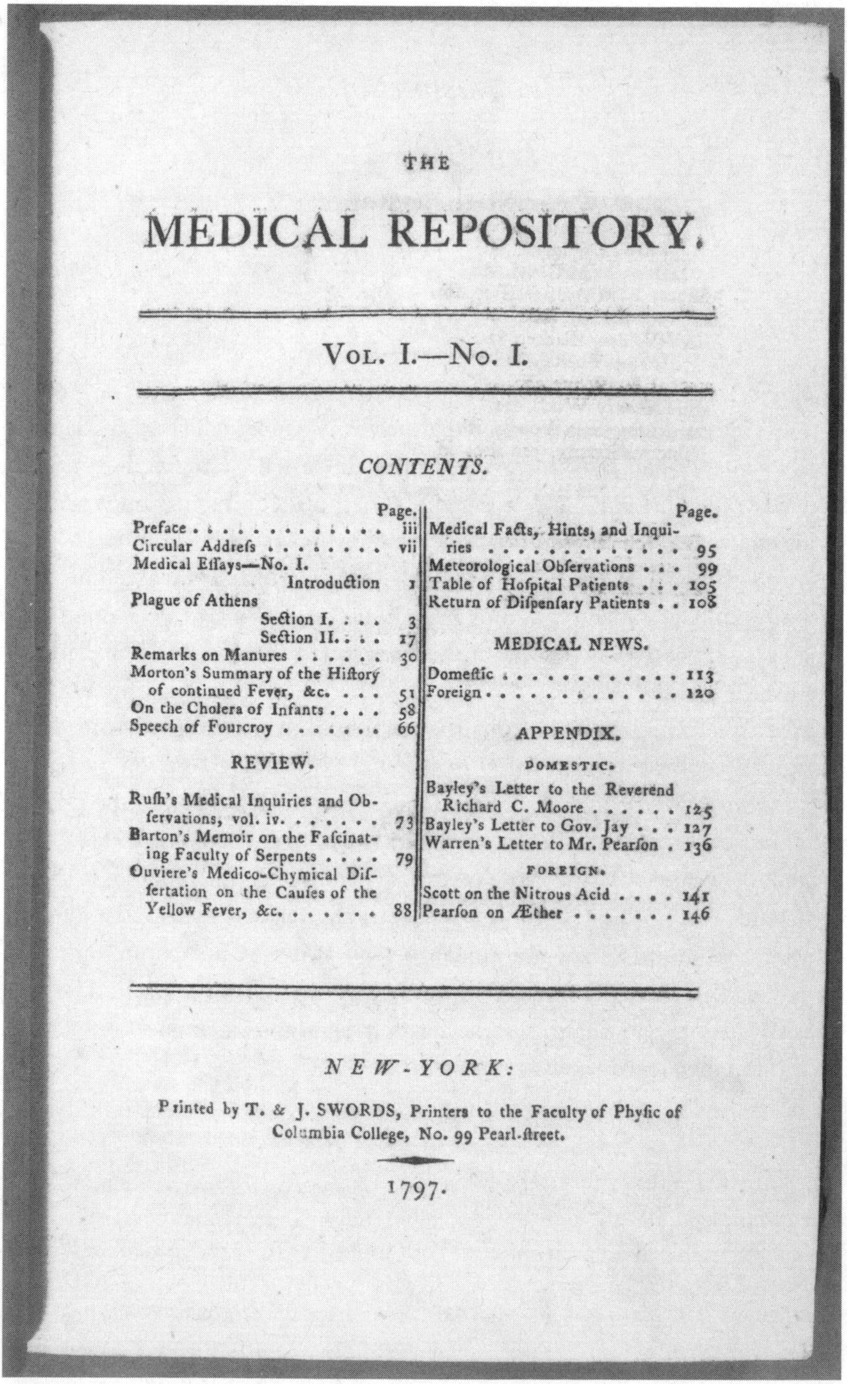

THE

MEDICAL REPOSITORY.

VOL. I.—No. I.

CONTENTS.

NEW-YORK:

Printed by T. & J. SWORDS, Printers to the Faculty of Physic of Columbia College, No. 99 Pearl-street.

1797.

FIGURE 2. *Medical Repository*, I, no. 1 (August 1797).
By permission, American Antiquarian Society, Worcester, Mass.

the creation and circulation of knowledge so that health and virtue, at the level of the individual, the community, the nation, and the world, might triumph. "Who shall say to the intellectual tide, 'thus far shalt thou go, and no farther'?" Smith demanded in a diary passage he wrote as the 1795 yellow fever crisis receded as mysteriously as it had begun. "Hitherto, men seem to have been groping in the dark, in search of they know not what. . . . False observations, false relations, false reasoning, false applications, have continued the deception and the distress." But humanity was advancing in knowledge: "A ray of light darted from the school of Leyden, a serene and steady luster shone from the university of Gottingen, a dazzling glory beamed from the hills of Scotland," Smith effused. And more work was needed. "Who is he," Smith demanded urgently, "that shall hold up the convex and transparent glass, and cast upon the mental eye the pure, un-wavering, lovely, and eternal beam of truth?"[2]

Smith hoped that he would be among those who would hold up that "convex and transparent glass." He did not expect to become a great scientist. Instead, he served "truth" by marshaling the practices of Shaftesburian sociability to the cause of science. During the same years that he read and discussed philosophy and brought literary texts into circulation, Smith and his fellow cultural networkers Samuel Latham Mitchill and Edward Miller established the nation's first long-lived medical and scientific periodical, the *Medical Repository*.[3]

The quest for scientific and medical knowledge was part of cultural life in the eighteenth century. Samuel Latham Mitchill was one man whose interests encompassed almost every field of investigation. "Ancient and modern languages were unlocked to him," a contemporary remembered, "and a wide range of physical science the pabulum of his intellectual repast." "He was now engaged with the anatomy of the egg, and now deciphering a Babylonian brick; now involved in the nature of meteoric stones; now in the different species of brassica. . . . In the morning he might be found composing songs for the nursery; at noon dietetically experimenting and writing on fishes, or unfolding to admiration a new theory on terrene formations." Science and medicine were of interest to intellectually ambitious individu-

2. Cronin, ed., *Diary*, Oct. 17, 1795, 74.

3. Victor Robinson, "The Early Medical Journals of America Founded during the Quarter-Century 1797–1822," *Medical Life*, XXXVI (1929), 552–585; James H. Cassedy, "The Flourishing and Character of Early American Medical Journalism, 1797–1860," *Journal of the History of Medicine and Allied Sciences*, XXXVIII (1983), 135–150.

als such as Mitchill throughout England and America. In Newcastle, Birmingham, Edinburgh, Manchester, and Norwich, merchants and artisans attended scientific lectures and participated in societies devoted to scientific inquiry as well as to literary and philosophical discussion. In Philadelphia, the American Philosophical Society began in the late 1760s to offer a forum for scientific inquiry and conversation, and by the 1790s the society's local members had come to include both men of science, such as Benjamin Rush and Benjamin S. Barton, and others, including the painter Charles Willson Peale, the lawyer and Supreme Court justice James Wilson, and the financier Robert Morris; the philosophers Dugald Stewart and the marquis de Condorcet were among the society's elected foreign members. Massachusetts boasted the American Academy of Arts and Sciences, and New York City saw not only the Friendly Club, whose members often discussed scientific subjects at their meetings, but also the development of the Society for the Promotion of Agriculture, Arts, and Manufactures. In 1792, the latter organization petitioned the legislature to establish at Columbia College a professorship of natural history, chemistry, agriculture, and "the other Arts depending thereon," a position first filled by none other than Samuel Latham Mitchill.[4]

Science and literature mingled in print as they did in conversation circles, clubs, and individual careers. Denis Diderot and Jean Le Rond d'Alembert's famed *Encyclopédie*—a collaborative project undertaken by a "society of men of letters"—was subtitled *A Systematic Dictionary of Science, Arts, and the Trades;* its accounts of natural history and new mechanical processes were as central to its Enlightenment worldview as were its entries by Voltaire and Jean Jacques Rousseau titled "Men of Letters" and "Style." The scientist Erasmus Darwin sought in his 1791 work, *The Botanic Garden*, "to inlist under the banner of Science"; Darwin's versification of the Linnaean scheme of classification so enchanted Smith that he brought out the first American edition of the work in 1798. Samuel Latham Mitchill edited and

4. Dr. John W. Francis, quoted in "Samuel Latham Mitchill," *Appleton's Cyclopedia of American Biography*, ed. James Grant Wilson and John Fiske (New York, 1887–1889); John Brewer, *The Pleasures of the Imagination: English Culture in the Eighteenth Century* (New York, 1997), 509–513; Jenny Uglow, *The Lunar Men: Five Friends Whose Curiosity Changed the World* (New York, 2002), 1–2, 33–34; Henry F. May, *The Enlightenment in America* (New York, 1976), 212–215; I. Bernard Cohen, *Science and the Founding Fathers: Science in the Political Thought of Jefferson, Franklin, Adams, and Madison* (New York, 1995), 19–23; John C. Greene, *American Science in the Age of Jefferson* (Ames, Iowa, 1984), 40–43, 95.

wrote a preface to the first American edition of another work by Darwin, *Zoonomia*, in 1796. The British periodicals that Smith and his collaborators read contained medical statistics and scientific essays, and American news-papers published such information as well.[5]

Inspired both by the fever crisis and by the confluence of scientific and literary interests among his peers, Elihu Smith decided to devote his skills as editor and networker to an enterprise uniting physicians, scientists, and men of letters in the cause of human health. His friend Noah Webster had earlier in the decade written to physicians requesting their views about the transmission of disease, and Smith helped to enlist authors for Webster's 1796 *Collection of Papers on the Subject of Bilious Fevers*. When Webster declined to compile a subsequent volume on the subject, Smith conceived his own, more ambitious project. "I think," he wrote to his friend William Buel, "as Mr. Webster has relinquished his plan of continuing his Collec-tion, of taking it up myself, on a far more extensive scale, and publishing an annual volume; the principal object of which will be the preserving and collecting of the materials for a History of the Diseases of America." In pur-suit of this goal, Smith quickly began enlisting friends and acquaintances to make observations in their areas regarding disease and health.[6]

5. Roger Hahn, "Science and the Arts in France: The Limitations of Encylopedic Ideology," *Studies in Eighteenth-Century Culture*, X (1981), 77–93; James Llana, "Natural History and the *Encylopédie*," *Journal of the History of Biology*, XXXIII (2000), 1–25; "The *Encyclopédie* of Diderot and D'Alembert, Collaborative Trans-lation Project," http://www.hti.umich.edu/d/did (accessed June 6, 2007); [Erasmus Darwin], *The Botanic Garden: A Poem in Two Parts . . . with Philosophical Notes* (Lon-don, 1791) (see "Advertisement to the London Edition"); Darwin, *Zoonomia; or, The Laws of Organic Life*, I (New York, 1796); [Darwin], *The Botanic Garden: A Poem in Two Parts . . . with Philosophical Notes; the First American Edition* (New York, 1798); William K. Beatty and Virginia L. Beatty, "Sources of Medical Information," *Journal of the American Medical Association*, CCXXXVI (1976), 78–82. For a discussion of Darwin's appeal to Smith and his collaborators, see Fredrika J. Teute, "The Loves of the Plants; or, The Cross-Fertilization of Science and Desire at the End of the Eigh-teenth Century," *Huntington Library Quarterly*, LXIII (2000), 329–332.

6. Noah Webster wrote a preface and summary to his *Collection of Papers on the Subject of Bilious Fevers, Prevalent in the United States for a Few Years Past* (New York, 1796) in which he confessed his lack of medical expertise but argued that yellow fever originated locally and could be controlled through improved public hygiene. In 1797, Webster wrote twenty-five letters in New York's *Commercial Advertiser*, disputing the foreign origin theories of William Currie, a Philadelphia physician. From his efforts emerged *A Brief History of Epidemic and Pestilential Diseases . . .* , 2 vols. (Hartford, Conn., 1799). The *Advertiser* essays are collected in Benjamin Spector, ed., *Noah Web-*

Smith shared his former teacher Benjamin Rush's view that *"there is but one fever in the World,"* and he believed that the human body was a single system in which the mental and physical were entwined. "All diseases," in this view, "were due to a single cause, a state of excessive excitability or disordered excitement." Smith also drew inspiration from Darwin's argument that a unified medical theory "founded upon nature, that should bind together the scattered facts of medical knowledge," would allow "men of moderate abilities" to be competent physicians and would, perhaps more importantly, "teach mankind . . . the knowledge of themselves." Smith thought that, if enough observations could be created and collected, the cause not just of yellow fever but also of all illness might be discerned and eradicated. Inspired by this belief and confident in his ability to create a large community of inquiry, Smith collaborated with Miller and Mitchill to found the *Medical Repository.* The *Repository* was a response to the immediate yellow fever crisis, a practical use of Shaftesburian sociability, and a part of the larger late-Enlightenment quest for information of all kinds and for human progress on every front.[7]

_____

ster: *Letters on the Yellow Fever Addressed to Dr. William Currie* (Baltimore, 1947). Smith explained his initial involvement in Webster's *Collection* to his friend William Buel, whose "Communication" was to be included in Smith's project, and later wrote of his subsequent plan (Smith to Buel, May 13, Aug. 11, 1796, in Cronin, ed., *Diary,* 167, 201). On Smith's thoughts regarding yellow fever and work to alleviate it, see Bryan Waterman, "Arthur Mervyn's *Medical Repository* and the Early Republic's Knowledge Industries," *American Literary History,* XV (2003), 213–247.

7. Rush had developed his ideas while studying in Edinburgh; he was particularly influenced by William Cullen, and Smith's ideas accordingly show Cullen's influence as well. See L. H. Butterfield, ed., *Letters of Benjamin Rush,* 2 vols. (Princeton, N.J., 1951), I, 584–585 n. 1 (the language is from notes of a student of Rush). Lizbeth Haakonssen analyzes Benjamin Rush's medical views in *Medicine and Morals in the Enlightenment: John Gregory, Thomas Percival, and Benjamin Rush* (Atlanta, Ga., 1997), chap. 4. Smith's views are evident throughout his diary as well as in the pieces he wrote for the *Repository* before his sudden death. His "Introduction" to his series, "The Plague of Athens," for example, explains that "the study of the histories of those wide-wasting diseases which pass under the name of Epidemics . . . is calculated to excite a suspicion, that they all have one common origin." "Should a minute inquiry into every thing which relates to these pestilential maladies justify such a suspicion, we should, probably, discover their hitherto hidden cause, and be enabled to prevent its future operation" (*Medical Repository,* I, no. 1 [August 1797], 1). Elsewhere in this series, Smith makes clear his view that mental and physical causes of disease are linked as well; explaining the death of Pericles, he writes, "It is probably that the calumnies of his enemies, the ill success of some of his enterprises, the ingratitude of one of his

The *Medical Repository* was an assertive American entry in a long tradition of transatlantic scientific cooperation. Americans had long corresponded with British scientific societies and British authors, and the *Repository*'s editors now sought to draw both American and British scientists and men of letters into a collaborative periodical centered in America. The painstaking network building at which Smith excelled was precisely what was needed for the task. Smith diligently solicited subscriptions, essays, observations, and logistical assistance from an ever growing array of individuals at home and abroad. These included, among many others, Benjamin Rush, Benjamin Smith Barton, the English author and physician Robert John Thornton, the Bermudian physician Francis Forbes, the author and politician Jedediah Morse, and Thomas Beddoes, an English physician who sought to put Joseph Priestley's theories of gases and vapors to practical medical use. Coeditor Samuel Mitchill's combination of Tammany Society connections and intellectual heft helped him to secure the invaluable participation of the controversial British scientist and philosopher Joseph Priestley. Priestley, who came to New York in 1794, had provoked a lively debate not only for his political and religious views but also for his insistence on the existence of phlogiston, a supposed property of materials released through burning. Mitchill opposed the theory and had published his *Nomenclature of the New Chemistry* (1794) in order to publicize Antoine-Laurent Lavoisier's opposing system. Opening the *Medical Repository* to both sides of the debate inspired more than forty pieces in the periodical's first six years.[8]

─────

sons, and the death of the one most worthy of his love, and of whom he was doatingly fond, predisposed him to be affected" (26). See Erasmus Darwin, "Preface," *Zoonomia; or, The Laws of Organic Life,* I (Dublin, 1794), 2. Jenny Uglow describes Darwin's tendency to "envisage the improvement of society through medicine, rather than politics," in *The Lunar Men,* 462. Edward Miller studied at the University of Pennsylvania and was a physician at New York's College of Physicians and Surgeons, and he practiced at New-York Hospital. The better-known Samuel Latham Mitchill studied medicine at the University of Edinburgh and law in New York. As well as being a professor of natural history, chemistry, and botany at what would later become Columbia College, he served in a variety of political posts, including terms in the New York state legislature during the 1790s. Both Mitchell and Miller participated not only in the *Repository* but also in Smith's less formal cultural and scientific pursuits. See Richard J. Kahn and Patricia G. Kahn, "The *Medical Repository*—The First U.S. Medical Journal (1797–1829)," *New England Journal of Medicine,* CCCXXXVII (1997), 1926–1930; Alan David Aberbach, *In Search of an American Identity: Samuel Latham Mitchill, Jeffersonian Nationalist* (New York, 1988).

8. Smith to Robert John Thornton, Aug. 29, 1797, Smith to Benjamin Rush, Dec.

In keeping with the entanglement of literary, philosophical, and scientific inquiry, Smith urged all men of letters to "furnish us, either quarterly, semi-annually, or annually, as may best suit with your convenience, with such information . . . as may be in your power." The editors' efforts to draw in a wide range of educated Americans bore fruit: almost one-quarter of the subscribers to the first volume were merchants, lawyers, or judges, and close to three-quarters were physicians, and the rest were booksellers.[9]

Smith and his fellow *Medical Repository* editors created a more permanent incarnation of the fleeting associations Smith used to market freestanding texts such as *Alcuin* and *Edwin and Angelina*. Like those communities, the one that created and circulated the *Medical Repository* had roots in child-

---

1, 1797, Smith to Benjamin Smith Barton, Dec. 11, 1797, Smith to Jedediah Morse, Jan. 7, 1798, Smith to Thomas Beddoes, Jan. 18, 1798, Smith to Francis Forbes, Feb. 24, 1798, all in Cronin, ed., *Diary*, 352, 400, 403–404, 416–417, 420, 426–427; Denis I. Duveen and Herbert S. Klickstein, "The Introduction of Lavoisier's Chemical Nomenclature into America," *Isis*, XLV (1954), 285–286. John C. Greene describes the participation of Americans, including John Banister, John Brickell, Cadwallader Colden, Cotton Mather, and Manasseh Cutler, in transatlantic intellectual exchanges, noting that their work appeared in European periodicals and contributed to such foundational texts as John Ray's *History of Plants* and Carolus Linnaeus's *Systema Naturae* (*American Science*, 253–254).

9. "Circular Address," *Medical Repository*, I, no. 1 (August 1797), ix. The following is only a sampling of the many letters Smith wrote, some of which were in response to criticism or encouragement from those already aware of the *Repository*: Smith to William Eustis, Dec. 18, 1797, Smith to Thomas O'Hara Croswell, Dec. 20, 1797, Smith to Josiah Quincy, Dec. 20, 1797, Smith to Nathaniel Dwight, Dec. 26, 1797, Smith to Jedidiah Morse, Jan. 7, 1798, Smith to Charles Brockden Brown, Jan. 9, 1798, Smith to Francis Forbes, Feb. 24, 1798, Smith to Samuel M. Hopkins, Mar. 16, 1798, all in Cronin, ed., *Diary*, 405, 407, 408, 410, 417, 427, 431. Smith's one great disappointment was Benjamin Rush's lack of interest in the project; when his friend and mentor failed him, he turned, characteristically, to printers to seek the subscribers he had hoped Rush's good offices would bring (Cronin, ed., *Diary*, Dec. 25, 1797, 410). By the time of the publication of the first volume of the *Repository*, the periodical listed 268 subscribers, several of whom were booksellers taking more than one copy. There were 195 subscribers listed as "Dr.," "m.d.," or as a medical student. But there were also 9 "Reverends" and 23 subscribers listed as "esquire." Other subscribers included a member of Congress (Samuel W. Dana of Connecticut) and a judge of the superior court of Connecticut (Tapping Reeve) ("List of Subscribers," *Medical Repository*, I, no. 1 [August 1797], 9–16). Toby Appel describes Smith's involvement in Connecticut's world of doctors and fledgling medical associations in "Disease and Medicine in Connecticut around 1800" (paper presented to the Connecticut Academy of Arts and Sciences, January 1999; revised July 1999).

hood friendships as well as transatlantic ambitions. Subscribers were likely to come from states associated with the editors, such as New York, Connecticut, and Delaware, and Smith relied on the assistance of friends such as Thomas Croswell, William Dunlap, and Josiah Quincy as he worked to find contributors and purchasers. Old friendships could provide considerable reach: Smith wrote to the traveling Samuel Miles Hopkins, asking him to "leave the Nos. of the [Medical] Repository with the Proprietor of [England's] Monthly Review" and, if possible, to send them to Paris as well.[10]

Smith insisted that he and his coeditors "had no expectations, nor scarcely any wish, to make money by" the periodical, but he knew that the *Repository* needed to circulate as a purchased text if it was to circulate as a compendium of ideas. Achieving a large circulation for the *Repository* was necessary to its intellectual success: only if enough people read and wrote would enough data be collected that the project could function as intended. Thus, just as he did when he circulated literary texts, Smith sought to merge the resources and goals of professional men of culture with those of his network of friends. Smith knew of the popularity of Joseph Dennie's *Farmer's Weekly Museum,* and he sent a *Repository* prospectus to Dennie when he sought to place the *Medical Repository* in the public eye. Dennie, happy for the material and, it seems likely, happy for the chance to do a favor for the well-connected Elihu Smith, referred to the periodical in the *Farmer's Weekly Museum* in May 1797 and directed readers to Smith's printer for further information. That printer was none other than T. and J. Swords; no doubt because of the Swordses' continuing relationship with Smith and confidence in his ability to create markets for texts, they had agreed to publish the periodical, although no American scientific periodical had ever achieved a long life. Smith also urged other booksellers to stock the periodical, hoping that the quest for reform and the quest for profit could serve each other.[11]

10. Smith to Hopkins, Mar. 16, 1798, in Cronin, ed., *Diary,* 430–432. Subscribers to the first volume of the *Medical Repository* (1797–1798) came from fourteen states — with disproportionate numbers from New York and Connecticut — as well as from Martinique, Nova Scotia, and London. See "List of Subscribers," *Medical Repository,* I, no. 1 (August 1797), 9–16.

11. Cronin, ed., *Diary,* Dec. 10, 1797, 402; *Farmer's Weekly Museum: Newhampshire and Vermont Journal,* May 23, 1797. Kahn and Kahn, in "The Medical Repository," *NEJM,* CCCXXXVII (1997), 1928, write: "The booksellers ordered a total of 119 copies, with Philadelphia (50 copies) and Boston (36 copies) leading the sales. We have been unable to locate later subscription lists or business records. The cost, as

The mundane fueled the visionary; while endlessly copyediting and soliciting contributors and subscribers, the *Repository*'s editors hoped for world transformation. They wanted to stitch together a national and international observatory of the human condition, a kind of enormous, ever growing scientific panopticon. They believed that to observe was to know, and to know was to master. Collecting the knowledge and insights of myriad individuals would conquer disease, and participating individuals themselves would be improved by the labor. "What incalculable benefits would result," Smith wrote to his friend Joseph Strong, "from converting the great mass of physicians, thro'out the Union, into rational, observing, reflecting, prac[ti]tioners?" Just as the Shaftesburian club was understood both to elevate its participants and to allow for the pursuit of truth, so, too, would creating the *Repository* be both a means of collecting and sharing information and a means of creating individuals who craved and therefore pursued such collection and sharing. What was most important, Smith wrote to his friend, the poet Richard Alsop, "was to generate a habit of observation and communication among our countrymen."[12]

Editors of the *Medical Repository* expected that the periodical would collect observations about matters extending far beyond physical health. "No plan," Smith wrote in his "Circular Address" explaining the *Repository*'s purpose and design, "seems more happily calculated to mark and explain the influence of different states of society, occupations, institutions, manners, exposure, air, modes of living, etc. etc. on health; and thus indirectly, on morals, industry, and happiness." Throughout the eighteenth century, observation was believed to be the key to understanding humanity's social and political arrangements. Scottish philosophers such as Adam Ferguson and Henry Home, Lord Kames, proposed that civilization progressed in stages, from societies reliant on hunting and gathering through those engaged in modern commerce, and that each stage was accompanied by changes in culture. Influenced by Scottish "conjectural histories" and intrigued by developments in the new United States, individuals on both sides of the Atlan-

---

published in the journal itself in 1800, was '. . . a dollar to be paid on receipt of the first number, and a half a dollar on delivery of each succeeding number. . . . Copies shall be sent, regularly, to Subscribers, by any conveyance they shall point out, they being at any charge which may so arise.' There were occasional advertisements in the *Medical Repository*, mainly for other books and journals, but we have no information about whether advertising was used to recover costs."

12. Smith to Joseph Strong, Feb. 14, 1797, Smith to Richard Alsop, Sept. 29, 1797, in Cronin, ed., *Diary*, 291, 370.

tic turned their eyes to America's distinctive landscapes, communities, and inhabitants. In *Notes on the State of Virginia*, written in 1781 and 1782 and published in 1787, Jefferson described institutions as well as terrain, offering information about "Colleges, Buildings, and Roads," "Manners," and "Laws." Addressing a similarly broad range of issues were Samuel Williams's *Natural and Civil History of Vermont* (1794), Gilbert Imlay's *Topographical Description of the Western Territory of North America* (1792), and Jeremy Belknap's third volume of *The History of New-Hampshire* (1792), which offered, as its subtitle reads, *A Geographical Description of the State; with Sketches of Its Natural History, Productions, Improvements, and Present State of Society and Manners, Laws and Government.*[13]

The influence of Scottish philosophy ensured that in some texts observations of specific locales blended with efforts to create general theories of social and political development. Having pondered Pennsylvania's history, Benjamin Rush argued in 1786 that settlement of frontier territory occurred in waves, with the first wave being frontiersmen who adopted the ways of the indigenous population and the last being true "farmers" who supported social and governmental institutions and possessed the civic virtue necessary to the Republic. Just as the specific could lead to the general, so could description lead to prescription: exploring patterns of settlement led some to hope that reason, rather than chance, could guide the development of a community. The vastness of the United States offered an arena in which such hopes could be put to the test. The impulse to impose order on the wilderness and on human nature itself is evident in the Enlightenment grid the Northwest Ordinance of 1787 placed on the wilderness; both Ohio Company associates and Congress wanted to turn settlement into an orderly process that would quickly promote productive American communities and avoid creating a ragged frontier. Some Europeans conceived of the United States as the potential site not simply of planned settlement and social improvement but also of communities and individuals entirely freed of superstition and pernicious traditions. Joseph Priestley sent his son Joseph, Jr., and son-in-law Thomas Cooper to America in search of land on which to start a community of "English friends of freedom." That plan failed, but

13. "Circular Address," *Medical Repository*, I, no. 1 (August 1797), viii; Henry Home, Lord Kaims [Kames], *Sketches of the History of Man . . .* (Dublin, 1774–1775); Adam Ferguson, *Essay on the History of Civil Society* (1767), ed. Duncan Forbes (Edinburgh, 1966); Gladys Bryson, *Man and Society: The Scottish Inquiry of the Eighteenth Century* (Princeton, N.J., 1945), chap. 4; Thomas Jefferson, *Notes on the State of Virginia* (1787), ed. William Peden (Chapel Hill, N.C., 1954).

Cooper wrote a book detailing Priestley's efforts, *Some Information respecting America* (1795), and Cooper's book might have influenced the British poets Robert Southey and Samuel Taylor Coleridge, who imagined a pantisocratic society that was to be located, like Priestley's community, on the banks of the Susquehanna. French author and abolitionist J. P. Brissot de Warville dabbled in utopianism in his 1792 *New Travels in the United States of America* (Joel Barlow's translation of which was published in the United States, in the same year, by T. and J. Swords). Brissot proposed a society—a "colony" as he styled it in tone-deaf fashion—to be founded in America. "If men of wisdom and information should organize the plan of a society before it existed, and extend their foresight to every circumstance of preparing proper institutions for the forming of the morals, public and private," he wrote, "it is my opinion, even that the love of gain, the love of novelty, and the spirit of philosophy, would lend a hand to an enterprise, which, before the American Revolution, might have been judged impracticable."[14]

By the next chapter, Brissot had abandoned his utopian idea as "but a dream." He was traveling in America, not simply thinking about it, a fact that might have made him less prone than Priestley, Southey, or Coleridge to conceive of the new nation as a blank canvas on which to draw his perfect world. Elihu Smith, for his part, lived in America, and his life reveals an oscillation between believing he could shape the new nation into an ideal state and believing that such shaping was already—and perhaps always had been—impossible.[15]

Like many of his contemporaries, Smith was drawn to the task of imagining a place in which environment, social institutions, and political institutions produced a virtuous and happy people. His conversations, work with printers, and labors for the *Repository* demonstrate a hope that America itself could be improved through hard work, open-ended inquiry, and exacting observation. But Smith longed for a way to achieve progress more quickly. Hoping that government could be harnessed to the cause of enlightenment, Smith wrote to his friend John Allen while the latter served in the

14. Andrew R. L. Cayton, *The Frontier Republic: Ideology and Politics in the Ohio Country, 1780–1825* (Kent, Ohio, 1989), 24; Greene, *American Science,* 164; Samuel Taylor Coleridge to Robert Southey, Oct. 21, 1794, in Earl Leslie Griggs, ed., *Collected Letters of Samuel Taylor Coleridge,* I (Oxford, 1956), 114; J[acques] P[ierre] Brissot de Warville, *New Travels in the United States of America; Performed in 1788,* trans. Joel Barlow (New York, 1792), Letter 3, May 21, 1788, 35.

15. Brissot, *New Travels,* trans. Jordan, Letter 4, May 21, 1788, 39.

Connecticut legislature. Smith proposed a "few Hints" for improving Connecticut's education system, including annual surveys of schools' conditions and the establishment of small school districts. After Smith failed in this effort to reshape Connecticut, he began to write a description of an imaginary western state called, straightforwardly enough, Utopia, "between the 39th and 41st degrees of north latitude." Within Utopia's imaginary borders, Smith's longed-for cultural and intellectual vanguard had "real" influence. But Smith was not satisfied with escapism. As he wrote the utopia, he imagined it might serve as a blueprint for reforming the United States as a whole. "The flourishing condition of the State of Utopia, lately admitted into the Union," he wrote, "renders it an interesting subject of inquiry." "Herein, the author has endeavored," he continued, "by a careful history of the Institutions of the Republic of Utopia, to expose to every inquirer the causes of it's rare felicity." Smith wanted to believe his "Institutions," which he never published, was no mere indulgence but instead was—like the *Medical Repository*—a tool for promoting moral and physical health.[16]

Complete with numerous "chapters," schematic diagrams, and painstaking descriptions of Utopia's "civil and political divisions" and natural resources ("Veins of Lead and Copper . . . Plumbago. . . . Several salt-springs"), the "Institutions" limned a physical, social, and political world Smith believed would create citizens sound in mind, body, and morals. Smith's imagined state was "Sixty miles square" and "divided into Nine Counties,—each twenty miles square; each County is subdivided into nine Towns, of equal size," and so on, down to the smallest division, the "District." Smith sketched these neatly nesting subdivisions in geometrically precise drawings; on the originals, one can still see the pinholes he used to align the markings. With its right angles and nesting squares, Smith's Utopia brings to mind the Enlightenment landscape of Jefferson's Northwest Ordinance and of Pierre Charles L'Enfant's Washington designs, but Smith could even ensure that, in Utopia, the population was a perfect square, 360,000. And, because Smith's description was, in fact, invention, the natural landscape could also be rendered improbably orderly. Describing Utopia's topography, climate, and settlement pattern at some length,

16. Smith to John Allen, Mar. 30, 1796, in Cronin, ed., *Diary*, 15. Smith's "Institutions of the Republic of Utopia" is not included in the edition of the diary edited by James Cronin. The work is reproduced in Catherine Kaplan, "Elihu Hubbard Smith's 'The Institutions of the Republic of Utopia,'" *Early American Literature*, XXXV (2000), 294–333 (quotations on 309, 310) (hereafter cited as "Institutions").

Smith invented a state "nearly equi-distant from the Atlantic and the Mississippi," one possessed of land neither too bountiful nor too barren and blessed by mountains neither too tall nor too short.[17]

The "Institutions" was a prescription for humanity's physical and moral health, one written, like all prescriptions, in the face of disease. Smith undertook his utopia project in the same month he began his "History of Mankind's Plagues" and in the same year he worked on "Letters on the Fever." Flowing through all of these complementary projects was a vision of circulation—of air, of water, and, especially, of information—as the key to curing moral, social, and physical ills. Almost every element of Smith's imaginary land, from its lack of marshes and lowlands to its "pure and healthful air" to its orderly systems for collecting and sharing information, offered the precise inverse of the features Smith had come to associate with New York's ghastly yellow fever epidemics. Even Smith's odd little note that, in Utopia, "storms of wind and rain . . . are as frequent and as violent here as elsewhere" was a quiet response to his observation that in New York City's terrible fever season of 1795 there was "but one thunderstorm, and this was very gentle." Smith also described a man-made landscape in Utopia; lovely hand-drawn diagrams depict wide, straight boulevards—"grand roads," in his words—which were the opposite of the "streets narrow, crooked, and unpaved" that he believed collected the water and filth that rendered New York's summers so deadly. Stagnation of water or intellect meant death. And, in his plans for Utopia's roads, Smith's theory that observation could master disease was borne out; although he had not discovered the vector of yellow fever transmission, he had accurately discerned that pools of water fostered that transmission. The paved, well-maintained roads he prescribed for Utopia would have fostered fewer pools in which mosquitoes could breed, and so would have slowed the spread of yellow fever.[18]

17. "Institutions," 309–311. Smith's description places Utopia in the Northwest Territory, just west and south of the Connecticut Reserve, on land that would now form part of northern Ohio and Indiana. The area had been well mapped by the time of Smith's writing; his description, although not egregiously inaccurate, renders the area more like Connecticut and less accessible by water than was in fact the case.

18. "Institutions," 310, 317; "On the Fever of 1795; Letter Third," as drafted in Smith's diary, March 1796 (between Mar. 4 and 5), Harvey Cushing/John Hay Whitney Medical Library, Yale University, New Haven, Conn. Peter Gay argues that, during the Enlightenment, "medicine was philosophy at work; philosophy was medicine for the individual and for society" ("The Enlightenment as Medicine and as Cure," in W. H. Barber et al., eds., *The Age of the Enlightenment: Studies Presented to Theodore Besterman* [London, 1967], 380).

Just as yellow fever and its breeding places were the foil to Utopia's healthful expanse, America's developing party system was the foil to Smith's imagined government. A critical aspect of Utopia's exemplary civic virtue was its "absence of party-spirit" and "the harmony with which all the internal affairs of that Commonwealth are conducted." On one level, Smith's insistence on the absence of factions in Utopia was quite conventional; parties were mistrusted in post-Revolutionary America even by those who were creating them. Smith's "Institutions," however, reveals something more intriguing than a standard eighteenth-century fear of faction. It suggests a profound impatience with politics itself, an impatience that emerged both from the cacophony of partisan rhetoric in the 1790s and from Smith's Shaftesburian understanding of what true communication and problem solving should look like. In his diary entries, Smith decried "disputatious argument" as unproductive. Partisan argument was as stultifying as the anxious murmurings about yellow fever; it generally "ended . . . without the conviction of either party; and with no clearer ideas on the subject, than before." Seeking "conversation," Smith was frustrated by what seemed to him to be the parallel monologues of endlessly reiterated and endlessly opposed partisan convictions. Government rooted in partisanship, Smith believed, was an extension and formalization of this stagnant and isolating form of communication; it was a failure to connect, and so necessarily a failure to progress. Debate, compromise, and competing interests, traditional foundations of a political paradigm, would in Utopia be replaced by what Smith sought in his many cultural projects: open inquiry, true conversation, the mutual discovery of truth, and a harmonious oneness of purpose.[19]

Smith's Utopian government pursued these Shaftesburian ideals from within structures resembling the existing states' political institutions. Utopia had frequent elections, a governor, and a two-house legislature. But the Uto-

19. "Institutions," 309. "Much talk; very little conversation" was a representative Smith complaint (Cronin, ed., *Diary,* Dec. 24, 1796, 275). "A long and disputatious argument, 'On the difference between poetry and prose,'" he wrote on another occasion, "ended, as such discussions usually do, without the conviction of either party; and with no clearer ideas on the subject, than before" (Dec. 19, 1796, 273). A particularly scathing description of the Friendly Club occurred after a night spent in political discussion. "The late city election, the Treaty, etc. etc. occupied most of the time," Smith wrote, "during which, one yawned, another stretched himself, a third dozed, and all were stupid. I can not but regret that we do not give a higher and efficient character to this little association, which certainly is not wanting in capacity and information, and ought to be devoted to something better than mere amusements" (Apr. 30, 1796, 160).

pian government was primarily a tool intended to foster knowledge, virtue, and health through systematized observation and disclosure. Information was the chief resource Utopia's government was designed to make and circulate, extract from its citizens and bestow on them. Information was that which Utopia's citizens craved and created, and that which they were entitled to demand. Smith's imagined government was populated by numerous clerks and committees, and the major purpose of an entire political unit, the county, was "the administration of Justice, the communication of instruction to youth, the collection and circulation of Moral, Medical, Agricultural, Jural, and Literary information" and "the transmission of every kind of intelligence, and prosecution of every plan of improvement." Smith notes that Utopian officials' desks were equipped with writing implements: the pen, not the gavel or the sword, was the proper symbol of the Utopian state. The collection and circulation of knowledge would reveal and destroy the source of social ills just as they did physical ills, and thus a unitary truth, not a two-party establishment, would emerge. Utopia's government was the *Medical Repository* in civic garb.[20]

As central to Smith's conception of Utopia as the idea that citizens would continually create and revel in knowledge was the idea that Utopia's government would know a great deal about its citizens. Smith planned for a yearly census whose detail outstripped not only the state censuses of his day but also the federal one; his plan for a printed census form preceded the use of such a system by more than thirty years, and it extended the era's Linnaean impulse toward description and classification to include America's human inhabitants.[21]

Smith's state of Utopia, then, was both paradise and panopticon. As such,

20. "Institutions," 313, 325.

21. The federal government would begin to use printed census forms in 1830 (Margo J. Anderson, *The American Census: A Social History* [New Haven, Conn., 1988], 14). Smith's census is not only more frequent than censuses of existing states but also more detailed than the only federal census taken during his lifetime. The 1790 census reported only the name of the head of household, the number of free white males over sixteen and under sixteen, the number of free white females, the number of any other free persons, and the number of the enslaved. Smith wrote a sample census form for a Utopian household; the form gives the names and ages of all household inhabitants, lists their occupations, and includes a space for remarks such as, in the case of one imagined female inhabitant whose occupation was listed as "Wife," "takes in weaving." For a discussion of the appeal of Linnaean science to early national Americans, see Laura Rigal, *The American Manufactory: Art, Labor, and the World of Things in the Early Republic* (Princeton, N.J., 1998), 4–5.

it illuminates elements of the real personal and social world through which Smith moved. Smith's networks of friendships involved not only exchanges of information and affection but also mutual surveillance and regulation. Smith spent days writing a letter explaining his deism because his friend Theodore Dwight had essentially demanded such an accounting of him; the letter was circulated, as Smith knew it would be, to the many friends who also felt entitled to know and to judge his views. Smith accepted and welcomed such exchanges, which he believed offered him a chance to enlighten others even as he himself was improved by the scrutiny. Smith also believed in the power of government surveillance to reform individuals, and his Utopian government is reminiscent of the reformist prisons developed in late-eighteenth-century America by Smith's former teacher Benjamin Rush and Smith's fellow participant in the Manumission Society, the wealthy New York Quaker Thomas Eddy. Prison reformers believed that the causes of criminality could be discerned and controlled in individuals and in populations, and they designed prisons intended to benevolently surveil their inhabitants. "Observation and regulation," Michael Meranze has noted, marked inmates' experiences in Philadelphia's reformed Walnut Street Jail during the 1790s, and it was observation and regulation that marked the lives of inhabitants of Smith's Utopia as well. Smith, of course, imagined himself creating, not a prison house, but an enlightened state. But his goal, like the goal of those designing prisons, was that inhabitants be shaped by surveillance and education so that they internalized the rules of their governors.[22]

22. Cronin, ed., *Diary*, November 1796, Nov. 19, 1796 (Smith to Dwight), 241–253; Michael Meranze, *Laboratories of Virtue: Punishment, Revolution, and Authority in Philadelphia, 1765–1835* (Chapel Hill, N.C., 1996), 181–189; Christopher Adamson, "Evangelical Quakerism and the Early American Penitentiary Revisited: The Contributions of Thomas Eddy, Roberts Vaux, John Griscom, Stephen Grellet, Elisha Bates, and Isaac Hopper," *Quaker History*, XC, no. 2 (Fall 2001), 35–40. The coercive power lurking in Smith's utopian plan to remake institutions to cure the ills of American society and state also finds illumination in Michel Foucault's description of early modern plague towns. "This enclosed, segmented space, observed at every point," Foucault writes, "in which the individuals are inserted in a fixed place, in which the slightest movements are supervised, in which all events are recorded, in which an uninterrupted work of writing links the center and periphery, in which power is exercised without division, according to a continuous hierarchical figure, in which each individual is constantly located, examined and distributed among the living beings, the sick and the dead—all this constitutes a compact model of the disciplinary mechanism" (*Discipline and Punish: The Birth of the Prison,* trans. Alan Sheridan [London, 1977], 197).

Unlike Philadelphia's prison, Utopia was a republic, and its inhabitants chose the governors to whose direction they then acceded. Smith wanted that choice to be both free and harmonious. He was well aware that the appearance of consent could be manufactured through the kinds of electoral procedures followed in his home state of Connecticut. In the "Land of Steady Habits," as Connecticut was known, there were unusually frequent (for some positions, even annual) elections, but influential elites, byzantine procedural rules, and resultant voter apathy led to extraordinarily high rates of incumbent reelection. From 1783 to 1801, only one official was voted from office, and town meeting votes were scheduled for the afternoon, when they could occur largely unencumbered by voters, most of whom had already gone home. Smith, however, wanted more than the appearance of consensus. He wanted its reality. In the "Institutions," he mandated that settlers in Utopia must live there for ten years before being allowed to vote; this would allow them to be remade by Utopia's powerful institutions so that they could correctly exercise their freedom of choice and, presumably, converge on the proper candidate. Smith also conceived harsh laws to ensure voter turnout. As the logic of Smith's vision of internalized discipline required, however, all of those harsh laws were irrelevant: "There has occurred no instance," Smith wrote, "wherein it has been necessary to enforce these laws for several years." "As it is probable they had some influence, originally, in bringing about that strict attendance which is now common on occasions of this nature, I tho't it proper to notice them."[23]

In Smith's Utopia, that is, institutions and laws were in some sense unnecessary, just as Godwinian thought suggested they would be in a perfected society. In Smith's imagined polity, however, institutions and laws were nonetheless still present. "The laws are still in force," Smith carefully explained, "tho' the virtuous habits of the people have long since rendered them unnecessary." Smith had written his utopia "for the purpose of shewing what improvements are compatible with the present condition of man, in our country." In that condition, Smith made clear, there was still a need for the "force" of law. Indeed, Smith longed for a government of startling power. In his 1796 letter to Representative John Allen, Smith explained his belief that governments needed actively to promote citizens' welfare. "It is not sufficient," he wrote, that the Government of a Nation should not place

23. Chilton Williamson, *American Suffrage: From Property to Democracy, 1760–1860* (Princeton, N.J., 1960), 166; Richard J. Purcell, *Connecticut in Transition, 1775–1818* (Washington, D.C., 1918), 195; "Institutions," 314.

any obstacles in the way of each citizen to happiness, but it is the duty of every Government to do all in it's power to augment that happiness." "For the design of all Political Institution should be to *assist*, as well as *protect;* a design never accomplished where encouragement does not go hand in hand, with restraint." Government should have the right to use all property as it saw fit. "In my view," Smith wrote, "the whole property comprehended in a state, is the State's property; and ought to be apportioned to the necessities, and capacities of doing good, of each citizen." Thus, Smith's Utopian government had the power "to erect or pull down a market-place, to lay out and pave a street, to supply itself with water, to convert certain of its grounds to purposes of pleasure, or improvement, to build mills, *to restrain any citizen from the wasteful disposition of his property,* to regulate the mode of building, etc. etc. etc."[24]

A strong government with the ability to coerce virtuous activity—even if that ability usually lay dormant—was necessary if individuals and society as a whole were to advance toward knowledge and harmony. Smith shared William Godwin's hope that reason might one day make the enforcement of laws unnecessary. But Godwin asserted, "Since government, even in its best state, is an evil, the object principally to be aimed at is that we should have as little of it as the general peace of human society will permit." Smith, by contrast, believed that, in America, a republican government designed by enlightened (Godwin-reading) men such as himself could be a benevolent force. Government's power could be used to create citizens who one day would render the exertion of governmental power unnecessary.[25]

Education

Smith envisioned an extensive government-supported school system through which Utopia would create virtuous and useful citizens. Most Americans of the day believed that a successful republic required an educated populace; John Adams, James Madison, Benjamin Rush, Thomas Jefferson, and New York governor George Clinton all proposed ambitious, publicly financed systems of primary and secondary education.[26]

24. Smith to John Allen, Mar. 30, 1796, in Cronin, ed., *Diary*, 149–150; "Institutions," 323 (emphasis added).

25. William Godwin, *Enquiry concerning Political Justice, and Its Influence on Modern Morals and Happiness*, ed. Isaac Kramnick (Harmondsworth, 1976), 253.

26. Jefferson's Bill for the More General Diffusion of Knowledge, drafted in 1779,

Smith's "Institutions" proposed an extraordinarily extensive and intensive public education system. Unlike most of his contemporaries' plans for public education, including those of Jefferson and Rush in America and Mary Wollstonecraft in England, Smith's offered no sense that fewer and fewer people would attend each progressively higher level of education. And Utopian education, which was paid for by the state, was to be deep as well as broad. "The expence of Education being so inconsiderable, to the immediate subject of it," Smith wrote, "few men in Utopia are ill-educated." "It is unusual for men to enter into public life, or into the exercise of a profession, till after having passed thro' the University: I mean thro' that division of it which relates to his particular business. A general idea of all science is obtained at College—particular instruction is perfected at the University.—It is common for men to continue there till they are twenty-seven, eight, nine, or thirty." Such a system would prevent what Smith believed was a common problem: the truncation of professional education owing to financial constraints and social pressure. After offering his services

------

had set forth a system of common schools for Virginia that proposed free tuition only for three years and that expected only boys of "the best and most promising genius and disposition" to advance beyond the primary level (Roy J. Honeywell, *Educational Work of Thomas Jefferson* [Cambridge, 1931], Appendix A). This bill was finally passed in 1796, but an amendment that left it to each county to determine for itself when to carry out the bill's provisions rendered it meaningless (Charles Flinn Arrowood, ed., *Thomas Jefferson and Education in a Republic* [New York, 1930], 23). Wollstonecraft believed that "after the age of nine, girls and boys, intended for domestic employments, or mechanical trades, ought to be removed to other schools, and receive instruction, in some measure appropriated to the destination of each individual" (*A Vindication of the Rights of Woman: An Authoritative Text, Backgrounds, the Wollstonecraft Debate, Criticism*, 2d ed., ed. Carol H. Poston [New York, 1988], 168). Rush put forth his thoughts on education that might "convert men into republican machines" in *A Plan for the Establishment of Public Schools and the Diffusion of Knowledge in Pennsylvania* . . . (Philadelphia, 1786). Smith's description of the University of Utopia is also not unlike Rush's 1787 proposal for a national university; Smith's insistence on nominal or free tuition, however, and his apparent wish that all or almost all of Utopia's young men attend college and university differentiates his vision from Rush's more elitist one. In fact, the only other American to propose a truly inclusive system of public schools was none other than Smith's Federalist-allied friend, Noah Webster (David W. Robson, *Educating Republicans: The College in the Era of the American Revolution, 1750–1800* [Westport, Conn., 1985], 229–231). For a discussion of Americans' interest in educating citizens during this era, see Richard D. Brown, *The Strength of a People: The Idea of an Informed Citizenry in America, 1650–1870* (Chapel Hill, N.C., 1996), chap. 4.

as an unpaid physician at New York's public hospital in 1796, Smith was overcome by what he called "the consciousness of my own ignorance which constantly oppresses me—especially of my professional ignorance." "Could I trace out a correct and comprehensive method of study," he wrote the next week, "were my situation favorable to the putting of it in operation; could I clearly discern what knowledge was most important to be obtained . . . my happiness would gain a good deal of stability." Smith also deeply resented the experience of his friend James Kent, whose lectures on the law at Columbia were poorly attended, Smith felt, because young law clerks were discouraged by rapacious employers from continuing their education. Such limits on education were to Smith both sources of personal anguish and threats to the nation as a whole. Utopia and Utopians would not suffer from such failures.[27]

The lifelong education system Smith described was intricately gendered. Both boys and girls were to study "reading, writing, the elements of geography, arithmetic, morals, and Physics" until the age of twelve and to continue those studies while adding "Natural Philosophy and Natural History," "Elocution," "first principles of Politics—as connected [with Morals]— and Economics." Boys and girls were not only to study similar subjects but also to study together through the age of twelve, to continue to do so "under particular regulations" through the age of seventeen, and to do so "under certain regulations" through the age of twenty-two. In Smith's imagined western state, women could attend college, where they would study "French, German, Italian, Latin, and Greek . . . Algebra, Geometry, Trigonometry . . . Natural Philosophy and Astronomy . . . Rhetoric and Logic." Despite this striking gender inclusiveness, however, Smith also noted that boys and girls would be taught different "mechanical employments." More important, women were absent from Smith's Utopian university and thus could not pursue professional careers. Nor were women allowed to vote in Utopia (perhaps as a nod to Charles Brockden Brown's Mrs. Carter, Smith departs from the American Constitution's silence on the issue of women's suffrage and bans them from voting, not once, but twice). Smith's imagined state, like the cultural network in which he participated, was a place where women could exercise their intellects with considerable freedom and assertiveness. But political and economic enfranchisement did not follow directly from intellectual, nor did Smith wish them to. He imagined a world in

27. "Institutions," 317; Smith to John Allen, Jan. 24, 1796, "General Preface to the Month," June 1796, "Preface," June 5, 1796, in Cronin, ed., *Diary*, 127, 173, 174.

which individuals would be transformed for the better while the structures of society—familial as well as governmental—were maintained.[28]

Smith's desire for sublimated but powerful institutions, for transformation without disorder, and for freely achieved but absolute harmony all become evident in his discussions of Utopian religion. Christianity was integral to eighteenth-century theories of government and arguments over legitimate and illegitimate authority, and those who pondered social and political bonds pondered religion as well. Anthony Ashley Cooper, third earl of Shaftesbury, had advocated a reduction in the power of the church and the monarchy, and the philosopher David Hume warned that priests and princes understood the power each could gain through an alliance: "All princes that have aimed at despotic power have known of what importance it was to gain the established clergy," he wrote, "as the clergy, on their part, have shown a great facility in entering into the views of such princes." English Dissenters, including Dr. John Aikin—whose son John Aikin served as editor of the *Monthly Magazine*—and Joseph Priestley, worked in the 1780s to expand the civil rights of Dissenting Protestants; the campaign failed, but their intellectual circle came to overlap with the circle of radical reformers around Godwin, and together they discussed and modeled the sympathetic and rational social bonds that they believed made the political and clerical power of the English establishment unnecessary and harmful. Edmund Burke, by contrast, opposed repeal of the Test Acts (which imposed civil disabilities on those not professing the established religion) and argued that Christianity was the foundation of order and true social bonds; in his *Reflections on the Revolution in France*, he attacked both French anticlericalism

28. "Institutions," 315–317. This plan is, like much in Smith's "Institutions," a testament to both his cosmopolitan reading and his New England experience. In her *Vindication of the Rights of Woman*, a favorite of Smith's, Mary Wollstonecraft had proposed a similar scheme for the youngest children. Boys, she argued, learned "nasty indecent tricks" when shut up with each other, and girls learned "bad habits"; "were boys and girls permitted to pursue the same studies together," she concluded, "those graceful decencies might early be inculcated which produce modesty without those sexual distinctions that taint the mind" (*Vindication of the Rights of Woman*, ed. Poston, 164–165). In his "Notes from Recollections of My Life from My Birth till the Age of Eleven," written in 1797, Smith deplored "the physical as well as moral debasement" that resulted because, in Connecticut schools, "children of all ages, and educated at home in the most different habits, mingle without restraint." It was to this early influence that Smith traced his own habit of "self-pollution," a "pernicious practice" from which he did not succeed in "emancipating" himself until he was eighteen (Cronin, ed., *Diary*, 26).

and what he deemed the *"hortus siccus,"* or dry garden, of English Dissenters' rationalism.[29]

In America, even weak establishments attracted opposition, often from deeply religious Dissenting Protestants. During the years of the imperial crisis, resentment of the Anglican Church's goal of establishing an American bishopric helped drive colonial mistrust of the British government as a whole. By the 1770s and 1780s, some Americans came to believe political liberty must include liberty of conscience and disestablishment of religion. Despite the movement toward disestablishment at the state and federal level, however, politics remained entangled with religion. For some Federalist politicians, the French Revolution was evidence that their policies and style of citizenship must triumph over those of Democratic-Republicans for religion to be preserved. Politicians and clergy, seeking to bolster their influence, merged patriotic sentiment, Christianity, and Federalism, attacking Jefferson as an atheist and turning the tradition of fast days into occasions for professing fealty to Federalist policies. It was a potent alignment of cosmology and electoral strategy.[30]

Ideas about organized religion, however, could no more be contained by partisanship than they could escape becoming entangled with partisanship. Despite the efforts of some Federalists to claim the mantle of orthodox Christianity, some of those who sympathized with the party held unorthodox or even deist views. Such was true of leaders such as Timothy Pickering, John Adams, and Josiah Quincy, and it was true of Elihu Hubbard Smith. In New York City during the late 1790s, Smith gradually abandoned his

29. Lawrence E. Klein, *Shaftesbury and the Culture of Politeness: Moral Discourse and Cultural Politics in Early Eighteenth-Century England* (Cambridge, 1994), 21; David Hume, "Of the Parties of Great Britain," in Charles W. Hendel, ed., *David Hume's Political Essays* (New York, 1953), 87; Anne Janowitz, "Amiable and Radical Sociability: Anna Barbauld's 'Free Familiar Conversation,'" in Gillian Russell and Clara Tuite, eds., *Romantic Sociability: Social Networks and Literary Culture in Britain, 1770-1840* (New York, 2002), 62–63; Daniel E. White, "'The Joineriana': Anna Barbauld, the Aikin Family Circle, and the Dissenting Public Sphere," *Eighteenth-Century Studies*, XXXII (1999), 511–533; Edmund Burke, *Reflections on the Revolution in France*, ed. J. G. A. Pocock (Indianapolis, Ind., 1987), 12.

30. Gary B. Nash, "The American Clergy and the French Revolution," *William and Mary Quarterly*, 3d Ser., XXII (1965), 392–412; Harry S. Stout, "Rhetoric and Reality in the Early Republic: The Case of the Federalist Clergy," in Mark A. Noll, ed., *Religion and American Politics: From the Colonial Period to the 1980s* (New York, 1990), 62–76; David Waldstreicher, *In the Midst of Perpetual Fetes: The Making of American Nationalism, 1776-1820* (Chapel Hill, N.C., 1997), 145–152.

belief in the validity of Christianity as traditionally practiced. He rejected what he impatiently described as "the Atonement, Regeneration, Election, the Fall, Original Sin, etc. etc." Smith admired the French author C.-F. Volney, whose 1791 *Ruins* portrayed Christianity as an outdated shackle on the human mind, and, by the time of his death, he had not only stopped attending church but had also stopped his lifelong habit of daily prayer. Christianity, Smith calmly predicted, would one day fall away with all the other detritus of human ignorance. Smith's expectation paralleled that of Thomas Jefferson, who believed that orthodox Christianity would fade as Americans freely exercised their reason. But it was not to Jefferson but to Godwin that Smith claimed allegiance. "It has been said," Smith wrote, "that [Godwin's] morality is drawn from the New Testament. I should call it more pure." Smith argued that Godwin's belief that mankind could advance toward perfection was simply a secular version of the Protestant optimism of divines such as the Reverend Timothy Dwight. "'Dr. Dwight says that man may as easily become an angel, as continue a brute'—There is no difference between him and Godwin, but that one calls in the aid of religion, and the other rests on morality. In every other point of view, they agree."[31]

Smith's comparison was extraordinarily tendentious—Timothy Dwight urgently rejected Godwin and all whom he deemed "visionary" philosophers. But Smith was pointing to a true confluence between the minister's hopes for mankind and his own. Nor did Smith believe Dwight's Christian leadership was obsolete. Smith shared the view, common among deists on both sides of the Atlantic, that most individuals required the constraints of Christianity. "Think how great a Proportion of Mankind consists of weak and ignorant Men and Women," Benjamin Franklin cautioned, "and of inexperienc'd and inconsiderate Youth of both Sexes, who have need of the Motives of Religion to restrain them from Vice, to support their Virtue, and retain them in the Practice of it till it became *habitual*, which is the great Point for its Security." "If Men are so wicked as we now see them *with Religion* what would they be *without it?*" Sharing Franklin's view, Smith ignored the presence in New York City of Elihu Palmer, who sought to spread deism

31. Herbert M. Morais, *Deism in Eighteenth Century America* (1934; rpt. New York, 1960), 142–143; Smith to Theodore Dwight, October 1796, in Cronin, ed., *Diary*, 249, 251. Smith joined Coleridge in pondering the relationship between Godwin's ethical system and that of Christianity. See Nicola Trott, "The Coleridge Circle and the 'Answer to Godwin,'" *Review of English Studies*, n.s., XLI (1990), 212–217.

to the masses. Religion, like government, was a necessity in an imperfect world.[32]

Rather than removing orthodox Christianity from Utopia, Smith imagined a system in which state-supported Christian ministers rendered the Republic's citizens moral. "The complaints that have been made against religion, liberty and learning," Smith's former teacher Benjamin Rush wrote in 1786, "have been made, against each of them in a separate state." "Perhaps like certain liquors, they should only be used in a state of mixture. They mutually assist in correcting the abuses, and in improving the good effects of each other. From the combined and reciprocal influence of religion, liberty, and learning upon the morals, manners, and knowledge of individuals, of these, upon government, and of government, upon individuals, it is impossible to measure the degrees of happiness and perfection to which mankind may be raised." Smith adopted a similar position. Thus, Utopians were free to choose their clergymen, but choose them they must. "Each [Utopian unit called a] Society maintains a clergyman. He may be of what denomination they please." With religion as with government, current strength could hasten future obsolescence. In his utopian plan, Smith wove together church and state to create citizens who would one day need neither.[33]

Smith realized that state-supported ministers—like establishments in the real United States—would displease Dissenting evangelical Protestants and others whose piety did not find expression in the established church. His response was to write such people out of his imaginary world. "No Quakers, no Methodists, no Catholics are in Utopia. The law, therefore, is not oppressive, but springs out of the condition of Society." The law did not interfere with Utopians' freedom of conscience, that is, because anyone

32. Franklin to ———, [Dec. 13, 1757], in Leonard W. Labaree et al., eds., *The Papers of Benjamin Franklin*, VII (New Haven, Conn., 1963), 294–295; Elihu Palmer, *Posthumous Pieces . . . to Which Are Prefixed a Memoir of Mr. Palmer, by His Friend John Fellows of New York, and Mr. Palmer's "Principles of the Deistical Society of New York"* (London, 1824), 8–12. For an account of Palmer and New York as well as of the Deistical Society, see Morais, *Deism in Eighteenth Century America,* 130–132; Roderick S. French, "Elihu Palmer, Radical Deist, Radical Republican: A Reconsideration of American Free Thought," *Studies in Eighteenth-Century Culture,* VIII (1979), 87–108. Henry F. May describes "the view, widespread in the skeptical Enlightenment, that religion is necessary for the vulgar" (*Enlightenment in America,* 129).

33. "Institutions," 323; Benjamin Rush, "Of the Mode of Education Proper in a Republic," in Rush, *Essays, Literary, Moral, and Philosophical* (Philadelphia, 1798), 20.

with whose conscience the law interfered simply was not there. In this, Smith's late-eighteenth-century Utopia bore echoes of early Connecticut. New Haven had been intended as a new Jerusalem, a place in which moral authority emerged from a seamlessly unified church and state. Like Smith's tidy Utopia, New Haven's original settlement consisted of neat squares formed by roads meeting at perfect right angles, and it was populated by families who shared religious beliefs. Self-consciously seeking to create a new society, Smith partook of an old New England dream and, despite himself, dreamed of old New England.[34]

Yet Utopia was not simply Connecticut. Whereas Smith had been schooled by a minister and had read the New Testament, by his estimate, six times by the age of eleven, students in Utopia were to have no religious teaching in their schools until college. At that point, one presumes, Smith believed they could evaluate the proffered religious teachings on their own. Utopian children were instead taught "Morals," a word Smith used to describe the works of Scottish moral philosophers but also controversial texts by William Godwin and unrestricted investigations into the legitimacy of Christianity itself. Thus, in Utopia, Christian ministers would keep society in good order while individual minds freed themselves from Christian orthodoxy. By the time the scaffolding of tradition was removed, the new ethical system based on Enlightenment philosophy would be strong enough to hold up the structure of society unchanged.

The great mystery of Smith's utopia is the apparent secrecy in which he held it. Smith loved to discuss his writings and translations with others, and he published both literary and medical offerings in newspapers and journals. More important, the framing device of Smith's utopia suggests that he wished to believe that this text offered a way to cure the real world of disorder, intellectual barrenness, and contagion. But Smith never mentioned plans to publish the "Institutions." Nor, even more strikingly, does he seem to have shared it with the Friendly Club. Perhaps he wished to complete it and then present it fully formed to the "statesman" he hoped, as he wrote in its introduction, would use it as a model. Perhaps he thought his disenfranchisement of women or his positing of a religious establishment would disappoint friends who—at least in an imaginary world—might hope for more radical change.[35]

34. "Institutions," 323.
35. Ibid., 309.

Most likely, Smith realized he could treat the text as a practical model for improvement only while he was writing it. Once completed, and particularly once published, it would melt into a work of fiction. The "Institutions" describes a state that both is and is not part of the nation, and a landscape that is and is not that of the United States; it does so in a format that is both a blueprint for change and a concession that Smith had no real mechanism for achieving the kind of controlled transformation he desired. Both the specifics of Smith's text and the act of his writing a utopia at all demonstrate the tension between the hope that intellect and sociability could transform America and the fear that intellect and sociability could only truly reign in clubs, conversations, and the realms of the imagination.

Ultimately, Smith's "Institutions," with its lists of mineral deposits and its proposals for census forms, was a fantasy cloaked in the sober garb of order, fact, and reason. In it—in Smith's ideal vision of the real nation in which he lived—inquiry, choice, and investigation always led to consensus, knowledge flowed freely without overrunning its proper channels or washing away familiar landmarks, and an educated and enlightened populace willingly allowed itself, because of its very education and enlightenment, to be governed and instructed by a still more educated and enlightened few. Smith longed for such a place, but he committed himself to confronting the problems of the world in which he lived. In the last months of his life, Smith set aside his utopia and devoted more and more time to the *Medical Repository*. That periodical was a practical application of fellowship, education, and inquiry, and Smith believed it could month by month chip away at disease and ignorance, even in the absence of perfect boulevards, geometrically precise towns, and pens on all the legislators' desks.

CHAPTER 4

He Summons
Genius to His Aid
Joseph Dennie and the Farmer's
Weekly Museum, *1795–1800*

During the 1790s, while Elihu Hubbard Smith labored in New York City, Joseph Dennie used his own considerable rhetorical and logistical skills to summon a far-flung cadre of readers and writers. As editor of Walpole, New Hampshire's *Farmer's Weekly Museum,* Dennie offered a forum in which readers and contributors participated in civic life outside formal politics. As he did so, he contributed to the development of the partisan system whose dominance of American life he disdained.

When Dennie left Harvard College in 1790, still too angered by his rustication to participate in commencement, he secured a clerkship in the office of a Charlestown, New Hampshire, lawyer. But he was convinced that his exquisite sensibility suited him to a life in letters. "The same [nervous] irritation, which sometimes hinders me from pronouncing my part on Life's stage," he wrote, "will enable me so to act at another as to challenge the *Spectator*'s applause." Adopting the *Spectator*'s critical, bemused persona, Dennie began contributing essays under the title "Farrago" to a Windsor, Vermont, paper called the *Morning Ray; or, Impartial Oracle.* Even as he completed his required three-year clerkship and started a law practice in New Hampshire, Dennie continued his belletristic efforts. His writing began to be printed not only in the *Morning Ray* but also in the *Eagle; or, Dartmouth Centinel* and in the *Newhampshire Journal; or, The Farmer's Weekly Museum,* the latter published by Isaiah Thomas and David Carlisle, Jr., at Walpole, New Hampshire. Working with the playwright Royall Tyler, Dennie created a column, "Shop of Colon and Spondee," that offered poetry, prose, and jibes at Democratic-Republicans.[1]

1. "The last acts of pigmy despotism exercised," Dennie wrote to his friend Roger Vose, "I forsook Cambridge with bitter execrations, and repaired to Lexington to snuff sweet air" (Aug. 17, 1790, Dennie-Vose Papers, Massachusetts Historical Society, Boston). See also Harold Milton Ellis, *Joseph Dennie and His Circle: A Study in American Literature from 1792 to 1812,* Bulletin of the University of Texas, no. 40 (Austin, Tex., 1915), 40–42; Dennie to Joseph and Mary Green Dennie, Nov. 6, 1791,

Dennie maintained his legal practice but made less and less effort to hide his distaste for the law. Jeremiah Mason, a friend to both Dennie and Elihu Smith, later marveled that Dennie's "legal knowledge consisted wholly in a choice selection of quaint, obsolete, and queer phrases from 'Plowden's Commentaries,' the only law book he had ever read with any attention, and this was read for the sole purpose of treasuring up these quaint phrases." "These he often repeated in ridicule of the law." During the spring of 1795, Dennie traveled to Boston, hoping to found a literary periodical that would bring him the renown he craved and that would add to—or perhaps someday replace—his meager revenues as a lawyer. Expecting to find an audience among the wealthy and educated families of the city, Dennie started the *Tablet,* a weekly, four-page belletristic magazine for which he wrote most of the content. Despite the presence in Boston and Cambridge of friends such as Josiah Quincy, of money, and of citizens who had seemed to Dennie such likely patrons of his talents, the *Tablet* failed in thirteen weeks. Years later, Dennie recalled the pain he felt at the "death" of the project he called "my child," a death he blamed on the "dullness of the Bostonians" and the "inconvenience of being poor" and therefore unable to sustain the *Tablet* from his own purse.[2]

After the failure of the *Tablet,* Dennie moved himself and his would-be

<hr />

Joseph Dennie Papers, Houghton Library, Harvard College Library, Harvard University, Cambridge, Mass. "Farrago" essays (nos. 2 and 3) by Dennie appear in the Feb. 21 and Mar. 6, 1792, issues of the *Morning Ray; or, Impartial Oracle.* See also Ellis, *Joseph Dennie and His Circle,* chaps. 4, 5; J. E. Hall, *Philadelphia Souvenir: A Collection of Fugitive Pieces from the Philadelphia Press; with Biographical and Explanatory Notes* (Philadelphia, 1826), 34. Royall Tyler contributed to the *Farmer's Weekly Museum* as well; see G. Thomas Tanselle, "Attribution of Authorship in 'The Spirit of the Farmers' Museum' (1801)," Bibliographical Society of America, *Papers,* LIX (1965), 170-176. He is better known as author of the play *The Contrast* (1787) and in his writing shared Dennie's mixture of social and literary interests; see John Evelev, *"The Contrast:* The Problem of Theatricality and Political and Social Crisis in Postrevolutionary America," *Early American Literature,* XXXI (1996), 74-97; Roger B. Stein, "Royall Tyler and the Question of Our Speech," *New England Quarterly,* XXXVIII (1965), 454-474; Ellis, *Joseph Dennie and His Circle,* 58.

2. G. J. Clark, ed., *Memoirs of Jeremiah Mason; Reproduction of Privately Printed Edition of 1873,* ed. George Stillman Hillard (Boston, 1917), 29; Ellis, *Joseph Dennie and His Circle,* 73-74; Dennie to Mary Green Dennie, Apr. 24, 1795, Apr. 26, 1797, Dennie Papers; Edmund Quincy, *Life of Josiah Quincy of Massachusetts* (Boston, 1867), 31. The *Tablet* was to be printed by William Spotswood, who would act as publisher by assuming the financial risk of the magazine; he agreed to share the profits with Dennie (Ellis, *Joseph Dennie and His Circle,* 79).

FIGURE 3. Joseph Dennie. *By James Sharples. Circa 1790.*
Museum of Fine Arts, Boston. Bequest of James Dennie.
Photograph © Museum of Fine Arts, Boston

law practice to Walpole, New Hampshire. This was not a shrewd choice for one truly bent on establishing himself as a lawyer. Walpole was the largest village in the northern Connecticut River valley, but it already had three lawyers to serve its population of fewer than fifteen hundred people. Dennie, however, moved to Walpole to further a literary career, not a legal one. In 1793, the print entrepreneur Isaiah Thomas had opened a printing office and bookstore in Walpole and had inaugurated the paper that would become the *Farmer's Weekly Museum*. Upon his arrival in fall 1795, Dennie sent a column to Thomas's partner, David Carlisle. "Without saying a word respecting a stipend," Dennie later explained, "I wrote [to Carlisle] and gave him an essay . . . and called it the *Lay Preacher*." "I determined, by the agency of my pen," Dennie wrote, "to convince him that I could be useful, and then—my humble knowledge of human agency taught me—I was sure he would encourage me when his own *interest* was the prompter." By writing a wide variety of pieces for the *Museum*, Dennie pursued his plan of making himself indispensable to the newspaper's printers. He also abandoned any pretense of interest in his law office. "On a day one [client] strayed in," Josiah Quincy later recalled, "but the interruption he caused to the leisure and favorite occupations of his counsel learned in the law was so great, that a repetition of the annoyance was carefully guarded against. Mr. Dennie thenceforward kept his office-door locked on the inside." In April 1796, David Carlisle, to whom Isaiah Thomas had turned over the *Museum*, made Dennie editor of the paper at a salary of £110 per year.[3]

Two years after the disheartening demise of the *Tablet*, Dennie declared the *Museum* a success. "The constant swell of our subscription book suggests a theme to our gratitude, and a motive to our industry," Dennie effused in an editor's column. "The *Farmer's Museum* is read by more than TWO THOUSAND INDIVIDUALS, and has its patrons in Georgia, and on the banks of the Ohio." Spurring on his readers, contributors, and himself to further efforts, Dennie asked that "the owners of London papers . . . promptly

3. Dennie to Mary Green Dennie, Aug. 6, 1796, Dennie Papers; Quincy, *Life of Josiah Quincy*, 31. Walpole benefited from its location on the Connecticut River and by the mid-1790s was becoming what David Jaffee describes as a provincial "print center." Nonetheless, as Jaffee notes, Walpole had no post office until 1795 and only acquired a weekly stage to and from Boston in 1801 (after Dennie's departure). Jaffee discusses Walpole's rapid development during the era in *People of the Wachusett: Greater New England in History and Memory, 1630-1860* (Ithaca, N.Y., 1999), 218–225. See also Clifford K. Shipton, *Isaiah Thomas: Printer, Patriot, and Philanthropist, 1749-1831* (Rochester, N.Y., 1948), 32–67.

answer the Editor's late" appeals for material; he dramatically announced that he had, "with a trembling hand," embarked on a new set of columns for the *Museum*'s back page; and he demanded that the *Museum*'s far-flung subscribers pay seventy-five cents in advance for the privilege of receiving his paper, lest Dennie summarily deprive readers of his editorial talents.[4]

Dennie's exuberance was not misplaced. His estimate of two thousand subscribers approached the upper limits of any early national newspaper's paid circulation. During Dennie's association with the *Museum*, which lasted until 1800, politicians and amateur literati were eager to have their offerings appear in his pages. Dennie's "Paper," Elihu Hubbard Smith noted in a July 1797 letter, "has acquired much reputation; and there are about 3,000 copies circulated every week; and it gains subscribers constantly."[5]

His Flowery Road You May Rely on: The Museum as Content

Turning the pages of the *Museum* during Dennie's association with the paper, readers came upon a varied and lively assemblage of essays, satires,

4. "To Readers and Correspondents," Dec. 4, 1797, *Farmer's Weekly Museum: Newhampshire and Vermont Journal*, 3.

5. Elihu Hubbard Smith to Charles Brockden Brown, July 11, 1797, in James E. Cronin, ed., *The Diary of Elihu Hubbard Smith (1771–1798)* (Philadelphia, 1973), 332; Jeffrey L. Pasley, *"The Tyranny of Printers": Newspaper Politics in the Early American Republic* (Charlottesville, Va., 2001), 422 n. 2. As is common for eighteenth-century papers, no direct proof of the number of Dennie's subscribers has survived, but circumstantial evidence tends to support his claims about numbers and geographical range. The Federalist *Columbian Centinel*, on Aug. 26, 1796, for example, attested to the *Museum*'s popularity throughout the Union, claiming that its "Lay Preacher" columns were copied "into over eighty different newspapers in the United States" and opining that "the library of every genuine federalist ought to be adorned with them; and our municipal officers ought to introduce them into our schools—as useful and convenient." Signed "A Friend to Merit," this piece is also an example of the symbiotic relationship between printers and the blur between editorial and advertising copy. Also suggestive is that Dennie was able to begin the *Port Folio* in 1801 with an immediate subscribership of fifteen hundred. For an estimate of the *Port Folio*'s subscribership, for which there are surviving circulation records, see Linda K. Kerber and Walter John Morris, "Politics and Literature: The Adams Family and the *Port Folio*," *William and Mary Quarterly*, 3d Ser., XXIII (1966), 462. For accounts of conversations about and awareness of Dennie, see, for example, Cronin, ed., *Diary*, Sept. 27, 1796, 223; Thomas Boylston Adams to Dennie, Mar. 16, 1799, Dennie Papers (in which he describes such a conversation and also instructs Dennie to bill "the President" for his *Museums*); and the accounts discussed below in this chapter.

letters from contributors, and poems. Sedate neoclassical poetry coexisted with gleeful attacks on Harvard (as he had predicted, Dennie's anger did not sleep), and stout avowals of Federalism shared the page with airy dismissals of partisanship. "The question of defensive operation is warmly agitated," Dennie wrote in one 1797 column; "Arm or slaves, says one party; arm and starve, says the other; and the necessity of uniting is urged in language better calculated to divide." But the *Museum* was no mere potpourri. Dennie presided over it in his editorial and Lay Preacher personas, and he turned the periodical into a forum for vigorous, lively criticism of America's devotion to commerce and politics.[6]

As the Lay Preacher, Dennie claimed age, wisdom, and an aversion to frivolity. He also subverted these claims at every turn. Many, if not most, of his interconnected readers knew of his youth, and it seems likely that word of his penchant for bright silks and silver buckles also would have got around, giving the lie to his injunctions against vanity and waste. Dennie, moreover, was known to write his "lay sermons" "at the village tavern, directly opposite to a chamber where he and his friends were amusing themselves with cards." All of these contradictions were not simply a matter of dissonance between Dennie and Dennie-as-Lay-Preacher. Even within his "Lay Preacher" columns, Dennie mingled stern moral pronouncements with confessions of his own "valetudinarianism." He deplored "restlessness" as "a capital defect in character, generally indicating, either a light mind, or a tainted heart," but delighted in darting from subject to subject. One 1796 column began with the confident dictum, *"On the first day of the first month—set in order the things that are to be set in order,"* only to progress quickly to the admission, "I confess with candor, that I loiter and slumber much, and while I preach industry to others, *am myself a castaway.*" In short, Dennie adopted a pseudo-Franklinian persona in order to mock the respectable moral advice he purported to give. Readers could delight in being in on the joke. One contributor, expressing an apt wish to "pull off the black coat of the Lay Preacher," teased:

> His flowery road you may rely on,
> Is but a crooked path to Zion
>
> . . . .
>
> His stile is smooth as lover's sonnet
> Not unadorn'd as quaker's bonnet
> But interlaced with quotation,

6. *Farmer's Weekly Museum*, Mar. 27, 1798.

Arranged with apt alliteration
On Lady's cheek may raise a dimple,
Please sentimental folks, and simple;
But, with submission much I doubt,
If wicked folks will turn about.

Dennie's true claim to authority lay, not in the Lay Preacher's transparently false pretensions to staid respectability, but in his insistence on independent judgment and fearless self-expression. In one mischievous column, Dennie suggested that no one in America really believed that the majority was ever in the right. "The minority ought, in all cases, to carry the vote," he wrote in a 1797 column, and then supported this counterintuitive assertion by observing that minority, rather than majority, rule was the one ideal on which everyone already agreed: "the democrat" scorns the majority who passed the Jay Treaty, "Mr. Federalist" loathes "the mob majorities," and the pious know that "the majority of mankind are reprobate in this world, and will be eternally damned in the next." No one believed that the majority's opinion was more valid than his own, the *Museum* insisted. Beneath the joke lay a real demand: the duty of an American citizen and the duty of the *Museum* reader lay in exercising independent judgment.[7]

Throughout the *Museum,* Dennie deplored Americans' pursuit of commercial success, bland respectability, and political power. In a "Lay Preacher" column taking as its inspiration the biblical phrase, "Issachar is a strong ass," Dennie bitterly compared attorneys and clergymen to slave traders. "Gold coast navigators" who captured enslaved laborers, the "little mercenary attorney" who collected every last shilling from his clients, and the uninspired clergyman who was "corpulent, red-faced, and a heavy leaner upon the cushion" all, Dennie asserted, "change humanity into a "strong ass" by devoting themselves to wealth and status in a way that robbed them and others of their humanity. The *Museum* also put the era's criticism of hypocritical sensibility to work against America's elites; one *Museum* essayist mocked the genteel swell who wept over the novels

7. *Farmer's Weekly Museum,* Jan. 5, 1796, June 12, 1797 ("Colon and Spondee"), Aug. 13, 1798 ("The Lay Preacher"). Joseph T. Buckingham describes Dennie's bright clothes and adds that his hair "in front, . . . [was] well loaded with pomatum, frizzled, or craped, and powdered; the earl-locks had undergone the same process; behind, his natural hair was augmented by the addition of a large queue . . . which, enrolled in some yards of black ribbon, reached half-way down his back" (*Specimens of Newspaper Literature: With Personal Memoirs, Anecdotes, and Reminiscences,* 2 vols. [Boston, 1850], II, 196).

of Laurence Sterne while being "a grinder of poverty's face," and another ridiculed as "sanctimonious wretches" the wealthy merchants who, from their "moldering mansions," oppressed widows, soldiers, and orphans. The paper even pricked self-congratulatory and hypocritical nationalist com-memoration: a 1796 column lambasted Bostonians for mourning "a dead mulatto"; "Would not you have cudgelled the same Crispus Atucks [sic] for accosting you civilly?" the *Museum* writer chided.[8]

Dennie cast himself as a foe of mindless radicalism as well as of mindless devotion to conventional success. Assaults on wealth and patriotic display shared the page with criticism of the "grinder of poverty's face." Dennie warned readers: "Trust me, he who jeers received truths, or who tells you that there is no distinction among men, and that all are equally qualified to govern, is an impostor more pernicious than Mahomet, and his Favor is deceitful." The man who advocated radical change and absolute egalitari-anism, that is, was as false as the man who wept at novels while caring noth-ing for people: neither nurtured the true social bonds that formed the basis of a good community. And radicals' greatest sin, in the *Museum*'s telling, was their courting of the crowd. In the same column in which he chastised mercenary attorneys and slave traders, Dennie excoriated the "candidate for Congress, [who] instead of studying the constitution at home, is constantly in a bar room with a mug of flip in his hand courting the suffrages of the populace. . . . Like Absalom he stands at the city gate, taking every stranger familiarly by the hand." Such raw need for approval destroyed personal dignity and social order as much as did sentimental hypocrisy and ruthless radicalism. All indicated failures of mind and heart, failures that Dennie combated with an irony fueled by true anger.[9]

Brothers in Print: The Museum as Process

The *Museum* succeeded not only because Dennie appealed to readers with his lively writing but also because he understood the powers of the nation's many amateur literati. Very early in his time in Walpole, Dennie

8. *Farmer's Weekly Museum*, Oct. 27, 1795 ("The Lay Preacher"), Nov. 3, 1795 ("The Lay Preacher"), Sept. 7, 1796 ("The Hermit"), Aug. 14, 1797 ("Beri Hesdin"); *Farmer's Museum; or, Lay Preacher's Gazette*, Aug. 5, 1799. On Harvard, for example, see Nov. 29, 1796: Harvard "is a mortifying instance of dronish life and of 'thought-less meditation'" that produces "nothing."

9. *Farmer's Weekly Museum*, Oct. 27 ("The Lay Preacher"), Nov. 3, 1795 ("The Lay Preacher").

began to piece together a creative and circulative network. That network included all those who read, wrote for, found subscriptions for, extracted, or even quoted the *Museum*. Their efforts brought Dennie readers, and some of those readers joined the ranks of those who wrote for and informally marketed the *Museum*. Both product and process, the *Museum* fed cultural hunger as it sated it and built the network that helped to make it.

Dennie cultivated readers and contributors through face-to-face sociability and through correspondence. He was far more hospitable to fellow literary sparks than he was to potential legal clients. Walpole was easily accessible along the Connecticut River, and, during Dennie's sojourn, it became the scene of convivial gatherings of young, literary-minded professionals. In the words of one nineteenth-century historian of the town, it "was the resort of a *coterie* of wags, wits, and literati from all the surrounding country," and its "old tavern . . . was turned into a *literary pandemonium*." Lawyers dominated this group, and Jeremiah Mason later recalled that they pursued their "amusement and recreation" not only at the tavern but also "at the sessions of the courts."[10]

Like Elihu Smith, Dennie linked his local circle to a geographically expansive network. Dennie's correspondence and the issues of the *Farmer's Weekly Museum* reveal his carefully crafted overtures to culturally engaged and ambitious Americans. "He summons genius of every description to his aid," Dennie wrote of himself; "His industry shall cooperate with the abilities of his friends." Dennie penned personal letters, asking for contributions and for assistance in gaining subscribers, to men such as George Richards Minot, whose history of Shays's Rebellion had been published by Isaiah Thomas in 1788; the Federalist politician Fisher Ames; the Connecticut poet Richard Alsop; David Everett of Boston, who wrote for the *Museum* and later for the *Port Folio;* two sons of John Adams, Charles Adams (who lost the first set of subscription papers and asked for replacements) and Thomas Boylston Adams, who offered logistical assistance throughout Dennie's editorial career; and Noah Webster. Webster's response suggests the tenor of Dennie's appeals. Writing from New York, he thanked Dennie for his "obliging letter" and added, "I acknowledge myself much honored by the terms of the letter; but hardly dare flatter myself that my hasty writings can have been a model for the ingenious author of the 'Lay Preacher.'" Court-

10. George Aldrich, *Walpole as It Was and Is, Containing the Complete Civil History of the Town from 1749 to 1879* . . . (Claremont, N.H., 1880), 81; Clark, ed., *Memoirs of Jeremiah Mason*, ed. Hillard, 27–32.

ing literary contributors suited Dennie's talents more than courting legal clients.[11]

One of Dennie's most productive relationships was with another man who understood the power of cultural networks, Elihu Hubbard Smith. Dennie appears to have sent an emissary to Smith and his associates early in the fall of 1796. Thomas Green Fessenden was a Walpole resident and young man of letters who arrived in New York City declaring his intentions to study law and asking to stay with a friend of Smith's. Fessenden, Smith noted in his diary, stayed only one week, during which time he probably progressed little in his legal studies. He did, however, manage to establish invaluable relationships with Smith and other members of the city's Friendly Club, and that was most likely the true purpose of the visit.[12]

Dennie and Smith adroitly furthered the association that Fessenden's brief visit had begun. Each man recognized the other as a fellow cultural impresario. Having learned of Dennie's interest in him and the Friendly Club, Smith wrote the editor a forthright critique of the *Museum,* suggesting it

11. "To Readers and Correspondents," *Farmer's Weekly Museum,* Aug. 30, 1796. Dennie's letters are evident in the responses: Fisher Ames to Dennie, Feb. 20, 1797, Charles Adams to Dennie, May 9, 1797, Richard Alsop to Dennie, May 9, 1797, Thomas Boylston Adams to Dennie, Mar. 16, 1799, Dennie Papers. In Minot's response, he takes a subscription for himself but begs off asking others. His explanation indicates both the perils of cultural work and its persistent appeal: "I once solicited one [a subscription sheet] on my own account, and received encouragement. This was so great a favour from *literary patrons* in our quarter, that I consider myself under obligations never to ask another, and I have come to a conclusion to attempt a little 12 mo. Publication in the historical line, (which I think will bring me in debt) without asking assistance, merely from the disagreeableness of receiving it, putting all uncertainty of its being granted out of the question" (G. R. Minot to Dennie, Mar. 25, 1797, Dennie Papers). See Webster to Dennie, Sept. 30, 1796, Dennie Papers. Webster continued: "I have occasionally read the numbers of the latter publication, as they appear in the papers, and would have republished them in our papers, could I have been favored with the whole in order, and had not a press of news continually crowded upon our hands. From what I have now, I think highly of the pieces, I am happy to find them held in high estimation by the public."

12. This incident is visible in Smith's entries of September 1796 (Cronin, ed., *Diary,* 211–223). Fessenden was the son of a Walpole clergyman, Thomas Fessenden; he began practicing as a lawyer in 1799 but continued to write verse, most notably his 1805 "Democracy Unveiled," a satiric attack on Jefferson. Later in his life, he worked as a newspaper editor. See Porter Gale Perrin, *The Life and Works of Thomas Green Fessenden, 1771-1837* (Orono, Maine, 1925), University of Maine Studies, 2d Ser., no. 4.

might be improved by more attention to economics and the lives of authors. The resourceful Dennie wasted nothing from this offering. He adopted some of Smith's recommendations for enlarging the paper's subject matter, and he not only published the letter Smith wrote but also divided it in two parts to create the illusion of one more contribution.[13]

As the weeks passed, the two men's association continued. "Since you have devoted a corner of the 'Museum' to the subjects pointed out by me," Smith wrote to Dennie in June, "I have laid aside several european papers which may not improperly come under the head of Economics." "I am pleased to see the lives of the Poets occupy a portion of your Journal." He continued, "I have a suggestion to make, on this head." Smith also provided Dennie with other forms of aid. He put the editor in correspondence with his own favorite New York City printers and booksellers, T. and J. Swords. He subscribed to the *Museum*—no small thing, given that Smith's roommate already had a paid subscription and that Smith, for reasons of purse and principle, was a habitual sharer of texts. Smith even found Dennie three new subscribers, John Roulet, William Woolsey, and Tunis Wortman. Whether Wortman, the young secretary of New York's Democratic-Republican Society, subscribed to this Federalist-leaning periodical because of respect for its literary merits or as a favor to Smith is unclear; what is certain is that the connections of the cultural networks had trumped the expected divisions of partisanship.[14]

Dennie, busy with his writing and editorial duties, found the time to sell twenty copies of Smith's libretto and to mention favorably in the *Museum* both it and the *Medical Repository*, the former of which he noted was "excellently printed on vellum paper." Dennie also praised the Erasmus Darwin volume that Smith shepherded to press: "Under the tasteful direction of Dr. Elihu H. Smith, Mess. Swords, Newyork Booksellers, have published a beautiful and portable edition of Dr. Darwin's Botanic Garden." Smith and Dennie's relationship served both men well, enabling each to expand the range of reading and audience.[15]

The success of the *Museum* also relied on—and attracted—contributions

13. Cronin, ed., *Diary*, Mar. 5, 1797, 299–300.
14. Elihu Hubbard Smith to Dennie, June 18, 1797, in Cronin, ed., *Diary*, 326–327. Smith's correspondence with Dennie continued the next month; see Smith to Dennie, July 27, 1797, ibid., 335.
15. *Farmer's Weekly Museum*, May 22, 1798. Smith notes that Dennie sold *Edwin and Angelina* in a letter to Dennie (Cronin, ed., *Diary*, July 24, 1797, 336). Dennie's praise of the opera in the *Farmer's Weekly Museum* appears on June 5, 1797.

from individuals to whom Dennie made no overtures. The Post Office Act of 1792, which admitted newspapers into the mail for a nominal fee and codified the printers' custom of exchanging papers without charge, created a web of relationships that could be woven into the existing web of amateur cultural exchanges. Editors had easy access to Dennie's writing and faced no copyright prohibitions against reprinting it in their newspapers. Far from robbing Dennie of subscribers, reprints attracted them. Writers coveting a broad audience, moreover, chose to send work to a newspaper likely to be extracted. "Having remarked, in other Newspapers, many ingenious extracts from the *Farmer's Museum*," a man writing as "The Meddler" explained: "I was induced to inquire into the state of that paper; and find a very considerable part of it is professedly devoted to polite literature. Upon this, notwithstanding my remote situation, I resolved to embark with those literary adventurers." The lawyer and man of letters Isaac Story, for his part, observed that Dennie's abilities and taste "have enriched and given energy to almost every newspaper in the Union." Story pulled his essays from the *Massachusetts Magazine* in order that they might find a place in the more widely read *Farmer's Weekly Museum*.[16]

Dennie was among America's first professional men of letters. His ability to earn money from literature, however, was entirely dependent on the eagerness of others to remain amateurs. The works he produced that did not include the writings of amateurs, works such as the *Tablet* and the collected volume of his "Lay Preacher" essays, sold poorly. Dennie realized that the survival of the *Museum* required that its publication and circulation be contributors' only reward; he never even answered Elihu Smith's letter proposing that Charles Brockden Brown be paid for contributions. He knew others would write for free: Dennie could increase by orders of magnitude the number of readers his contributors could have achieved through more

16. "The Meddler," *Farmer's Weekly Museum*, Nov. 29, 1796; Isaac Story to Dennie, n.d., 1797, Dennie Papers. Richard R. John explains that the Act "admitted newspapers into the mail on unusually favorable terms, hastening the rapid growth of the press," and "established a set of procedures that facilitated the extraordinarily rapid expansion of the postal network from the Atlantic seaboard into the transappalachian West" (*Spreading the News: The American Postal System from Franklin to Morse* [Cambridge, Mass., 1995], 31). William J. Gilmore explains that Walpole and other Upper Connecticut Valley towns in particular saw, between 1780 and 1835, "the creation of a new regional communications environment in the American Northeast, based on printed and written texts" (*Reading Becomes a Necessity of Life: Material and Cultural Life in Rural New England, 1780–1835* [Knoxville, Tenn., 1989], 17).

traditional practices of manuscript exchange. And, because of the eagerness of men such as Isaac Story to become members of what Dennie called the "*Corps* periodical," gaining content and gaining an audience were one and the same. With the *Tablet,* Dennie had sought an audience in a single city and had offered primarily his own voice. In the *Farmer's Weekly Museum,* by contrast, Dennie learned to cultivate, not a locale, but a cohort—not a geographic community, but a community of interest and ambition. And he learned to offer not only his own voice but also a forum for the voices of others.[17]

A Receptacle for Fugitive Good Things: The Museum as Object

Dennie believed that the quality of craftsmanship evidenced in a text's pages and design was an important element of its merit and a good reason to purchase it. So he worried over his inability to render the *Museum* as

17. Dennie blamed the failure of the *Lay Preacher; or, Short Sermons, for Idle Readers* (Walpole, N.H., 1796) on his printer's bankruptcy, lamenting: "To have the whole profits of my pen, the honorable and liberal source of my support, thus snatched away, you may easily conceive to be not only mortifying, but an embarrassing event" (Dennie to Mary Green Dennie, Sept. 6, 1799, Dennie Papers). Even the single-authored "Lay Preacher" columns emerged from Dennie's participation in the practices of his cultural network: "While I was mingling in the crowd on 'change, lounging in booksellers' shops, arguing in a coffee house, in defence of the Executive, or chatting with sensible women round a supper table," Dennie wrote in the *Museum,* "I was in fact composing Lay Preachers" ("The Lay Preacher," *Farmer's Weekly Museum,* June 19, 1798). David Jaffee has noted the mixture of amateurism and professionalism in Dennie's career but sees amateurism as a facade for Dennie's individualist professionalism. "Dennie," Jaffee argues, "affected the pose of a genteel amateur," although he "in fact was a canny professional, who relied upon his editorial and authorial efforts to support himself" (*People of the Wachusett,* 227). Jaffee also focuses on what he believes to be the disadvantages of Walpole as a location, suggesting that "the effort to establish a literary journal in Walpole, when even cosmopolitan Boston could not sustain one for long, required great effort and brought out the contradictory strains of literary entrepreneurship in Dennie and his circle" (228). "I do not hear any thing from Dennie," Smith wrote to Brown on September 16, 1797; "I do not know that my first letter ever reached him. I have written again; and shall communicate the result, as soon as known. Meantime, 'Alcuin' rests with me" (Cronin, ed., *Diary,* 364). This exchange resulted in a stalemate: Dennie knew that he could get contributions for free and so remained silent in the face of Smith's suggestions; Smith knew enough about cultural commerce's sharp practices to realize that he should forward Brown's manuscript only when he had received a commitment that Brown would be paid, and so he kept *Alcuin* with him.

an object of beauty. In April 1797, Samuel Eliot of Boston wrote to re-assure the editor, in response to Dennie's apparent queries, that people did not complain about "the small sheet, and ordinary quality" of the news-paper: "I have heard none as yet," Eliot wrote, "tho' I have been attentive to every syllable of conversation which your Museum has furnished." Physical beauty, however, was not the only quality that could make a text desirable. Dennie knew that texts could be tokens of membership in cultural com-munities—he praised *Edwin and Angelina* not only for its vellum sheets but because it was "'a parlour window book' among the Newyork amateurs," suggesting it was an object proudly displayed within a certain circle. Dennie rendered the *Museum* as a similar marker of cultural community. He did so by making visible to his readers the continuing acts of creativity, collection, and assembly that "built" each issue of the newspaper. In its "small sheets," they found, not conventional visual beauty, but rather the coveted evidence of their own activities and communities.[18]

Like an Arts and Crafts table of a later century, the *Museum* bore as an essential part of its artistry the marks of its creation. Dennie habitu-ally recounted how information made its way to him, and he appealed for readers' help not only in private letters but also in the *Museum* itself. He encouraged Dartmouth students to send submissions, for example, and in-sisted that "the Boston and Newyork amateurs must not only read, but adorn the *Museum*." Readers could imagine themselves not simply as pur-chasers of the text, nor even simply as participants in an "imagined com-munity" of simultaneous readers. They could understand themselves, when reading, as links in a chain of information, emotion, and judgments. "I saw, in a late *Museum*," wrote one correspondent, "that among other things, a few bundles from the shrubbery of Parnassus were wanted. I have therefore taken the liberty to send you a small bundle of dry sticks" written in a "season of pleasing melancholy." Extracts as well as original contributions were valued. In late 1797, Dennie offered an explicit vision of readers' col-lecting the "things" necessary to the assemblage of the *Museum*. "Men of literary leisure," Dennie coaxed, could "greatly extend the wide and useful designs of this paper by suggesting things to the Editor, and by keeping a kind of letter box, as a receptacle for those fugitive good things, which occur in the course of much and various reading. These extracts [will] . . . prove of singular service to that *Museum*, which professes to exhibit 'what-

18. Samuel Eliot to Dennie, Apr. 11, 1797, Dennie Papers; *Farmer's Weekly Museum*, June 5, 1797.

soever things are lovely and of good report.'" The letter boxes on readers' desks would serve both as a kind of advertisement for the newspaper and as a symbol of their owners' participation in the *Museum*'s endeavors. Even those who might not have had the time, inclination, skill, or nerve to send in an original piece for Dennie's perusal could still, if they heeded this invitation, find themselves part of the *Museum*'s creation. And he who marketed also served. John Pintard of Newark, New Jersey, wrote in January 1799 to inform Dennie that he had read excerpts of the *Museum* in the *Newark Gazette,* that he wanted a subscription, and that he would encourage others to subscribe. "It is the duty of everyone who is anxious to elevate our national character," he opined, "to throw in their mite, literary or pecuniary, into some common fund where it is most likely to be improved to our advantage."[19]

The paper offered not only the possibility for literary renown but also an intellectual and even artisanal companionship potentially more satisfying than that offered by people brought together only by proximity or shared status. The Bostonian John Sylvester John Gardiner, a prominent Episcopalian clergyman, sent Dennie not only his thoughts on theater but also dismissive assessments of the educated gentlemen with whom he socialized. Authorizing Dennie to print his remarks "dressed in any language or introduced in any manner you please," Gardiner was more than willing to serve up his actual neighbors for the delectation of his print community. A letter from 1797 perhaps best expresses the intensity of the connection readers could feel to Dennie and to his print world and the excitement with which they embarked on the "adventure" of contribution. The twenty-six-year-old David Everett wrote to the editor that he had purchased a collection of Dennie's "Lay Preacher" writings. He had saved the money to do so, he explained, by abstaining from cutting his hair. "I carried it to bed with me and read till my candle fell asleep," he wrote Dennie. "The remainder was finished on the top of Beacon Hill just as the sun rose this morning. Every

19. *Farmer's Weekly Museum*, June 5, Dec. 4, 1797, Dec. 17, 1798; John Pintard to Dennie, Jan. 20, 1799, Dennie Papers; Benedict Anderson, *Imagined Communities: Reflections on the Origin and Spread of Nationalism*, rev. ed. (New York, 1991). My discussion is influenced by Michael G. Ketchum's exploration of the *Spectator* in *Transparent Designs: Reading, Performance, and Form in the "Spectator" Papers* (Athens, Ga., 1985), esp. 9. See also Neil McKendrick, John Brewer, and J. H. Plumb, *The Birth of a Consumer Society: Commercialization in Eighteenth Century England* (New York, 1984); and Ann Bermingham and John Brewer, eds., *The Consumption of Culture, 1600–1800: Image, Object, Text* (New York, 1995).

. . . idea was worked to sociability, with the Lay Preacher; my social feelings vibrated in unison with his." This imagined sociability, intense as it was, was not enough. In an earlier letter, Everett had sent an essay to the *Museum,* the first of what would become his long-running "Common Sense in Dishabille" series. Dennie introduced the essay to his readers by proclaiming warmly that its author "is considered a member of the *Corps* periodical, and is saluted as a Brother." The *Farmer's Weekly Museum* offered a real community built from imagination.[20]

Vocations and Avocations, Revisited

Like Elihu Smith, Dennie needed money to sustain his projects; unlike Smith, Dennie wished to support himself entirely from his literary labors. Dennie also understood, perhaps even better than did the young New York physician, the potentially symbiotic relationship between the network of unpaid literati and printer-booksellers. During the same months that he wrote to potential contributors to his newspaper, Dennie began a correspondence with the Boston printer Joseph Nancrede.[21]

Dennie was trying to create a virtual metropolis from his readership to compensate for America's lack of a center such as London. That virtual metropolis needed to be a market as well as an audience. Dennie appealed for advertisers to market "large parcels of land" to his far-flung readers, but he seems to have been forced to rely heavily on purely local advertisements for general stores and schools. It was really only cultural and political productions that could claim a national appeal. Nancrede offered the former, asking Dennie to publicize texts he had printed. Nancrede's advertisements were one element of a complex relationship. Dennie flamboyantly deplored pandering to mass taste, and Nancrede scorned the "fraternity of booksellers" he felt cared only about their profits. Such views did not mean the men disdained all audiences and all markets, however; on the contrary, they cooperated in an extended effort to gauge, affect, and benefit from what Nancrede referred to as "public opinion." The public opinion they cultivated was not that of an undifferentiated mass of Americans, nor that of an

20. John Sylvester John Gardiner to Dennie, Feb. 7, Mar. 26, 1797, David Everett to Dennie, May 9, 1797, Dennie Papers; "To Correspondents," *Farmer's Weekly Museum,* May 9, 1797.

21. Born in France, Joseph Nancrede had worked as an editor before establishing himself in Boston as a printer-bookseller. See Madeleine B. Stern, "A Salem and a Boston Publisher: James Tytler and Joseph Nancrede," *NEQ,* XLVII (1974), 292.

abstract and invisible nation. It was instead the half-found and half-created public of interconnected readers and writers, circulators, borrowers, acquaintances, relatives, strivers, and friends.[22]

Dennie's *Museum* network was accessible to him in its entirety but from a distance, as a far-flung collection of correspondents; it was visible to Nancrede up close but partially, as a store filled with, as he described them to Dennie, the "lounging Gentlemen, who often inundate bookstores." Each man needed the vantage point, as well as the products, of the other. Knowing that each additional subscriber to the *Museum* was an additional pair of eyes for any material he placed therein, Nancrede helped the young editor to gain subscribers in Boston. He first placed the blank subscription papers Dennie had sent him, not at his own store, but at an office that he deemed "a place of general resort, and where it was more immediately important to make a beginning, *by a good number of names.*" After that success, Nancrede explained to Dennie, "I too began to put my subscription paper out." The printer also warned Dennie to get his productions to booksellers and printers during the first flush of excitement and interest, and he copied down and forwarded to Dennie the "flying opinions" of the young Bostonian gentlemen who discussed Dennie's paper and who vowed to offer him their assistance. "That's a charming paper, says one," reads Nancrede's record of one conversation. "She's the best in the United States, says another. Sir, says a third, I know the young fellow who conducts it, and I assure you, he holds the prettiest pen in America." "He shan't want my help," offered another, "let his paper be in any shape whatever."[23]

Dennie reciprocated by fulfilling Nancrede's requests that he "mention" and excerpt works for which Nancrede was eager to find readers. "William Spotswood and Joseph Nancrede have issued proposals at Boston for pub-

22. Joseph Nancrede to Dennie, July 6, 1797, Dennie Papers. The following notice, for example, appeared in the June 5, 1798, issue of the *Farmer's Weekly Museum:* "The *Museum,* which now has a general circulation through the United States, will be found a cheap medium for many kinds of advertisements. Venders of large tracts of land, in particular, and publishers of new works, may find it advantageous to make this paper the vehicle of such communications."

23. Nancrede to Dennie, Mar. 14, 1797, Dennie Papers. Nancrede included a list of seven new subscribers who had signed for the paper at his store (Nancrede to Dennie, July 6, 1797, Dennie Papers). Lawrence C. Wroth describes colonial printing shops as centers of practical conversation and of "contact with the outside intellectual world" in "The First Press in Providence: A Study in Social Development," American Antiquarian Society, *Proceedings,* LI (1941), 379.

lishing by subscription two very valuable and novel works," reads one of Dennie's glowing passages: "It is almost superfluous to remark that, from the known professional ingenuity of the Printer, they will be executed in a good style of *Press* neatness. A Prospectus of these works and a specimen of their intended type and paper may be seen, by applying to the Publisher of this paper. Gentlemen would do well no less as *patriots*, than scholars to encourage correct *American* editions of valuable books." This relationship foreshadowed the way a modern magazine's editors might excerpt a book published by a corporate affiliate to create excitement and enhance sales— and might listen in to online chat rooms to determine what texts created a buzz. Nancrede and Dennie, however, couched their savvy dealings with one another in the sentimental, even anticommercial language prevalent in their eighteenth-century world. "Benevolence is the flower of friendship," Nancrede effused, and then went on to explain that he had once again been "cruelly disappointed" by fellow booksellers and needed Dennie's aid. Like Smith and his collaborators, Dennie and Nancrede turned commerce to their own purposes while criticizing its degrading effect on others' judgment.[24]

The Museum *as Political Text*

In politics as in culture, the story of the *Museum* mingles the assertion of individual judgment with the creation of community, claims of intellectual independence with the assiduous gauging of opinion, and the work of professionals with a wider network of the more casually interested. Federalism has often been described as conservative in its message and maladroit in its use of formal and informal communication systems. Federalists did express disdain for the opinion of the crowd, for "the swinish multitude," in Burke's instantly famous and infamous phrase. But disdain for the opinion of the crowd was an effective and entertaining way of attracting one. More precisely, it was an excellent means of appealing to the particular— and potentially powerful—form of "public opinion" to which Nancrede referred: a group that was neither an undivided American populace nor a

---

24. *Newhampshire and Vermont Journal; or, The Farmer's Weekly Museum*, July 12, 1796; Nancrede to Dennie, Mar. 14, 1797, Dennie Papers. A request regarding *Studies of Nature*, which Nancrede deemed "a very heavy undertaking," appears in Nancrede's letter to Dennie of July 6, 1797, and a request regarding *St. Pierre's Appeals* is in Nancrede to Dennie, Mar. 14, 1797, Dennie Papers.

handful of impotent "anglophiles" and chauvinists but that was instead a potential network of talkers, writers, readers, and circulators, elitist but not necessarily conservative, eager to be taken seriously but not always willing to keep a straight face.[25]

Dennie's love of England and disdain for what he saw as Republicans' capitulation to the views of the crowd led him to sympathize with the Federalist Party, and he even allowed his name to be put forward for a congressional seat in 1798. But Dennie's use of Federalist politics arose from a lesson he learned as editor of the *Tablet*. Recalling his time in Boston, Dennie observed to his mother: "The Aristocracy were pleased that the satires of Colon and Spondee were leveled against the foes of Federalism. Such is the state of parties here that this apparently trivial circumstance has procured me a host of friends, not like Dennie friends but such as will render me pecuniary service." Political engagement furthered Dennie's career as a man of letters. Dennie has long been portrayed as an exemplar of those who "retreated" to literature after the national failure of Federalist politics. In fact, however, the reverse was true. Along with contemporaries such as Noah Webster, Philip Freneau, and James Callendar, Dennie turned to politics, temporarily or permanently, after literature alone failed to gain for him an

25. Pasley, whose main focus is on Republican newspapers, argues that the Federalist press lacked the networking capabilities and inclinations of their Republican foes, and he passes along the erroneous view of a distraught Federalist, writing after Jefferson's election, that Federalist editors failed even to reprint one another's stories (*Tyranny*, 231). Joanne B. Freeman portrays the Federalist Party of the 1790s as a similarly inept group. "Federalist strategy and spirit," she writes, "revolved around the industrious Hamilton"; as a result, "Hamilton's political style restricted the scope of national Federalist activity to the limits of his energies and interests." Arguing that Federalists "were too confidently situated in office, too sure of their success" to believe they needed "a network of passionate believers," Freeman concludes that "it was their staggering loss in the election of 1800 that taught Federalists their error" (*Affairs of Honor: National Politics in the New Republic* [New Haven, Conn., 2001], 88, 90). Older treatments, such as, among many, James M. Banner, Jr., *To the Hartford Convention: The Federalists and the Origins of Party Politics in Massachusetts, 1789–1815* (New York, 1970), offer an even starker portrait of Federalists' alleged resistance to innovation and disdain for public opinion. David Waldstreicher's *In the Midst of Perpetual Fetes: The Making of American Nationalism, 1776–1820* (Chapel Hill, N.C., 1997) and Simon P. Newman's *Parades and the Politics of the Street: Festive Culture in the Early American Republic* (Philadelphia, 1997), by contrast, include Federalist efforts in their accounts of partisan displays, print culture, and the development of nationalist sentiment, although they focus on different processes of community formation and performance than those in which Dennie was engaged.

audience and a place in the world. Dennie put his newspaper to the service of Federalist politicians to pursue his own purpose of finding an audience and copy for that audience to read.[26]

Under Dennie's direction, the *Museum* did offer enough Federalist rhetoric and argument to make the newspaper acceptable to those who saw it as a party organ. The newspaper praised, for example, the electors of the state of New Hampshire who voted for John Adams and Oliver Ellsworth, and it congratulated the "real American citizens" in Vermont who supported the "federal" candidate. More important, the dual nature of the *Museum*, as a vessel of ideas and as a spur to networking, made the newspaper valuable to Federalist politicians. As with literary material, so with political: Dennie printed both the content and the relationships and exchanges that had produced the content. Both were equally the point. Thus, in the summer of 1798, readers would have found what Dennie called an "Extract of a Letter, Dated Philadelphia, June 18, 1798, from a Member of Congress to the Editor": "I have this morning enclosed to you a little pamphlet, entitled, 'The Cannibal's Progress, or a narrative of the atrocities of the French in the District of Suabia.' Perhaps some extracts from it, may, at this time, be serviceable. It will not add to the *elegance* of your paper; but the facts are of such a nature, that the most simple narrative will produce sufficient effect." "I will forward to you the answer of our Envoys to the French minister's memorial, a very excellent performance," the published letter continued,

26. Dennie's candidacy for the congressional seat was half-hearted and poorly received, with Dennie receiving 6 votes to the winner's 124. See Dennie to Mary Green Dennie, Apr. 24, 1795, Sept. 6, 1799, Dennie Papers; Ellis, *Joseph Dennie and His Circle,* 105–106. The argument for Dennie's so-called retreat to literature is most forcefully made by William C. Dowling throughout *Literary Federalism in the Age of Jefferson: Joseph Dennie and "The Port Folio," 1801–1811* (Columbia, S.C., 1999). "To read through *The Port Folio* during the years of Dennie's editorship," Dowling argues, "is to find oneself in the very midst of what I shall be calling the Federalist retreat from history, a long and complex withdrawal in which Federalism, banished from the civic sphere by a triumphant Jeffersonian ideology, seeks an alternative home in what we now call the public sphere but what the *Port Folio* writers called, in the usual eighteenth-century phrase, the republic of letters" (ix). See also Lawrence Buell's discussion of "Federalist writers" as "the first group of alienated American intellectuals" in *New England Literary Culture: From Revolution through Renaissance* (New York, 1986), 94 and chap. 4; Michael Durey, *Transatlantic Radicals and the Early American Republic* (Lawrence, Kans., 1997), 58–69; Marcus Daniel, "Ribaldry and Billingsgate: Popular Journalism, Political Culture, and the Public Sphere in the Early Republic" (Ph.D. diss., Princeton University, 1998).

"pray give it a place, as early as possible." In the final extracted passage, this "Member of Congress" appealed to Dennie and through him to readers in a Dennie-inflected tone of ebullient melancholy. "At this moment, my friend, we should have our lamps trimmed and burning, for we know not the day nor the hour, when the Sans Culottes will come upon us."[27]

In such passages, the *Museum* drew readers into an imagined Federalist community of beleaguered conviviality. It also invited them into a real partisan community in which they participated not only by voting but also by retelling Federalist-inflected anecdotes, by sending in their own political information, and simply by interpreting events in the way the *Museum* guided them to do. Not all Federalist politicians understood the usefulness of Dennie's ability to reach and engage his readers: as late as 1801, the editor was still writing to Alexander Hamilton, plaintively urging that the politician "take some notice of a young man, who has long been anxious for the privilege of your friendship." Other Federalist politicians and sympathizers, however, many of them young enough to be connected in some way to the world of youthful cultural exchanges and well placed enough to have information to offer and ambitions to fulfill, were quick to see in the *Museum* precisely what the printer Joseph Nancrede had: efficient access to a sympathetic and dynamic—but far-flung and not otherwise easily reached—audience. Representative Jeremiah Smith sent the *Museum* a flurry of letters in 1796 and 1797. In one, he provided "my friend Mr. Ames's speech on the British treaty" and added that "the printed copy [others had access to] is far inferiour to what he delivered." In another letter, Representative Smith offered "sketches by a friend of mine which are at your service to dish up for our sovereign lord, the people, if you think they can digest them"; he also asked Dennie whether the editor might send along any political information he had gathered so that Smith might have it published in Philadelphia. In still another letter, Smith asked that Dennie put to use the enclo-

27. *Farmer's Weekly Museum*, June 19, 1797, July 3, 1798. Politicians eagerly participated in all aspects of the *Museum*'s community, not just the overtly political issues. Lewis Richard Morris, son of the chief justice of New York and elected to Congress from Vermont in 1798, took it upon himself to attend to the subscription of "Mr. Meredith of Philadelphia" (July 1797, Dennie Papers), and one unnamed provider of political essays was greeted, when he opened the *Museum*, with a request that he send more "political communications" and also that he "lodge" "'Madame Roland's Memoirs'" "at the bookstore of Mr. James White, whence it can have a ready conveyance to the Editor" ("To Readers and Correspondents," *Farmer's Weekly Museum*, Dec. 4, 1797).

sures he'd sent along, and then forward them to Oliver Wolcott, so that they could finally "probably be transcribed into N. Webster's paper." It was the political incarnation of the correspondence chains Elihu Smith used to gather and circulate scientific and literary information.[28]

Other politicians participated in the *Museum*'s community as well. In 1797, Fisher Ames wrote that he was "happy" to accept Dennie's offer of a subscription, "if it can avail as even a small encouragement to a man of taste, genius, and federal principles to prosecute a design which has my best wishes." Lewis Richard Morris, son of the chief justice of New York and himself a member of Congress, sent Dennie his copies of addresses by members such as Robert Goodloe Harper as well as accounts of "Civic Feasts" and even, in one missive, the news that "the Spanish Minister has been roughly handled by a Philadelphian for being found in bed with the Citizen's Wife." "The upright and Federal politics, I have aimed to inculcate," Dennie wrote proudly to his mother, "have procured the attention of Government, and in letters from members of Congress I have been warmly thanked for my services."[29]

As a weekly rather than as a daily, Dennie's newspaper did not offer the earliest accounts of major stories. Moreover, because Dennie was committed and eager to print literature as well as politics and was unable to print "extras," he could not offer the most complete coverage of political events and controversies. Instead, what Federalist politicians found in the *Museum* was a vehicle that wrapped their proffered bits of information and argument in its air of au courant intimacy. *Museum* readers, for their part, felt included in the highly personal political world. Dennie and his readers and contributors, in short, were participating, not in a backward-looking politics of elitist nostalgia, but instead in an interactive, dynamic attempt to shape opinion. So successful was the project that Dennie scoffed in June 1798 that Thomas Jefferson had to solicit subscriptions for the *Aurora* to stave off its collapse. It was Federalist expression, in Dennie's view, that

28. Jeremiah Smith to Dennie, n.d., 1796, Dec. 26, 1796, n.d., 1797, Dennie to Alexander Hamilton, May 6, 1801, Dennie Papers. Timothy Pickering had rather wearily written a letter to Hamilton, noting: "Mr. Joseph Dennie, now of Philadelphia, has more than once observed to me, that he had never the happiness of being known to you. He repeated the observation, as I lately passed thro' that city. And manifesting an earnest desire to be introduced, requested me to write to you for that purpose" (copy of Pickering to Hamilton, Apr. 29, 1801, Dennie Papers).

29. Dennie to Mary Green Dennie, Aug. 29, 1796, Fisher Ames to Dennie, Feb. 20, 1797, Morris to Dennie, June 29, 30, July 1, 2, n.d., 1797, Dennie Papers.

emerged spontaneously and Republican rhetoric that needed to be propped up by party elites.[30]

Dennie scoffed at Republicans but readily acknowledged that he needed them. Republican and Federalist editors needed one another at least as much as they needed their own party leaders. Given the lack of a metropolis such as London, editors needed their papers to be widely circulated if they were going to be truly influential. Gaining national circulation, in turn, required being talked about and reprinted. Intense partisan claims, rumors, and animadversions were talked about, forwarded, and excerpted. There was, therefore, an incentive for editors to produce highly colored partisan language. Dennie himself cheerfully acknowledged that newspapering opponents fueled the fires on which both relied for warmth. "Since the Editor has been splashed with the mud of Chronicle obloquy," he wrote of the Republican paper, "he has gained upwards of seven hundred subscribers. He therefore requests of the Ropemaker and his journeymen the honour and the profit of their future abuse. He even thinks he can afford them a small reward, say fifty cents, for every lampoon." The desire of both Federalist and Republican editors to project their own voices to a dispersed, literate, politically engaged population merged with the real political differences among them and among politicians and with the newspaper exchanges made feasible by the postal law of 1792 to create a virtual echo chamber of partisan outrage. Some of it was calculated, some of it sincere, some entertaining, and much of it all three. Men of letters such as the Federalist Dennie and the Republican Philip Freneau helped to create a party divide, an emotional and rhetorical, aesthetic and strategic division that emerged in the mid-1790s and that nurtured, rather than simply drew on, the tangible, competing party infrastructures.[31]

Dennie's theory of the partisan press differed dramatically from Thomas Jefferson's view that information diffused as widely as possible would bring all to the correct—Republican—conclusion. Dennie gained readers and contributors by creating a community that offered a viscerally powerful sense of insiders and outsiders, friends and enemies. In doing so, Dennie moved toward a modern understanding of American politics, openly embracing the inevitability of dissent in the new Republic. The *Museum* had another

30. *Farmer's Weekly Museum*, June 19, 1798.
31. Ibid., Jan. 16, 1798. Jeffrey A. Smith describes both Republican conceptions of the role of newspapers in the new nation and some of the interaction between Republican and Federalist newspapers in *Franklin and Bache: Envisioning the Enlightened Republic* (New York, 1990), chaps. 5–8.

effect as well. Its Federalism rendered political affiliation an individual act of reading, buying, or feeling rather than something requiring public action. The duties of its form of citizenship did not require electoral or legislative triumph; they could be fulfilled in a burst of sardonic laughter or a quick flood of tears. The *Museum*, moreover, posited as its ideal reader the man who reveled in his sense of difference and discomfiture rather than tried to change the world. Dennie helped to create a Federalism that heightened the emotional connection between partisan and party but attenuated the civic requirements of that connection. He created a Federalist identity politics.[32]

Despite his success in Walpole, Dennie longed to travel back down the Connecticut River toward one of the nation's cities. By 1800, he had many options. He had received requests from printers and editors in New York, Philadelphia, and Baltimore to take over or join their newspapers. Most temptingly, the shrilly Federalist editor William Cobbett had sent urgent letters begging him to embark on a joint venture. Accepting Cobbett's proposal would have united two of the most powerful voices in Federalism just before the climactic election of 1800. From Dennie's perspective, however, such a move meant merging two intensely idiosyncratic editorial personas (and editorial judgments), and it meant as well losing the support of the Adams family, who, though admirers and supporters of Dennie, were steadfast opponents of the fearless Cobbett. Dennie refused Cobbett's overtures and set off for Philadelphia, where he had been promised the assistance of Representative Morris, Thomas Boylston Adams, and the attorney William Meredith and where John Ward Fenno had offered him the editorship of the *Gazette of the United States,* eight hundred dollars per year, and a return on new subscriptions.[33]

32. Pasley, *Tyranny,* 34, 41. Dennie's creation of a community grounded in difference departs from Anderson, *Imagined Communities,* as well as Michael Warner, *The Letters of the Republic: Publication and the Public Sphere in Eighteenth-Century America* (Cambridge, Mass., 1990), with its highly influential vision of the way an early American citizen "incorporates into the meaning of the printed objects an awareness of the potentially limitless others who may also be reading," thereby imagining himself part of an "abstract public" and therefore part of a unified American nation (xiii, 61). My discussion is informed by John Brewer, "Commercialization and Politics," in McKendrick, Brewer, and Plumb, *Birth of a Consumer Society,* 197–262.

33. John Ward Fenno to Dennie, February–June 1799, Dennie Papers (terms in Feb. 12, 1799, letter). Cobbett's letters began in January 1799, when he claimed, "I would not ask you to advance a single farthing, and should think myself happy in having to pay you a thousand dollars," and they reached culmination in the spring of 1800; warning that Dennie would not earn money from a magazine or from the "Lay

Federalists who understood the value of Walpole's *Farmer's Weekly Museum* and the networks that nurtured it were determined to make Dennie more widely read; Dennie proudly informed his mother that in Philadelphia he would also be private secretary to the Federalist secretary of state Timothy Pickering at a salary of one thousand dollars. Pickering, Dennie contentedly noted, had clearly hinted that Dennie was wanted not only for his clerical skills but also for his potential as a useful Federalist voice: "I received official notice from Mr. P. that if, with my genius and taste, I quote *his* words, I could, in some degree relinquish the pursuits of literature, and submit to the drudgery of political business he would be glad to employ me, and congratulate himself upon being the instrument in availing the public of my talents." In fact, Dennie submitted only minimally to the demands of his post, as a letter Pickering wrote in June 1800 attested. By then, Pickering had lost his secretaryship owing to his opposition to President Adams's conciliatory policies toward France, and he was trying to help Dennie find a new post. While acceding to the request of Dennie and Lewis Morris that he recommend Dennie to the "department of State," Pickering felt compelled to issue a mild warning. "I cannot," he wrote, "because I ought not, to conceal from you, that Mr. Dennie's habits and literary turn—I should rather say, his insatiable appetite of knowledge, useful as well as ornamental, render his service as a clerk less productive than the labours of many dull men."[34]

Preacher" columns, he demanded: "Why, in God's name, will you not come to New York, and talk with me? Are you afraid to see the road—I will not say to fortune, but the road to competence, comfort, and fame?" (Cobbett to Dennie, Jan. 30, 1799, Apr. 11, 1800, Dennie Papers). Cobbett later offered Dennie his services as a "London Bookseller" and finally congratulated him on the success of the *Port Folio* (Cobbett to Dennie, May 7, 1800, Apr. 4, 1801, Dennie Papers). Cobbett's politics might also have been too much even for Dennie, and his apparent taste for confrontation as an end in itself differed from Dennie's root desire to use disagreement to create useful relationships; in one letter, Cobbett, who had apparently asked that Dennie write a critical piece on James Madison, found it necessary to reassure him: "I never did, so I never shall, propose to you, or to any one else, to say or to write any thing, that can possibly amount to a breach of 'an oath to support the Constitution and laws of the United States.' . . . What could more effectually lend to their support, than 'The Real Character,' well drawn, of their great founder?" (Cobbett to Dennie, May 7, 1800, Dennie Papers). Ellis describes the end of Dennie's tenure and the life of the *Museum* after his departure in *Joseph Dennie and His Circle*, 102–104.

34. Dennie to Mary Green Dennie, Sept. 6, 1799, Dennie Papers; Pickering to John Marshall, June 27, 1800, Timothy Pickering Papers, XIII, no. 557, Massachusetts Historical Society, Boston.

Dennie's literary turn and appetite for knowledge were in fact the well-spring of his productive labors; it was not his services as a clerk that had brought him to Philadelphia, but rather it was his abilities as writer, networker, cultural critic, and partisan provocateur. And, although he penned diatribes against Republican editors for the *Gazette*, he was already looking beyond that newspaper and dreaming of a periodical he could make entirely his own. In October 1800, he announced his plans for the *Port Folio*.[35]

35. Ellis, *Joseph Dennie and His Circle*, 124–125.

CHAPTER 5

Ungentle Readers
The Port Folio, 1801–1805

In December 1800, Philadelphia bookseller Asbury Dickins printed a footnote-bedecked *Prospectus*. Its five pages announced the latest project of "a young man, once known among village-readers, as the humble historian of the hour, the conductor of a *Farmer's* Museum, and a *Lay Preacher's* Gazette." In this *Prospectus,* Joseph Dennie revealed his new nom de plume—"Oliver Oldschool"—and appealed to "men of affluence, men of liberality, and men of letters" to take subscriptions to his new weekly paper. Dennie intended to marshal the talents of the educated Americans he had cultivated since his first days in Walpole and to put his new paper to the service of political and cultural ambition. "It must be apparent to the most heedless observer," he informed readers, "that it is the object of this undertaking, to combine literature with politics, and attempt something of a more honorable destiny, than a meagre journal. To accomplish this purpose, the co-operation of many minds is requisite." The asking price was "five dollars annually, and it is requested of subscribers that the money be paid in advance." He left the last page of the *Prospectus* blank in anticipation of signatures. By the end of April, Dickins and Dennie reported that the appeal seemed to be succeeding. "One thousand copies, constituting the first edition of the Prospectus of the *Port Folio*, having been distributed," they announced, "a *second edition* of a like number has been printed, and is nearly exhausted."[1]

In the *Port Folio*, Dennie founded a successful periodical in one of the new nation's leading cities. In an era in which the average lifespan of a periodical was fourteen months, Dennie's *Port Folio* carried on under his editorship for eleven years and continued for another fifteen years, in various formats, after his death. The *Port Folio's* surviving financial records give evidence of subscribers not only throughout New England and the mid-

---

1. [Joseph Dennie], *Prospectus of a New Weekly Paper Submitted to Men of Affluence, Men of Liberality, and Men of Letters* (Philadelphia, 1800).

Atlantic but also in the South and as far west as Kentucky. As editor of the *Port Folio,* Dennie became an early, if fickle, American champion of William Wordsworth as well as an inspiration to the young Washington Irving; he received letters of praise from William Cobbett and from Robert Anderson, the Scottish biographer of Tobias Smollett.[2]

Dennie and his many contributors celebrated individual contrarian aesthetic and political judgment. They asserted the splendor of male friendship and claimed that from such friendships and the larger communities built upon them—and not from the interest-based bonds of politics or commerce—emerged beauty and a just society. The *Port Folio* created a profoundly oppositional community, one opposed not only to Jeffersonianism but also to a society grounded in contractualism and false equality rather than in affective ties and the organic hierarchy of traditional society. Across the numbers of the periodical, Dennie pieced together a dystopian vision of an America in which individuals desperately pursued money, sex, and political power and in so doing debased themselves and failed to create beauty, stability, or meaning. Dennie drew expertly on Federalism, the literature of sensibility, Augustan literature, and the tradition of melancholia to nurture an immunity to the desire for political power, wealth, and the acclaim of the crowd. That distance, that immunity to desire, offered the vantage point Dennie proffered to and demanded from his readers. He sought a constructive disengagement, a sometimes sad, sometimes merry sense of difference that made public criticism and personal expression possible.

Building the Port Folio

To create the *Port Folio,* Dennie wrote original columns, reprinted columns from earlier projects, and selected from other newspapers extracts

2. Incomplete subscription files are contained in the Meredith Family Papers, Historical Society of Pennsylvania, Philadelphia, and reveal subscribers in these areas. See William Cobbett to Joseph Dennie, Apr. 4, 1801, Robert Anderson to Dennie, Apr. 24, 1805, both in Joseph Dennie Papers, Houghton Library, Harvard College Library, Harvard University, Cambridge, Mass. Anderson notes that "some of the articles, as might reasonably be expected by a reader on this side of the Atlantic, want novelty" but that the periodical "contains specimens of genius and harmony" as well as history, criticism, and poetry "highly creditable to the talents and industry of the editor." See also Michael Gilmore, "The Literature of the Revolutionary and Early National Periods," in Sacvan Bercovitch, ed., *The Cambridge History of American Literature*, I, *1590–1820* (New York, 1994), 560.

THE PORT FOLIO.

BY OLIVER OLDSCHOOL, ESQ.

"........................" "VARIOUS, THAT THE MIND
OF DESULTORY MAN, STUDIOUS OF CHANGE,
AND PLEAS'D WITH NOVELTY, MAY BE INDULGED."
COWPER.

VOL. I.]   [No. 46.

PHILADELPHIA, SATURDAY, NOVEMBER 14th, 1801.

BIOGRAPHY.

THE LIFE OF BARETTI.

Joseph Baretti, a man of letters of some distinction, was born at Turin, about the year 1716. His father was an architect, employed under Don Philip Invata, a Sicilian, who built several considerable edifices, in and near Turin. Young Baretti received a good education, and some paternal property, which last, from his own confession, he squandered in gaming. Of his early life very little is known. It appears to have been rambling and desultory, and, probably, often subjected to pecuniary distress. In 1748, we find him at Venice, a teacher of Italian to some English gentlemen. Two years afterwards, he came to England, chiefly, as it is said, at the instigation of lord Charlemont; and this island was thenceforth, except with a short interval, his constant residence. A wonderful facility in acquiring languages, together with a critical knowledge of his own, peculiarly fitted him for the profession of a language-master, in which he engaged.

As early as 1753, he ventured to become a writer in English, in which tongue he published "A Defence of the Poetry of his native country against the censures of Voltaire." About this time his acquaintance commenced with Dr. Johnson, then engaged in the compilation of his dictionary. It appears to have been attended with extraordinary kindness and cordiality on the part of Johnson, probably conciliated by equal deference and veneration on that of Baretti, who omits no occasion in his works, of testifying his profound admiration of his illustrious friend.

Some works which he wrote at that period, on the Italian language and literature, contributed to raise his reputation; and he availed himself of his friend's English dictionary, to compile a dictionary of the Italian and English languages, much more complete than any hitherto published, which first appeared in 1760, and still maintains its superiority over other works of the same kind. His industry was, indeed, exemplary; for his love of independence led him to rely chiefly on his own exertions, notwithstanding all advantages of temporary patronage. But he himself acknowledged that his performances partook too much of the imperfection, consequent upon haste and necessity.

In 1760, he revisited his native country, where, as appears from a letter of Johnson's to him, he had hopes of preferment, and had thoughts of forming a matrimonial connection; but neither of these took place. Soon after his arrival he projected, and published at Venice, a periodical work, under the title of "Frusta Literaria," in the character of an old querulous soldier, who was returned to his country after a long absence. This work met with great suc-cess, but the severity of its criticisms raised a storm of enmity against the author, which rendered his abode in that country unpleasant, if not unsafe. After an absence of six years, he returned through Spain and Portugal to England, where he resumed his literary occupations.

In 1768, he published "An Account of the Manners and Customs of Italy," principally intended as a reply to the severe strictures contained in the "Letters from Italy," by Mr. Sam. Sharp, the surgeon. Sharp had indeed written like a prejudiced Englishman, incapable of making due allowances for the difference of tastes and habits, and strongly impressed with the importance of all the more serious matters in which his own country claims a superiority over most of those on the continent. Baretti, on the other hand, was a citizen of the world, treating lightly not only differences in modes of living and fashionable manners, but the most essential diversities in morals, religion, and government. He was, however, successful in exposing many of Sharp's mistakes and misrepresentations, which he attacked both with humour and argument.

He retained the warm attachment of Dr. Johnson, who introduced him to the family of Thrale, a connection equally useful and agreeable to him, both as a teacher and a literary guest. In 1769, he visited part of Spain, probably for the purpose of completing his account of a tour in that country.

Soon after his return, an incident happened, which involved him in very disagreeable consequences. As he was returning, early one evening in October, from a coffee-house, he was accosted in the Haymarket, by a woman of the town, whom he repulsed with some roughness. An angry altercation ensued, which brought on the interference of three men, who endeavoured to push Baretti into the kennel. Alarmed for his safety, he took out a pocket French dessert-knife, and struck one of the assailants. The man pursued and collared him; upon which Baretti repeated his blows with the knife, in such a manner, that he died of his wounds the next day. Baretti was immediately taken into custody, and was tried for murder at the Old Bailey. The trial excited great interest in the public, and perhaps no person in his circumstances, had ever such an appearance of men of literary eminence to bear testimony to his character. Among these were the names of Johnson, Burke, Goldsmith, Garrick, Reynolds, and Beauclerk. Baretti rejected the privelege of having a jury of half foreigners, and confidently threw himself upon the generosity of Englishmen. He had no cause to repent this measure, for their verdict was self-defence. Yet he did not escape censure for the readiness, with which he had recourse to a mortal weapon to repel an assault, which, in so public a place, and at so early an hour (between six and seven), could scarcely have endangered his person; and the fact was thought an unfortunate example of that propensity to stabbing, which he had taken pains to refute, when brought as a charge against the Italians, by Mr. Sharp. It is asserted too, that, so far from showing any remorse for the fatality of the action, he was brutal enough once to present his knife to a young lady, for the purpose of cutting fruit, with the preface—This is the weapon that stabbed the villain!

In 1770, he published his "Journey from London to Genoa, through England, Portugal, Spain, and France," 4 vols. 8vo. a sprightly and entertaining performance, replete with lively traits of manners and sentiment, and every where maintaining the character of the good-humoured traveller, accommodating himself to all petty diversities, and superior to trifling difficulties. He continued to publish introductory works for the use of students in the Italian and some other modern languages, and superintended a complete edition of the works of Machiavel. About this time he was domesticated in the Thrale family; and, in 1775, he accompanied them and Dr. Johnson in a trip to Paris. He left Mr. Thrales in 1776, "in some whimsical fit of disgust or ill-nature, without taking leave" (Johnson's letter to Boswell); and it appears that the latter part of his life passed in struggles against difficulties.

In 1779, in conjunction with Mr. Philidor, and under the patronage of Dr. Johnson, he attempted to introduce to the public a classical entertainment, the "Carmen Seculare" of Horace, set to music; but it proved too refined for the national taste, and failed of success. He had for some time enjoyed the post of foreign secretary to the Royal Academy; but this was a source of honour, rather than emolument, and his circumstances now led him to be solicitous for the means of maintenance. A pension from government of 80l. per annum, which he obtained under lord North's administration, fell into arrear during the urgency of public wants, and he was scarcely able to preserve himself from absolute indigence.

In 1786, he published a work with the singular title of "Tolondron. Speeches to John Bowle about his Edition of Don Quixote; together with some account of Spanish Literature." This was his last performance. His constitution was broken by uneasiness of mind, and repeated attacks of the gout, and he died on May 5, 1789. He retained some respectable friends to the last, who attended him to the grave.

Baretti had a rough and somewhat cynical appearance, yet he was well fitted for society, and particularly delighted in the company of young persons, with whom his conversation generally took an instructive turn. He had seen much of the world, and had imbibed that

FIGURE 4. *Port Folio*, Nov. 14, 1801.

By permission, American Antiquarian Society, Worcester, Mass.

that shared the ethos of the *Port Folio*. As he had with the *Farmer's Weekly Museum*, Dennie also printed contributions from readers near and far. An informal circle quickly formed in Philadelphia around the editor, dubbing itself "the Tuesday Club"; its young professionals and their cultured wives wrote for the periodical, convened for dinners, and provided Dennie with the companionship and admiration he coveted. The average age of the club's participants in 1802, the year after the *Port Folio* began publication, was twenty-four. Many came from prominent local families and were beginning to follow fathers or other male relatives into respectable professional or merchant careers, even as they engaged in literary pursuits. Among the Tuesday Club's ranks were Samuel Ewing, a young lawyer who wrote poetical satires as well as the poetic series "Reflections in Solitude" for the periodical; the young minister and author John Blair Linn; the lawyers Charles Jared Ingersoll and Horace Binney, the latter of whom not only contributed satires to the *Port Folio* but also memorialized many of its contributors; and Joseph Hopkinson, a young lawyer and friend of Charles Brockden Brown who had written the popular patriotic song *Hail Columbia* in 1798 and who would go on to serve as congressman, judge, vice president of the American Philosophical Society, and president of the Academy of Fine Arts. The Tuesday Club also came to include the Scottish naturalist and author Alexander Wilson as well as Nicholas Biddle, who, long before his struggles with Andrew Jackson, was a contributor to the *Port Folio* and, after Dennie's death, its editor. The lawyer William Meredith, another scion of a prominent Philadelphia family, wrote for the *Port Folio*, hosted many of the club's dinners along with his wife Gertrude, and provided Dennie with a place to live on his arrival in Philadelphia. Thomas Boylston Adams, son of the president, friend of Elihu Hubbard Smith, and a former Harvard classmate of the editor, helped Dennie with the *Port Folio* for years; in 1803, Dennie proudly wrote to his mother that he was boarding with this "constant friend," "the second son of the *former* President." Adams both wrote for the periodical and tried to manage its logistics and finances.[3]

3. Dennie to Mary Green Dennie, June 15, 1803, Dennie Papers. For the average age of the Tuesday Club's participants, see Albrecht Koschnik, "Voluntary Associations, Political Culture, and the Public Sphere in Philadelphia, 1780–1830" (Ph.D. diss., University of Virginia, 2000), 201, 252. Koschnik, in "Fashioning a Federalist Self: Young Men and Voluntary Association in Early Nineteenth-Century Philadelphia," *Explorations in Early American Culture*, IV (2000), 220–257, also examines the Tuesday Club as an important form of fellowship for young Federalist lawyers, placing it in the context of the Philological Society, a student debating society created

The Tuesday Club functioned, like New York's Friendly Club and Dennie's Walpole coterie, within a larger, interconnected network of literary strivers closely tied to the for-profit world of printers and booksellers. The English author and traveler John Davis described Asbury Dickins's

---

at the University of Pennsylvania in 1807, and Federalist volunteer militia companies that flourished during the War of 1812. The list of those associated with the *Port Folio* and the circle around Dennie also includes the Philadelphians Nathaniel Chapman (1780–1853, physician), Richard Rush (1780–1859, lawyer and son of Benjamin Rush), Thomas Cadwalader (1779–1841, an agent for the Penn family and major general in the Pennsylvania militia), Thomas Wharton (1791–1856, lawyer and scion of the prominent merchant family), Richard Peters, Jr. (1779–1848, son of the prominent politician and lawyer Richard Peters), Dr. John Edmonds Stock (1774–1835), and Robert Walsh (1784–1859, lawyer). Contributors are identified and described in Linda K. Kerber and Walter John Morris, "Politics and Literature: The Adams Family and the *Port Folio,*" *William and Mary Quarterly,* 3d Ser., XXIII (1966), 450–476; Harold Milton Ellis, *Joseph Dennie and His Circle: A Study in American Literature from 1792 to 1812,* Bulletin of the University of Texas, no. 40 (Austin, Tex., 1915), 158–163, 202–205; Ellis Paxon Oberholtzer, *The Literary History of Philadelphia* (Philadelphia, 1906), 176–177; Randolph C. Randall, "Authors of the *Port Folio* Revealed by the Hall Files," *American Literature,* XI (1940), 379–416. I rely on each of these sources for attributions throughout this chapter. Identification of Clement Clark Moore is found in Linda K. Kerber, *Federalists in Dissent: Imagery and Ideology in Jeffersonian America* (Ithaca, N.Y., 1970), 53. Dennie himself authored the series "The Lay Preacher," "The Farrago," and "Literary Intelligence," many of which were reprinted in the *Port Folio* after appearing in the *Farmer's Weekly Museum,* the *Morning Ray; or, Impartial Oracle,* the *Eagle; or Dartmouth Centinel,* or the *Tablet* (Ellis, *Joseph Dennie and His Circle,* 236–244). With a few exceptions penned by Royall Tyler, Dennie also wrote the columns titled "An Author's Evenings" (Ellis, *Joseph Dennie and His Circle,* 174–215; Randall, "Authors of the *Port Folio,*" *American Literature,* XI [1940], 392 n. 46, 411). Because of Dennie's role as editor, I have also assumed him to be the author of "To the Public," "To Readers and Correspondents," and otherwise uncredited introductions; this assumption accords both with the style of these pieces, which strongly suggests Dennie's hand, and with scattered attributions of similar material in Randall, "Authors of the *Port Folio,*" *American Literature,* XI (1940), 379–416. In the case of other correspondents, the real name, when known, appears in brackets, with any uncertainty noted. If an author's name appears that is not bracketed, the author has been identified in the *Port Folio* text itself. Morris and Kerber describe Thomas Boylston Adams's stalwart assistance to Dennie in "Politics and Literature," *WMQ,* 3d Ser., XXIII (1966), 461–465. Adams's involvement is evident as well in letters between him and John Quincy Adams. See, for example, Jan. 5, 12, 1803, Adams Papers microfilm (APm 402), Massachusetts Historical Society, Boston. Printers' receipts signed by Thomas Boylston Adams give further evidence of his involvement and are to be found in the Meredith Family Papers.

bookstore as "the rendezvous of the *Philadelphia* sons of literature" and complained that young men gathered there in such numbers that Dickins "could scarcely find room to sell his wares." Far from obstructing Dickins's business, however, the young men undoubtedly collected and passed on to the printer valuable information. And, as Davis himself discovered, printer and literati alike eagerly welcomed new literary sparks into their shared community. "At Philadelphia," Davis wryly recounted, "I found Mr. [Charles Brockden] *Brown*, who felt no remission of his literary diligence, by a change of abode. . . . Mr. *Brown* introduced me to Mr. *Dickins*, and Mr. *Dickins* to Mr. *Dennie*; Mr. *Dennie* presented me to Mr. *Wilkins*, and Mr. *Wilkins* to the Rev. [James] Mr. *Abercrombie*, a constellation of *American* genius, in whose blaze I was almost consumed."[4]

These Philadelphians participated in the larger cultural web that the *Port Folio* spun in the eastern United States. Members of the Adams family involved themselves in the *Port Folio* much as they had contributed to Elihu Smith's various projects and to the *Farmer's Weekly Museum*. The *Port Folio's* first issue introduced a series of letters by John Quincy Adams (perhaps offered up, unbeknownst to their author, by Thomas Boylston Adams). This

4. Davis, however, was hardly in a position to criticize those who frequented bookstores to do something other than purchase books: earlier in his travels through America, he had stopped at the New York City shop of Elihu Hubbard Smith's printers, T. and J. Swords, and happily read the Edward Gibbon he found "lying on the counter" (John Davis, *Travels of Four Years and a Half in the United States of America during 1798, 1799, 1800, 1801, and 1802* [1803], ed. A. J. Morrison [New York, 1909], 218, 222–223, 225). The Reverend James Abercrombie was parson at Saint Peter's Episcopal Church, and Charles Brockden Brown was then attempting to make his own career as an editor and using Dickins as a printer and bookseller; Brown also occasionally wrote for the *Port Folio*. See Brown, "The Water Drinker," *Port Folio*, May 2, 1801, 143. Kerber and Morris also identify Brown as the "*small*, sly Deist, a disguised but determined jacobin," whom Thomas Boylston Adams claimed Dennie briefly installed as editor of the *Port Folio* during an 1802 yellow fever epidemic ("Politics and Literature," *WMQ*, 3d Ser., XXIII [1966], 563 n. 50). Brown did not maintain an intense association with the *Port Folio*, despite this episode, and Gertrude Meredith, writing during that fever season, queried her husband about "who carries on the paper in the absence of its Editor" and noted that she had seen "our friend Charles Brown in New York" (Gertrude Meredith to William Meredith, Aug. 29, 1802, Meredith Family Papers). Brown turned to Hugh Maxwell to publish his novel *Ormond*, but its title page noted that it was "sold by Thomas Dobson, Asbury Dickins, and the principal booksellers" (1799), and Dickins printed Brown's *Clara Howard; in a Series of Letters* (Philadelphia, 1801), although not *Jane Talbot, a Novel*, which was published the same year by another Philadelphia printer, Joseph Conrad.

series, "Letters from Silesia," continued throughout much of the periodical's first volume. The Adamses' cousin Josiah Quincy also contributed; his satirical series "Climenole" adroitly followed Dennie's rules for combining political and personal animadversion and anxiety. William Smith Shaw, nephew to Abigail Adams and secretary to John Adams, sent the *Prospectus* of the *Port Folio* to his friend Arthur Maynard Walter. "I wish you to obtain subscribers for him in Boston," Shaw wrote; "I feel a deep interest in the success of this periodical, not only as a friend to the proprietors, but also as an American." Other supporters included Boston's John Sylvester John Gardiner and Gouverneur Morris, who praised Dennie and invited him to stay at his elegant New York home, Morrisania. A letter Dennie received from the secretary of the Senate, Samuel Otis, makes clear that Dennie's paper was also read by members of Congress. Nor was the *Port Folio*'s readership confined to the northern United States. "Tell Joe," wrote Gertrude Meredith while visiting Baltimore, "that this vast city rings with his glory. . . . Mr. Welsh has been pointed out to me as the author of 'Florian,'" and a "Mr. Gray" of Norfolk, Virginia, as the author of the pieces signed "Fernando." The doctor Lemuel Kollock, a frequent participant in Elihu Smith's projects, helped to circulate a subscription paper for the *Port Folio* in Savannah, Georgia, and a bookseller in the same town wrote to Dennie that Charles Cotesworth Pinckney, a Revolutionary war general and well-known political figure, had "promised to give every encouragement in his Power to the circulation of the Port-Folio in Charleston." Dennie had succeeded in making himself read throughout the land.[5]

5. E. Jackson to Asbury Dickens, Feb. 28, 1801 (this letter is also the source of information about Lemuel Kollock's efforts on Dennie's behalf), Gertrude Meredith to William Meredith, Aug. 26, 1802, May 3, 1804, Samuel Otis to Dennie, Feb. 7, n.d., all in Meredith Family Papers; William Smith Shaw to Arthur Maynard Walter, Jan. 16, 1801, William Smith Shaw Papers, Boston Athenaeum. Shaw was a friend and correspondent of Dennie's close associate, Thomas Boylston Adams, and Adams thanked Shaw for his assistance and asked for more help (Adams to Shaw, Sept. 13, 1801, in Charles Grenfil Washburn, "Letters of Thomas Boylston Adams to William Smith Shaw, 1799–1823," American Antiquarian Society, *Proceedings*, n.s., XXVII [1917], 126). Both Shaw and John Quincy Adams were troubled—despite their admiration for Dennie, affection for Thomas Boylston, and interest in the *Port Folio*—by some of the periodical's more freewheeling content. John Quincy scolded Thomas Boylston for a piece he had written for the *Port Folio* in which he mocked Washington, D.C.'s southern character, and Shaw asked Thomas Boylston to avoid publishing the "observations of such *political heretics* as 'a native American,'" referring to a piece that had apparently praised the journalist James Thomson Callendar, whom Shaw deemed a

Four Rhetorical Frameworks

Dennie drew on Augustan literature and the literature of sensibility as he developed the *Port Folio*. English poets such as John Dryden, Alexander Pope, and James Thomson had deplored the destruction of traditional society in the face of impersonal market relations and social upheaval and had taken up their pens in "ideological warfare" against modernity. In America, Augustan writers such as Timothy Dwight, John Trumbull, and David Humphreys portrayed the modern world as an ugly and meaningless place in which individuals were bound only by interest rather than by bonds of emotion, duty, and tradition. All of these Augustan satirists presented themselves as critics whose heightened powers of perception enabled them to point out society's flaws. The literature of sensibility posited an equally perceptive individual but of a different kind. Rather than penetrating the mists of ideology with a keenness born of nostalgia and disdain, the man of sensibility perceived wounds and injustice others with less responsive minds and hearts could overlook. The *Port Folio*'s ideal reader possessed both kinds of perception and was therefore a kind of Augustan man of sensibility, an impassioned spectator who resisted the lures of society because, with his combination of sharp wit and tutored feelings, he could perceive both their absurdity and their cruelty.[6]

The *Port Folio* also bore the marks of an older tradition: melancholia. As understood from classical Greece through the Enlightenment, melancholia—known also as hypochondria—had as its central element sensitivity heightened to the point of danger. The melancholic suffered and risked psychic collapse, but he was capable of unusual insight and creativity. "The sun," Dennie wrote, placing himself in a proud but uneasy triad, "is the poet's, the invalid's, and the hypochondriac's friend." The torment of melan-

"hireling miscreant" (Shaw to Thomas Boylston Adams, Jan. 26, 1801, Shaw Papers). Federalist-inflected sociability flourished in Charleston, South Carolina; see Daniel Kilbride, "Cultivation, Conservatism, and the Early National Gentry: The Manigault Family and Their Circle," *Journal of the Early Republic*, XIX (1999), 221–256.

6. William C. Dowling, *Poetry and Ideology in Revolutionary Connecticut* (Athens, Ga., 1990), 6–8 (quotation on 7); Dowling, *Literary Federalism in the Age of Jefferson: Joseph Dennie and the "Port Folio," 1801–1812* (Columbia, S.C., 1999), 74–78; Colin Wells, *The Devil and Doctor Dwight: Satire and Theology in the Early American Republic* (Chapel Hill, N.C., 2002), 3. Jean-Cristophe Agnew describes English Augustan authors as conforming to a "Stoic ideal of detached and dispassionate contemplation of the world's follies"; see *Worlds Apart: The Market and the Theater in Anglo-American Thought, 1550–1750* (New York, 1986), 162.

cholic creatures was proof of their merit: "Who knows not to suffer, has not a noble soul," quoted one *Port Folio* columnist, from Fénelon's *Telemachus*. "A man of a superficial mind and little genius," read another extract, "has no diffidence arising from those delicacies and sensibilities, which often cruelly distress men of real ability." William Beckford's "Effects of the Atmosphere upon the Animal Spirits," reprinted in the *Port Folio* in 1802, archly noted that some men are constitutionally cheerful; their punishment is that they "know not those enjoyments, that proceed from melancholy, and are hence deprived of the highest rapture that can be sustained by rational and enlightened minds." The melancholic, in short, was the wild elder cousin of the man of sensibility and of the Augustan satirist. So acute was the psychic and physical pain he felt that he risked complete dissolution. The English poet William Cowper, who suffered that fate, was a particular favorite of the *Port Folio*. "The smothered flames of desire, uniting with the vapours of constitutional melancholy, and the fervency of religious zeal," reads a biography excerpted in 1803, "produced altogether that irregularity of corporeal sensation, and of mental health, which gave such extraordinary vicissitudes of splendour and of darkness to his mortal career, and made Cowper, at times, an idol of the purest admiration, and at times an object of the sincerest pity." In the *Port Folio*, such a man was a tragic hero.[7]

7. [Joseph Dennie], "An Author's Evenings," *Port Folio*, July 24, 1802, 231, William Beckford, "Effects of the Atmosphere upon the Animal Spirits," Aug. 7, 1802, 245, "Lewis Listless," "The American Lounger, No. XXXIX," II, no. 52 (Jan. 15, 1803), 409, "Character of William Cowper," Sept. 3, 1803, 283, [Dennie], "The Lay Preacher," May 5, 1804, 139. *Telemachus*, first published in 1699, told the story of the education of Odysseus's son by his tutor, Mentor. Tobias Smollett published a translation in 1776. "It may be remarked with truth, that not unfrequently those very foibles, which bring down men of the greatest capacity to a level with the common race of mortals, render them more interesting, particularly when they proceed from extreme sensibility, or from goodness of heart" ("The Life of Fenelon," *Port Folio*, July 9, 1803, 220). Beckford (1760–1844) was an English aristocrat who wrote about travel and art as well as writing miscellaneous essays and a gothic novel, *Vathek*. Such descriptions of the melancholic's character occur throughout these years of the *Port Folio*. For discussions of the changing nature of melancholia in the modern era, see Anne C. Vila, *Enlightenment and Pathology: Sensibility in the Literature and Medicine of Eighteenth-Century France* (Baltimore, 1998), chap. 3; Wolf Lepenies, *Melancholy and Society*, trans. Jeremy Gaines and Doris Jones (Cambridge, Mass., 1992); John Mullan, *Sentiment and Sensibility: The Language of Feeling in the Eighteenth Century* (New York, 1988), 202–240; Winfried Schleiner, *Melancholy, Genius, and Utopia in the Renaissance* (Wiesbaden, Germany, 1991). For discussions rooted more exclusively in literary analysis and psychoanalytic theory, see Lynn Enterline, *The Tears of Nar-*

Melancholia exaggerated the dangers of solipsism present in the literature of sensibility: even more than the man of feeling, the melancholic was likely to get lost in the intensity of his own responsiveness. Yet he, too, had the potential for insight because of his distance from the joys and purposes of the society around him. Rather than seeing, as did the satirist or the man of sensibility, the flaws of the world, the melancholic was gripped with an unsought awareness that all of human existence had become meaningless. In the *Port Folio*, Dennie cast the melancholic view of a lost dimension of meaning into geopolitical terms: England became the world of meaning, and America that of disorder and meaninglessness. Dennie portrayed himself as an unwilling exile from the British Empire and, throughout the *Port Folio*'s run, went so far as to print yearly birthday wishes to George III. This defiant, Anglophile melancholia offered Dennie a publicly recognizable framework in which to place an abiding and deeply personal sense of melancholy exile. It also had broader consequences. With its startling outbursts of Anglophile longing, the *Port Folio* urged readers to reject the loyalty demands of the new nation. Far from backward-looking, Dennie's flamboyant Anglophilia was a cranky declaration of spiritual independence, an insistence that Americans could have a public voice even while rejecting the most basic demand of the new nation: that citizens accept its legitimacy.[8]

---

cissus: Melancholia and Masculinity in Early Modern Writing (Stanford, Calif., 1995); Julia Kristeva, *Black Sun: Depression and Melancholia* (New York, 1989); Max Pensky, *Melancholy Dialectics: Walter Benjamin and the Play of Mourning* (Amherst, Mass., 1993); and Juliana Schiesari, *The Gendering of Melancholia: Feminism, Psychoanalysis, and the Symbolics of Loss in Renaissance Literature* (Ithaca, N.Y., 1992). A particularly useful study of literature and melancholia is Allan Ingram, *Boswell's Creative Gloom: A Study of Imagery and Melancholy in the Writings of James Boswell* (London, 1982). Dennie's own persona might have been influenced by that presented by Boswell in columns such as "The Hypochondriack." William C. Dowling argues that Dennie is "drawing on a tradition of literary valetudinarianism in which physical suffering brings with it a certain inescapable moral perspective on one's way of being in the world" (*Literary Federalism*, 50).

8. "The very image of meaninglessness, whose objects populate the melancholy landscape," Max Pensky has explained, "are themselves produced from a more hidden conviction, of an originary dimension of lost, destroyed, or withheld meaning" (Pensky, *Melancholy Dialectics*, 19). On birthday celebrations, see, for example, "Ode for His Majesty's Birthday, 1805," *Port Folio*, Sept. 7, 1805, 278. Sending birthday wishes to George III was a particularly mischievous practice, given the importance to Americans' self-conscious patriotism of occasions such as Washington's Birthday. See David Waldstreicher, *In the Midst of Perpetual Fetes: The Making of American Nationalism, 1776–1820* (Chapel Hill, N.C., 1997), 112–113, 119–120.

Even as he refused to lend his voice to patriotic nation building, Dennie craved civic respectability, contributors, and an audience. Federalism became a crucial means to achieving them. Dennie had first embraced partisanship to find an audience as a man of letters, and he continued to use Federalism in this way in the *Port Folio*. Moreover, Federalist rhetoric was most expressive of the oppositional stance Dennie sought to create precisely when Federalists were losing national influence. Far from trying to convert the majority to Federalism, Dennie used Federalism as a way to express discontent with the judgments of the majority and with the very idea that majority judgment should be assumed to be correct. Its rhetoric and usefulness in building an audience offered a way to oppose democratic conformity, to create a space for criticism, and to express difference, discontent, and unease.[9]

Despite the prevalence of Federalist rhetoric in the *Port Folio*, the questions that truly engaged Dennie and his contributors were not those of the comparative merits of partisan agendas. For Dennie as for Smith, the question of who should hold office was only a synecdoche for broader and deeper debates over what should be Americans' relation to their government, to literature, and to one another. Transatlantic arguments over sensibility shaped the *Port Folio* more profoundly than arguments over policy, and the French Revolution of the 1790s was almost as important a presence in the *Port Folio*'s first five years as were contemporary American events. The periodical's editor and contributors pondered whether beauty and truth could be pursued in the absence of the order provided by tradition and hierarchy, whether individual judgment could be developed and expressed in the face of a powerful crowd, and how human beings should be joined together in society. In its attention to such issues and in its fascination with the radical

9. In a brief discussion of Joseph Dennie's irritation at Benjamin Franklin's popularity, Grantland S. Rice argues, "Dennie fought against a whole nation which was redefining its writers as either the passive embodiment of the genius of a native spirit or the homogenous producers of useful intellectual property rather than participants in the public realm" (*The Transformation of Authorship in America* [Chicago, 1997], 69). Rice is analyzing an 1801 *Port Folio* column: [Joseph Dennie], "An Author's Evenings: From the Shop of Messrs. Colon and Spondee," Feb. 14, 1801, 53–54. For the argument that the *Port Folio* retreated from political engagement because of the 1800 triumph of Jefferson, see Dowling, *Literary Federalism*, esp. x. Pieces that support this argument were for the most part "Farrago" and "Lay Preacher" columns that were not written during the *Port Folio*'s run but were instead reprinted from the *Museum* and earlier efforts—they were written, that is, at a time of Federalist power, not decline.

phases of the French Revolution, the *Port Folio* was less a Hamiltonian or an Adamsian organ than it was a Burkean one. "Nothing is more just, nothing more true, and nothing more salutary than *all* the political doctrines of Mr. Burke respecting the accursed revolution in France," Dennie rhapsodized in a typical passage. Pitching his own rhetoric to Burke's piercing key, Dennie declared that Burke "derides the debility of republicanism, the pert loquacity and vile tampering of whig demagogues, and the madness of innovation; when he points to the beauty and the stedfastness of the Corinthian column, and when he indignantly strives, with all the energy of wisdom and virtue, to trample upon the reptiles who would subvert that column, and *dash and perplex maturest councils,* we approve every word, and would emulate every deed."[10]

Like Burke, Dennie insisted that the destruction of traditions led to a still more pernicious modern activity: the rejection of personal emotional bonds in favor of an ostensible commitment to the public good. It was to the French Revolution and French "philosophes" that Dennie turned for stark images of this critical failure. Jean Jacques Rousseau appeared in the magazine as "that eloquent lunatic, and splendid scoundrel, [who advocates] benevolence to the whole species, and want of feeling for every individual." The *Port Folio* printed an excerpt from the French playwright and essayist Jean François de La Harpe in which La Harpe, who had repudiated the French Revolution after being imprisoned in 1794, condemns "fanatics" and offers as an exemplar Horatius, "a fanatic of patriotism, [who] . . . killed his sister, because she cursed a victory, which deprived her of her lover." This choice of villain is telling; the revolutionary artist Jacques-Louis David turned to the same sequence of events in order to glorify the subjection of private affection to public duty. For La Harpe and by extension the *Port Folio,* Horatio was emblematic, not of patriotism, but of savagery. The revolutionary French provided his ideal and debased audience. "Among us," La Harpe continues sardonically, "the murderer would have been borne in triumph, and, before him the head of his sister, on the point of a pike." In the *Port Folio,* the violent phases of the French Revolution represented the nightmarish destination of America's current path. "With

10. [Joseph Dennie], introduction to "The Character of Edmund Burke," *Port Folio,* Apr. 9, 1803, 117. An extended treatment of the French Revolution came from John Adams, who pieced together paragraphs by classical historians and deemed them a chronicle of the French Revolution. See "A Translation of an Essay on the History of the French Revolution, by a Society of Latin Writers," Apr. 9, 1803, 114, Apr. 16, 1803, 121, Apr. 23, 1803, 129, May 7, 1803, 145.

regard to the decay of the Social Affections," read one "Miscellaneous Paragraph," "though some may consider it as a vice, yet our republicans glory in it, as arising from the spirit of patriotism, which teaches every citizen to postpone all private affections for the sake of the public." No good society, the periodical consistently argued, could be built on such a foundation. And yet devotion to the public good lay at the center of republican ideology. Lambasting that principle was as dramatic a rejection of the new nation as Dennie's flamboyant birthday greetings to George III.[11]

The *Port Folio* portrayed the republican citizen's devotion to the public good at the expense of private affections as the political version of the man who, in Oliver Goldsmith's mordant image, shed tears over the suffering of animals while happily "devouring the flesh of six different animals tossed up in a fricassee." Thomas Jefferson's combination of slaveholding and devotion to liberty are portrayed as the logical extension of the hypocritical sensibility at the center of republicanism. In a *Palladium* extract that Dennie reprinted in 1803, Jefferson stood writing at his desk: "This is a *self-evident truth.*—All men have an unalienable right to—(*here a black enters, and accidentally stumbling, strikes the extended arm of the patriotical speaker, and knocks the paper from his hand—which last kicks and beats him most unmercifully*)." Jefferson's insincere sensibility was then elevated to the level of immorality. "Oh you idle, impertinent, blundering scoundrel," Jefferson blurts out, "to break in upon me thus, when I had arrived at the most interesting, eloquent, and pathetic part of my speech, at the very instant when I was going to demonstrate the equality of all men." "Here was I gradually brought up to the right pitch of feeling, my heart expanded with philanthropy, and my voice was modelled to the sweetest tone," concludes this Jefferson, "when your—Oh, rascal, I'll thrash you, I'll—(*The negro runs out, and the master follows him, beating him continually.*" In the context of

11. [John Quincy Adams], "Letters, Literary and Political," *Port Folio*, Feb. 19, 1803, 58, "Miscellaneous Paragraphs," June 9, 1804, 182, [Joseph Dennie], "Literary Intelligence," Aug. 10, 1805, 245–246. Edmund Burke's condemnation of the "naked metaphysical abstractions" of the French Revolution also shaped the thinking of men of letters such as Timothy Dwight and David Humphreys (Dowling, *Poetry and Ideology*, 7–10). Many Americans were also troubled by the less dramatic but still disorienting losses of traditional hierarchies and roles that the American Revolution had caused. See Joanne B. Freeman, *Affairs of Honor: National Politics in the New Republic* (New Haven, Conn., 2001), xiii–xxiv; David S. Shields, *Civil Tongues and Polite Letters in British America* (Chapel Hill, N.C., 1997), xxi; Joan B. Landes, *Women and the Public Sphere in the Age of the French Revolution* (Ithaca, N.Y., 1988), 152–158.

the *Port Folio*, this was a satire that mocked Jefferson but mourned a deeper problem: Jefferson, who spouted benevolence and beat individuals, was a man dedicated to the public good but devoid of true social affections. He was creating a country in his own unfortunate image. Rejection of specific emotional ties was a mark of savagery, not enlightenment, and, if America promoted such rejection, it represented, not an advance in human society, but regression toward the primitive. "All the hordes of savages we have discovered are more or less formed into society," notes a *Port Folio* political essay, "and those who approach the nearest to a *state of nature* are, by far, the most wretched, as they are the most brutal, selfish, and unfeeling towards each other."[12]

By consistently portraying Jefferson in this way, Dennie channeled Federalist loathing of Jefferson into a transatlantic debate over the limits of benevolence. In his *Reflections on the Revolution in France*, Edmund Burke argued, "To love the little platoon we belong to in society, is the first principle . . . of public affections." Godwin, by contrast, contended in *Political Justice* that individuals should suppress all private and partial attachments and achieve a universal benevolence. Godwin's assertion provoked waves of criticism. Coleridge, for example, argued in response that private affections were necessary to the creation of any more generalized love of humanity. "The intensity of private attachments encourages, not prevents, universal Benevolence," he wrote in his 1795 *Conciones ad Populum*. In the same year, an essay in the *Monthly Magazine* asserted, "The rays of affection, which, while they are concentrated in private relations, are warm and vivid, diffused through the universe, become too faint and feeble to be seen or felt." Works such as Charles Lloyd's 1798 epistolary novel *Edmund Oliver* and Robert Hall's 1800 *Modern Infidelity* offered similar assaults on Godwin; in the latter, Hall argued, "Extended benevolence is the last and most perfect fruit of the private affections; so that to expect to reap the former from the extinction of the latter, is to oppose the means to the end."[13]

12. Oliver Goldsmith, "Letters from a Citizen of the World to His Friends in the East; Letter XV: Against Cruelty to Animals," in Washington Irving, ed., *The Miscellaneous Works of Oliver Goldsmith* (Philadelphia, 1830), 263; "Levity," *Port Folio*, July 30, 1803, 245, "Politics: Essay 1, Natural Rights," Nov. 20, 1802, 364.

13. Edmund Burke, *Reflections on the Revolution in France*, ed. J. G. A. Pocock (Indianapolis, Ind., 1987), 41; Samuel Taylor Coleridge, *Conciones ad Populum; or, Addresses to the People*, in Kathleen Coburn, gen. ed., *The Collected Works of Samuel Taylor Coleridge*, I, *Lectures 1795 on Politics and Religion*, ed. Lewis Patton and Peter Mann (Princeton, N.J., 1971), 46; William Enfield, "Enquirer," *Monthly Magazine*, I

By casting Jefferson as a Godwinian man and as a man of insincere sensibility, the *Port Folio* yoked partisan animosity to deeper qualms about late-eighteenth-century life. "If the lunatic Godwin could have his way," Dennie wrote angrily, "and realize his fantastic project of perfectibility, we should then behold such a Being, as the ensuing paragraph describes. Him the colds of winter and the heats of summer are equally incapable of molesting. To him a serene or cloudy sky are equally indifferent. Let the earth abound in fruits or be cursed with scarcity it has no influence on his welfare. He lives secure in rains and thunders, lightnings and earthquakes: He has no concern in the blossoms of Spring, or in the glowings of Summer, in the fruits of Autumn, or in the frosts of Winter." The *Port Folio's* exaggerated Godwin, like its exaggerated Jefferson, proffered to readers nightmarish versions of man and society. Godwin and Jefferson lacked the capacities to love and to feel and so were the precise opposites of the responsive social beings the *Port Folio* posited as its ideal readers and as the nation's ideal citizens. "Let crack-brained philosophers talk of obeying the noble impulses of sublimated nature, and regulating their conduct by the decisions of unbiassed reason," the correspondent Isaac Story snarled in another reference to Godwin, "whip me such muck-worm scoundrels, who put the soul into a retort, and measure the pulsations of the heart with a pendulum." Individuals should not be guided by "unbiased reason," the Burkean *Port Folio* consistently asserted; reason untethered to tradition, affection, and love would not allow men to perceive truth and could not create a good society. Of "philosophers" in France and America—by which he meant French revolutionaries and the Jeffersonians who believed in them— Dennie declared, "When they cast their blinking optics to heaven, [they] can discern nothing there but stones, hard as their callous hearts, cold and heavy, like their calculating heads, and rugged and senseless, like their republican system."[14]

In less earnest pieces, the *Port Folio* suggested that unfeeling individuals were not only destructive of society but also unmanly. The 1790s had witnessed growing skepticism toward the man of feeling's most dramatic

---

(1795), 275; Robert Hall, *Modern Infidelity Considered, with Respect to Its Influence on Society* . . . , 4th ed. (Cambridge, 1800), 51–53. For a discussion of this line of criticism, see Nicola Trott, "The Coleridge Circle and the 'Answer to Godwin,'" *Review of English Studies*, n.s., XVI (1990), 212–229.

14. *Port Folio*, Sept. 14, 1805, 287, [Isaac Story], "From the Desk of Beri Hesdin," Apr. 16, 1803, 123, Beatrice [Emily Mifflin Hopkinson], "The American Lounger, No. 107," Feb. 9, 1805, 33.

displays of emotion, but the *Port Folio* ardently defended them. A reprinted essay entitled "On the Unmanliness of Shedding Tears," by an unnamed "British essayist," decried how "hardness of heart, and insensibility of temper, conceal themselves under the appellation of manly fortitude." A correspondent styling himself "Senex" similarly complained that "sordid and stoical apathy . . . seems to me the characteristic of too many of the present generation of young men. Insensibility is, apparently, the fashion of the day." Like fashions of clothing, politics, and art, this fashion of insensibility was to be resisted.[15]

Dennie encouraged his readers to reject both Jeffersonian hypocrisy and Godwinian coldness and in their place to cultivate sincere, enlightened reason and feeling. The reader was invited to admire individuals who felt deeply and reacted profoundly, and he was encouraged to become such a person—more specifically, such a man—himself. Despite the importance of women contributors to the *Port Folio* and the Tuesday Club, the periodical associated true manhood with a refined sensibility. "A brave man," Dennie explained in one of the many "Lay Preacher" columns that he had reprinted in the *Port Folio*, "has, generally, 'a tear for pity.'" Emotional intensity and the capacity for unselfish love emerged, not from conventional heterosexual domesticity, but instead from male communities of reading, writing, and friendship. One of the series of columns entitled "An Author's Evenings" explicitly refuted an author's suggestion that men not exposed to women's civilizing touch were "brutal." "Though we are far from depreciating the numberless advantages, which arise from the company, conversation, and example of woman," it read, in a nod to the Humian conception of sociability, "yet the general position of this author, as he has here stated it, is not true." In the *Port Folio*, men of letters did not need women; they needed each other. The biographies that Dennie printed celebrated the symbiotic relationship between male friendship and literary prowess. "In the reigns of Elizabeth and James," began one anecdote, "the love of punning was exceeding great, and almost passing the love of women." Like participants in the Friendly Club, Dennie was determined to assert that cultural pur-

15. Senex [Dr. John Edmonds Stock], "The American Lounger, No. VI," *Port Folio*, Feb. 20, 1802, 49, "On the Unmanliness of Shedding Tears," May 25, 1805, 155. Dror Wahrman describes the "hasty retreat of the moist-eyed man of feeling" in the last decades of the eighteenth century; see *The Making of the Modern Self: Identity and Culture in Eighteenth-Century England* (New Haven, Conn., 2004), chap. 1. See also G. J. Barker-Benfield, *The Culture of Sensibility: Sex and Society in Eigtheenth-Century Britain* (Chicago, 1992), chap. 3.

suits were manly, even as he relied on and delighted in the contributions of women.[16]

The *Port Folio* did not just describe communities of men united through language; it also attempted to create one. Toward his readers, Dennie could be stern, teasing, or commiserative, but never impersonal. He appealed to his favorite contributors with a palpable warmth. Requesting another contribution from a correspondent signing himself "S," Dennie reprinted verse from William Gifford, the English writer who, Dennie remarked, "has well commemorated the friendship of men of letters." "I only seek, in language, void of art," the poem reads, "To ope my breast, and pour out all my heart; / And, boastful of thy various wroth; to tell / How long we lov'd, and thou canst add *how well*." Men's cultural labor not only produced friendships; it produced life. Creation was procreation, and Shakespeare, Joseph Hopkinson marveled in 1801, "carries within him all the rich and various stores of nature, and from him the world of genius has been peopled." Dennie himself offered to serve as a kind of mother for his fledgling writers. "The Editor will exercise great tenderness and lenity towards all who tempt the dangerous *ocean of ink*," he wrote in 1801. "The literary offspring of youthful and trembling authors shall, if possible, be fostered: 'Our natures merciful and mild, / Will, from fond pity, save the child.'"[17]

In the *Port Folio*, admirable literature and correct politics were to be united through fellowship. "Politicians, and men of letters," Dennie wrote in an early issue, "should be intimately connected, should, as it were, be *married*, with an affection, which, like the durable kindness of those fortunate couples, described by a Roman poet, is unbroken with bickering, and coeval with their existence." "If these be wanting," Dennie warned, "an editor cannot discharge his duty. His paper will be meagre and powerless. It will have a pale and cadaverous visage, and will quickly die." The union of men of letters and of politicians would instead create a powerful paper, one that would improve the world through observing its flaws in the way that

16. [Joseph Dennie], "The Lay Preacher," *Port Folio*, Oct. 10, 1801, 324, [Dennie], "An Author's Evenings," Oct. 10, 1801, 324, [Dennie], "An Author's Evenings," Nov. 21, 1801, 370.

17. [Joseph Hopkinson], "Criticism: Shakespeare, No. 11," *Port Folio*, Feb. 21, 1801, 59, [Hopkinson], "To Readers and Correspondents," Mar. 7, 1801, 79, [Joseph Dennie], "To Readers and Correspondents," July 17, 1802, 223. Gertrude Meredith wrote to her husband William: "Dennie says he loves you much and thinks of you often. I have persuaded him to write some marginal notes to you" (1805, Meredith Family Papers).

Smith's *Medical Repository* would improve the world through observing its plagues.[18]

Like the Augustan satires and traditional conversation circles on which it drew, the *Port Folio* posited an inside and an outside. Dennie divided the world into those who responded to it, like the sensitive and keen-eyed reader he himself hoped to be, and those who did not. "He who loves nothing but beef and beer will deride our sentimental bard," wrote Dennie before one poem. "He, whose nerves vibrate at the slightest touch of beauty, will acknowledge the justice of the ensuing picture." Dennie delighted in references to "frozen and strait-laced critics" and to readers possessed of the "frigid indifference of every true Indian." Such people neither understood the wit of satire nor felt the poignance of beauty, and their dullness sharpened the pleasures of those within the *Port Folio*'s circle. The ideals of sensibility and sociability had long looked both outward and inward; they could inspire sympathy for others and action to alleviate others' suffering, but, as critics noted, they could also promote a paralyzing satisfaction in one's own distinctive responsiveness. The *Port Folio* embraced the latter tendency and cast it as rebellion against America's crass demands.[19]

Despite their stolidity, the outsiders were not immune to the attractions of the world. On the contrary, the *Port Folio* depicted them as driven by greed, vulgar ambition, and lust, and thus dependent on those from whom they could obtain money, power, or sexual favors. A "Lounger" column from 1805 argued that "the two most predominant passions in the human constitution" were "revenge and sensuality—more especially the latter." The periodical implicitly commanded readers to laugh at those who succumbed to the lure of sex—and to laugh harder if their capitulation was thinly veiled by respectability. Wanting to be respected by the crowd and wanting carnal satisfaction were two manifestations of the same foolish dependence on unworthy others. Dennie printed extracts from Alexandre-Joseph-Pierre,

18. [Joseph Dennie], "To the Public," *Port Folio*, May 9, 1801, 150.

19. [Joseph Hopkinson], "Criticism: Shakespeare, No. 1," *Port Folio*, Feb. 14, 1801, 53, [Joseph Dennie], "To Readers and Correspondents," June 27, 1801, 207, [Dennie], introduction to "The Lover and the Friend," July 17, 1802, 224. Peter Stallybrass and Allon White explain that the Augustan writer established "a rhetorical inside which would gradually envelop his listeners in a symbolic community defined *implicitly* by those it rejects" (*The Politics and Poetics of Transgression* [Ithaca, N.Y., 1986], 88). See also Caroll Smith-Rosenberg, "Subject Female, Authorizing American Identity," *American Literary History*, V (1993), 481–485; and David S. Shields's discussion of wit in *Civil Tongues and Polite Letters*, 1–5.

vicomte de Ségur's history of women; during Louis XV's reign, one such passage noted: "Ladies got into grey carriages, with a plain equipage, that did not attract attention, and drove secretly to those Casini which belonged to their lovers, where all shame was forgot, and licentiousness reigned still more than voluptuousness. But the same women, as they went from these asylums of disorder, resumed at the door a composed mien, and even a sort of prudery peculiar to the morals of the times." Even religious art could be inspired by prurience. "The ingenious [Thomas] Cogan," an extract noted approvingly, explained that certain biblical stories are painted so often for a simple reason: "They pretend to give lessons of virtuous resistance . . . while, in reality, they are rendering themselves popular by inflaming concupiscence." *Port Folio* readers were to resist sexual lures and to resist as well the siren call of meaningless respectability.[20]

The *Port Folio* advocated benevolent relations between spiritually independent men. Sexual attraction offered a contrasting model of self-interested mutual dependence. Men attracted to women lost their judgment and dignity—and the women who sought to attract men did so too. Thus, face painting and women's fashion of wearing thin clothing were recurring themes in the *Port Folio;* their discussion neatly expressed Dennie's contention that desire was in the control of neither partner but rather arose in the space between and enmeshed both. Face painting embodied vanity, deceit, and the attempt to draw the gaze. The *Port Folio*'s jokes and stories about it sought to teach readers to penetrate the mask and to escape through harsh laughter the tyranny of desire. Face painting, hissed a column entitled "Festoon of Fashion," was a "vain and ruinous system of deception, practised by cheating coquettes, and by which no one is deceived." The fashion of wearing sheer muslins, in turn, appeared as outright "nudity," a nakedness that revealed naked desire. The proper response was disdain. "Let every lady therefore take care, that while she is displaying in public, a bosom

20. "Miscellaneous Paragraphs," *Port Folio*, Apr. 20, 1805, 117, "Polite Literature," July 20, 1805, 218, "The American Lounger, No. 143," Oct. 19, 1805, 321 (armies are motivated, the piece continues, by the idea that "they may criminally converse with the female relatives of the conquered"). The extracts are from Alexandre-Joseph-Pierre, vicomte de Ségur, *Les Femmes: Leur condition et leur influence dans l'ordre social chez différents peuples anciens et modernes* (Paris, 1803); Ségur's overall position, that the sexes are equal though different, also accords with some of the sentiments expressed in the *Port Folio*. See also "Polite Literature," *Port Folio*, July 27, 1805, 228, for further discussion of these "Casini." The reference is to T[homas] Cogan, *A Philosophical Treatise on the Passions* (Bath, 1800).

whiter than snow," read a representative passage, "the men do not look as if they were saying, 'Tis very pretty, *but we have seen it before!*'" The "gaze," here, did not empower the gazer; on the contrary, the object of the gaze, the woman, had the power to mesmerize, to ensnare, to humiliate. Only the abilities to look critically and to look away offered power, and they were abilities that most men lacked. A "letter," signed "Ichabod Flash, a captain in the milishee," implores the Lounger: "Do, squire, your a skoller, rite a logium on the buty of naked skins, or say sumthing to cumfort the ladies, whilst they are shivering in the cold to sho um to us." Ichabod and the ladies were locked in a stare that made fools of them both; the independent *Port Folio* reader looked upon them with withering glee.[21]

The *Port Folio* mocked commerce and politics by analogizing them to sexual courtships. A passage from the first year of the *Port Folio*, titled "Instructions for Shopkeepers, Apprentices, etc.," reads, "When [the shopkeeper] gets up in the morning let him dress off in the *sprucest style—* nankeen trowsers very wide, made *à la Turque—*as the size of a Turk's *inexpressibles* is very convenient, and much admired by the fair sex." Lest the allusions to sexual attraction somehow go unnoticed, the article continues at some length. "Your cravat should come up to your ears, and be filled out with a stiffener *large* and *strong,* which will give you the appearance of great strength, a natural qualification, and *useful* to the ladies in a *variety of ways.*" Far from enabling a manly independence, commerce rendered its participants absurdly in the thrall of women.[22]

21. "Festoon of Fashion," *Port Folio*, Jan. 21, 1802, 15, "Festoon of Fashion," Jan. 30, 1802, 26, Ichabod Flash, "The American Lounger, No. XXIV," June 26, 1802, 193. "The American Lounger, No. XV," Apr. 24, 1802, 121, describes the aged "coquette," who "never loses her desire to please, nor the good opinion of herself . . . and forgets that age is written on her own face." "The same dress, which formerly embellished her youth, now *disfigures* her person, and increases the imperfections of her old age. Preciseness and affectation accompany her in sorrow and sickness, and she dies full-dressed in ribbons of gaudy colours." See also [Joseph Dennie], "An Author's Evenings," Sept. 3, 1803, 282, in which a William Cowper poem claims of women that they are "insolent and self caress'd," "Curl'd, scented, furbelow'd, and flounced around, With feet too delicate to touch the ground: / They stretch the neck, and roll the wanton eye, / And sigh for every fool that flutters by." Dennie's introduction mockingly states, "I reverently presume that none of this species of women are to be found in America."

22. "Amusement," *Port Folio*, Oct. 24, 1801, 340. Despite Dennie's use of William Godwin as a symbolic archenemy, Dennie shared the philosopher's elitism and mistrust of the relationships created by trade. This passage is reminiscent of Godwin's

The *Port Folio* portrayed politicians' relations with voters as emerging from the same humiliating mutual dependence that yoked Ichabod Flash to the ladies and the shopkeeper to his client. Such a relationship was particularly damaging in the political realm: voter and politician needed each other in a way that rendered both incapable of independent judgment. The result was a stew of lust, self-interest, and corruption. Dennie quoted, "with fullest approbation," from a "wise and worthy writer: When I see a man of education and fortune put himself upon a level with the dregs of the people, mingle with the lowest vulgar, feed with them at the same board, and drink with them in the same cup, flatter their prejudices, expose himself to the belchings of their beer . . . I cannot help despising him, as a man guilty of the vilest prostitution." Jefferson was the *Port Folio*'s archetype of such a man. Josiah Quincy wrote in 1804 that Jefferson's prose resembled that of Quincy's maid, Betty. Quincy was not surprised, he wrote, "for Betty is a long-sided, raw-boned, red-haired slut, and, like Mr. Jefferson, always *hankering to have a mob of dirty fellows around her.*"[23]

Dennie's assault on Republicans aimed both at those whose desire for power and fame drew them into dependence and at the obtuseness of those who refused to perceive the mark of self-interest beneath the surface of patriotism. The *Port Folio* fellowship, by contrast, was protected by perspicacity from corruption and dependence. The *Port Folio* reader's eagle eye would not allow that "Virtue lend the mask to hide the basest crimes!" The speaker "Mercutio," in an original poem titled "Sketches from Nature," boasts: "My eye, like lightning, glances through the tribe" in order to see the "stain" of each "jacobin." This ability to penetrate deception extracted the reader from foolish bonds. Republicans and their public, by contrast, were trapped by their inability to see through one another's frauds; the Jacobin, Mercutio continues, manages to "beguile the herd" and so is "prais'd and courted, cherish'd and preferr'd." "Prudence avaunt!" Mercutio concludes defiantly, "the hate of fools I'll brave, / Remove the vizor from

essay, "Of Trades and Professions," which moved William Dunlap. In the essay, Godwin writes that the tradesman "exhibits all the arts of the male coquette; not that he wishes his fair visitor to fall in love with his person, but that he may induce her to take off his goods"; see *The Enquirer: Reflections on Education, Manners, and Literature; in a Series of Essays* (London, 1797), 218.

23. "Amusement," *Port Folio*, Oct. 24, 1801, 340, "From Paris, August," Nov. 6, 1802, 351, [Josiah Quincy], "Climenole, No. 11," Oct. 13, 1804, 321. Linda K. Kerber discusses Quincy and his series, placing them in the context of Federalist "Augustan" satire, in *Federalists in Dissent*, 15–18.

each crafty knave; / And when I cease to satirize through fear, / Dub me 'No Gentleman,' or 'Cavalier.'" In a final irony, the *Port Folio* reader's arrogant rejection of his peers' demands made him a better American than they; only a truly independent republican citizen would dare call himself a cavalier.[24]

Cajoling and even bullying his readers into penetrating masks and resisting lures, Dennie offered a perspective of manly self-control and power. To teach readers to resist the sexualized lures of democracy was to give them the gift of their own spiritual independence. Noting that the poet James Thomson, in "misplaced enthusiasm," wrote an ode to Liberty, the writer of one "Author's Evenings" declared that, by contrast: "Whenever I approach this same *Liberty*, I always feel under the influence of poppies and *drowsy syrups*. By a sort of mechanical impulse, I instantly close my aching eyes. Whenever this abused and cheating Liberty is praised I always *sit with sad civility*, and whenever I see the drab roaming the streets, I always wish that some *voice potential* would read the *riot*-act to her, and order her to disperse." Another paragraph took a similar tack. Describing Liberty as a woman, it read: "Before her coquetry, her fickleness, her perfidy, her whoredoms, and her rottenness, were notorious." "Men might be captivated by the leer and the smile, and the painted beauty of a courtezan Freedom. They might be fascinated with the snaky glare of her wild eyes, and discern in her desultory motion and her irregular gait, nothing but fresh provocatives to the enjoyment of so free and so independent a charmer. But, *at length, the morn, and cold indifference comes*." "We contrast the speciousness of promise with the hollowness of performance," concludes the paragraph, "and are indignant that our unrestrained rapture should be lavished upon nothing but a lackered and decorated skeleton." Look if you must, the *Port Folio* told its readers, but then look elsewhere.[25]

---

24. "A Modern Antique," *Port Folio*, Feb. 19, 1803, 64, Mercutio [probably Horace Binney], "Sketches from Nature," July 9, 1803, 224. The *Port Folio*'s "grand strategy in the symbolic warfare against Jeffersonian ideology," William C. Dowling writes, "becomes one of unmasking, dispelling the mists of visionary theory and 'darkness of delusion'" (*Literary Federalism*, 8). The *Port Folio* is turning a common motif, that of the association of vision and good citizenship, to partisan ends. Republican rhetoric used a similar trope but tended to focus on ferreting out crypto-monarchism and British conspiracy. On the subject of republican surveillance, or, in his terminology, "supervision," see Michael Warner, *The Letters of the Republic: Publication and the Public Sphere in Eighteenth-Century America* (Cambridge, Mass., 1990), 58–61.

25. "Miscellaneous Paragraphs," *Port Folio*, May 28, 1803, 175, [Joseph Dennie], "An Author's Evenings," June 4, 1803, 179.

A Brutal Theory

The *Port Folio*'s treatment of race exemplifies the power and the limitations of the periodical's critique of America. Racial slavery was America's most spectacular hypocrisy, the most dramatic evidence of the tangle of dependence, need, and power that lay beneath the claims of devotion to equality and liberty. The *Port Folio* returned to the subject again and again.[26]

Some *Port Folio* pieces participated in the transatlantic literary tradition of evoking readers' sorrow at slaveowners' inhumane sensibility. "Cease, unfeeling monster, cease," read the "Address to an Oppressor of the Enslaved Africans":

Let thy cruelty repose,
Let a transient gleam of peace,
Smile on wretched Afric's woes.
Let thy stern unfeeling soul
Yield to pity's pleading strain;
And humanity controul,
Thy insatiate thirst of gain.

One series, "Observations upon Certain Passages in Mr. Jefferson's Notes on Virginia," contrasted Africans' affectionate bonds with slaveowners' coldness. Drawing on the traveler and writer Mungo Park, the author argued that Africans "appear not only susceptible of the purest love, but many of them to possess hearts so generous and compassionate, that civilized nations might profit by their example." Thomas Jefferson, by contrast, argued that blacks were not "the same species with whites." It was, this author pithily noted, "a brutal theory."[27]

26. Allen Ingram singles out an issue of James Boswell's "Hypochondriack" in which Boswell notes his desire to expose the secrets of others and to "throw dirt." Ingram's explanation of the mischievous satisfaction such exposure provides suggests the pleasures of what is, in the *Port Folio*, both a personal and a political stance. Ingram writes: "One *would* like to throw the dirt, and one *does* enjoy seeing another completely exposed to the view of the world. There is a guilty fascination in showing the secrets of others, particularly their vices. This is partly because we are reassured that others, too, have inevitably a more furtive self than their appearances would indicate, and also because there is a not unpleasant thrill in being reminded of the possibility of our own humiliation by public exposure." See *Boswell's Creative Gloom*, 102.

27. "Address to an Oppressor of the Enslaved Africans," *Port Folio*, Jan. 7, 1804, 8,

Other pieces attacked the logic of racial distinctions in different fashion. Dennie printed an extract from Voltaire's *History of the Voyages of Scarmentado; a Satire*. The speaker, who has been taken prisoner by Africans, writes:

> Our captain railed against the captors, asking them the reason why they thus outrageously violated the laws of nations? they replied, your nose is long, and ours is flat; your hair is straight, and our wool is curled; you are white, and we are black; consequently we ought, according to the sacred and unalterable laws of nature, to be ever enemies. You buy us on the coast of Guinea, as if we were not human creatures, then treat us like beasts. . . . Therefore, when we meet with you, and are the strongest, we make you our slaves, and force you to till our ground, or else we cut off your nose or ears.

Reversing a racial hierarchy based on physical differences, this piece suggests, reveals that hierarchy to be unconvincing. Thus, America's new ordering principle of race was no less invented, only less fine-grained and aesthetically pleasing, than England's old hierarchy of monarchy, aristocracy, and commoners.[28]

Laughing at an unjust social order is not the same as building or even imagining an alternative to it. Despite the *Port Folio*'s mockery of race-based distinctions, Dennie relied on race to create the symbolic order of the periodical itself. The way in which the *Port Folio* manipulated racial hierarchy to score political points appeared clearly in a passage discussing the African American scientist Benjamin Banneker. The *Port Folio* suggested that Banneker's English was superior to that of the Republican secretary of the Treasury, Swiss-born Albert Gallatin. "The sooty astronomer, and *protegée* of Mammoth," read the passage, has been hired "for the purpose of '*correcting*' some part of this foreigner's 'procedure.'" "We think this would prove one of the most judicious of Mr. Jefferson's appointments; for the African *scholar*, if he could *correct* nothing else, might very easily correct Mr. Gallatin's English; nay, if Banneker had just arrived from the gold coast, or the

---

[Clement Clark Moore], "Observations upon Certain Passages in Mr. Jefferson's Notes on Virginia . . . ," Aug. 25, 1804, 268.

28. "The Adventures of Scarmentado: A Satirical Novel, Translated from the French," *Port Folio*, Apr. 17, 1802, 117. Not surprisingly, Dennie did not identify Voltaire as the author, referring to the text only as a "French classic." Voltaire wrote the original in 1756.

kingdom of Whidau, he would be superior to our imported financier, both in the pronouncing and writing of English." "The harmony and concert between the republican black, and the republican refugee, would be delightful," the piece continued. "The sound of Banneker's *banjo*, would be as tunable as Gallatin's broken French." In such a passage, the *Port Folio* turned to suggestions of black and white equality, or black superiority, only to insult Republicans. Rather than truly seeking to disrupt the symbolism of race—let alone the institution of slavery—the *Port Folio* used it to create hierarchies among whites: Federalist over Republican, English over French, and those who understand satire over those who do not.[29]

Dennie also used racial imagery to depict what he viewed as the horror of Republicans' desire for a public united in belief. Jefferson's famous declaration, "We are all federalists, we are all republicans," was in the *Port Folio* a nightmarish end to order and individual judgment. "The federalist and the democrat," read one passage, "are in a state of eternal hostility towards each other, as much as the dog and cat, and it is to be hoped they never will be more congenial." Dennie turned to the collapse of racial distinctions for an analogous vision of disorder. In an issue from 1802, he expressed disgust at a recently returned seafarer's claim: "The *best seaman* we had on board was a *black*, who discovered, in *no respect*, any mark of inferiority to men of a lighter complexion." Dennie linked this statement—so in keeping with other *Port Folio* passages—to the collapse of distinctions that so appalled him. "We are astonished that this writer . . . did not declare, that this sable worthy, now 'an *independent man*,' was not fully competent to any service in our church, or any office in our state." "As 'we are all federalists, all republicans,'" Dennie continued bitterly, "as we are all negroes, all white men." A remarkably similar unease appeared elsewhere in these volumes. A poem, supposed to be in the words of Jefferson's slave "Mungo," declared that "all white mans are all blackamoor." The satiric commentary that followed noted that Jefferson might not approve of the poem because the poet had "put an expression, very similar to one made by the president, into the mouth of Mungo; and although I do not think Jefferson could have got that beautiful paradox, of 'we are all federalists, we are all democrats,' from Mungo's 'all white mans are all blackamoor;' yet they resemble each other so much, that our antagonists might have an occasion to be merry at our expense." Jefferson's famous assertion of American unity was the *Port*

29. "Domestic Occurrences," *Port Folio*, Aug. 22, 1801, 270.

Folio's example of a failure to understand that it was from distinctions and differences that communities and selves were made.[30]

Dennie also turned to Haiti in order to link the social upheaval and political conformity he believed Republicans courted with the racial disorder he knew they feared. Early national Philadelphia had a close financial relationship with Haiti; almost one-quarter of the ships arriving in Philadelphia from foreign ports between 1789 and 1793 came from Haiti, and many of Philadelphia's prominent merchants were involved in the Haitian trade. Unrest in Haiti and the Haitian Revolution itself were of tremendous interest to Philadelphians, and the city's newspapers contained eyewitness accounts, written by sailors and supercargoes, of events on the island throughout the 1790s. Before the British and Spanish invasion of the rebellious French colony in 1793, those accounts tended to focus on the disruption of social order in Haiti and on the effects slave resistance might have on commerce. After 1793, Philadelphia newspapers increasingly wrapped their accounts of Haitian events into their arguments about the comparative merits of England and France and of the Federalist and Republican parties.[31]

For its part, the *Port Folio* portrayed Haiti as the logical end of Republicans' destruction of hierarchies. That Haiti's revolution destroyed the one hierarchy the periodical believed Jefferson wished to preserve, white over black, made the Haitian example irresistibly ironic. Thus, an article from the *Port Folio*'s first year titled "People of Colour" objected to that phrase as a creation of French revolutionaries. The phrase, according to the article, was coined to describe mulattoes—"the fruits," in its words, "of an obscene, but very fashionable commerce"—but the term had been expanded by Americans, the author claimed, to include all blacks. Such usage was dangerous, the writer explained, because "it leads to a confusion of ideas, and blends under one common name, two very distinct classes, which are as variant as midnight, and the dawn of day." The revolution in Saint Domingue had sent to Philadelphia white refugees who brought with them wives and mistresses of African descent; in the article, the use of the phrase "people of colour" encourages "carnal intercourse between whites and blacks" in Pennsylvania. Sex, commerce, and carelessness with language—"*Words are things,*" the au-

---

30. [Joseph Dennie], *Port Folio*, May 8, 1802, 139, "Levity: Duaneiana," Mar. 19, 1803, 92, "Miscellaneous Paragraphs," June 11, 1803, 191.

31. J. Alexander Dun, "'What Avenues of Commerce, Will You, Americans, Not Explore!' Commercial Philadelphia's Vantage onto the Early Haitian Revolution," *WMQ*, 3d Ser., LXII (2005), 473–504.

thor noted, quoting comte de Mirabeau—would dissolve Anglo-American society into French-Caribbean society, white into black, and self into other. "The geographers of the next century, will describe the complexions of one half the inhabitants of this country as olive, or copper-coloured," the writer of the article concluded. In short, the new nation's citizens would not be able to control the destruction of distinctions and social categories that they had begun. In such a piece, the dissenting identity the *Port Folio* held out to readers relied on racial distinctions the periodical elsewhere disdained.[32]

The most extended treatment of race offered by the *Port Folio* came in the series of poems and essays, some original and some extracted, discussing Jefferson's alleged relationship with Sally Hemings. The liaison between master and enslaved woman perfectly revealed the secret shame and dependence that Dennie hoped to find in all of his opponents. Jefferson's relationship with Sally offered the most extreme expression of two more general trends, the destruction of order and the creation of unsavory dependence. Jefferson the "patriot" and "sage," one verse noted, is "*serenely* pure, and wenching with a slave." Jefferson, claimed another, depended on his enslaved not only for sex but also for political power: "Mid loud hosannas of his knaves," this poem read, Jefferson will "from his own loins raise herds of slaves. / With numbers to outvote the free, / And smoke the yankies, five for three." Political and sexual lust devolved into each other, and Jefferson's apparent power, as slaveowner and president, was really the measure of his need. Josiah Quincy suggested that Jefferson depended on his enslaved even for the preservation of his reputation; the "Historiographer to the President" could defend Jefferson's chastity by using the testimony of "his cook, his waiting and chambermaid, his milliner and laundress." A more tangled mess of deceit, dependence, and inversion can scarcely be imagined: those most abused by Jefferson would paint him as virtuous to avoid still more abuse.[33]

32. "People of Colour," *Port Folio*, May 23, 1801, 163; Clare A. Lyons, *Sex among the Rabble: An Intimate History of Gender and Power in the Age of Revolution, Philadelphia, 1730–1830* (Chapel Hill, N.C., 2006), 194–195. Not all such *Port Folio* pieces were written by Philadelphians, of course, but Dennie's choice to reprint such pieces and to rely heavily on sexual imagery might have been fueled by Philadelphia's distinctive circumstances.

33. "The Metamorphosis," *Port Folio*, Dec. 18, 1802, 399, [Josiah Quincy], "Climenole, No. 6," Mar. 3, 1804, 66. See also "A Song, Supposed to Have Been Written by the Sage of Monticello," reprinted in the *Port Folio* from the *Boston Gazette*, in which Jefferson's relations with Sally are the function of his economic

As the *Port Folio* told it, Jefferson needed what he despised and despised what he needed. In his *Notes on the State of Virginia*, Jefferson evinced disdain for African Americans' physical appearance and cultural practices. The *Port Folio* reminded readers that this same Jefferson had been reared and even suckled by black women: an "Air" announced "Peaceful slumber in de cradle, / Lilly Tommy, Dinah nigh, / Stirring hominy wid de ladle; / Den sing, Tommy, lullaby," and a "Recitative" recalled "how bland the nutriment [Jefferson] drew / From Dinah's breast." Other poems went further, suggesting Jefferson disguised himself as a black man to woo the enslaved Sally Hemings:

If, scorning all his country's dames,
No tint, but jet, his blood inflames,
Why should our demi-god forbear
A transient veil of soot to wear,
Why not his godship put away,
Invest himself in Afric's clay,
Smear with lamp-black his pallid wax,
And look and smell like other blacks,
To charm the lovely Sally's eye,
And wallow in a negro-sty:

––––––

dependence; he needs "to breed a flock, of slaves for stock" (Oct. 2, 1802, 312). The *Port Folio* also delighted in satirizing the gift to Jefferson of a "mammoth cheese," and in one poem on the subject Samuel Ewing alluded to Jefferson's dependence on his enslaved as well (Mar. 6, 1802, 72). Irving N. Rothman tracks Ewing's classical references and political animus in "Structure and Theme in Samuel Ewing's Satire, the 'American Miracle,'" *American Literature*, XL (1968), 294–300. Linda K. Kerber describes the surprising number of poems on the Jefferson-Hemings liaison as an "excessive reaction," and Randolph C. Randall argues that Dennie's "sense of outrage" at contemporary politics "betrayed him" (Kerber, *Federalists in Dissent*, 52; Randall, "Joseph Dennie's Literary Attitudes in the *Port Folio*, 1801–1812," in James Woodress, ed., with the assistance of Townsend Ludington and Joseph Arpad, *Essays Mostly on Periodical Publishing in America: A Collection in Honor of Clarence Gohdes* [Durham, N.C., 1973], 60). Kerber also explains that the reaction "hints at the concern with which many Federalists viewed the mulatto, and points, by inference, to their distaste for the social arrangements implied by the mulatto's presence" (52). Winthrop D. Jordan discusses the Jefferson-Hemings scandal and white fears of racial mixing in *White over Black: American Attitudes toward the Negro, 1550–1812* (Chapel Hill, N.C., 1968), 461–469. On the latter subject, see also John Saillant, "Lemuel Haynes's Black Republicanism and the American Republican Tradition, 1775–1820," *Journal of the Early Republic*, XIV (1994), 311–324.

Then take his proper form again,
The pride of virtue . . . first of men.

Jefferson's liaison with Sally Hemings even resulted in a "transformation strange" into a black man: "His legs inflect; his stature shrinks, / And from his skin all Congo stinks; / Behold him now, by Cupid sped, / In darkness sneak to Sally's bed." Nothing could be more different from the *Port Folio's* distant, bemused stance than this transformed Jefferson, and Jefferson's transformation was a synecdoche for the larger problem of a democracy: he "became" black through his dependence on the enslaved just as Republican politicians became creatures through their dependence on the favor of the masses. The Hemings scandal provided the *Port Folio* with a racial metaphor for the vulgar transformation of the Republican politician and, beyond that, for the transformative power of uncontrolled desire.[34]

To Market, to Market

The *Port Folio* insisted that the man of letters distance himself from the demands of the crowd, and it deplored the judgments of the marketplace and their effects on writers and literature. If sales measured texts' virtue and if the desire for sales controlled authors' decisions about what and how to write, then the crowd would rule the literary world as it ruled the political. The result, the *Port Folio* suggested, would be the degradation of authors and of literature.

A story that appeared in the *Port Folio* in 1802 graphically presented the risks the marketplace posed to men of letters. Reprinted from the British periodical the *Microcosm,* "Frederic and Edmond" was the tragic story of a "romantic friendship" between two men, a friendship "cemented" at college by ties of "the most perfect unanimity of opinion." After a brief, blissful time together, Frederic is rendered penniless by the actions of a rapacious lawyer. Rather than accept Edmond's help, he retreats from their friend-

34. "Metamorphosis," *Port Folio,* Dec. 18, 1802, 399, "Levity: Duaneiana," Mar. 19, 1803, 92. Peter Stallybrass and Allon White have described the complexity of modern identity formation: a "mobile, conflictual fusion of power, fear and desire in the construction of subjectivity: a psychological dependence upon precisely those Others which are being rigorously opposed and excluded at the social level" (*Politics and Poetics,* 5). "A fundamental rule," Stallybrass and White note, "seems to be that what is excluded at the overt level of identity-formation is productive of new objects of desire" (25).

ship. "Hitherto we have lived together in the most uninterrupted union," Frederic mourns to his friend, "that we might have died as we have lived, was the fondest hope my imagination ever cherished: that hope is blasted." Edmond pleads that they might "encounter poverty together, and die as we have lived, *united*," but Frederic runs off, distraught, to London. There he takes "a miserable garret" and determines "to enlist himself among a tribe of translators." His intellect and body abused, Frederic soon discovers that there "is not so abject a slave as a hireling scribbler, nor so tyrannical a despot as an illiterate churl, who pays for learning and potatoes with the same remorseless stupidity." Confronted with such greed and insensibility, the young man begins to succumb to "famine, indigence, disease, and despair." Edmond, searching desperately, at last finds his friend, but only in time to witness him collapse at the foot of his bed. "Sinking into the arms of his friend," the story concludes, Frederic "groaned out his soul, and expired."[35]

The appeal to Dennie—and, we can imagine, to his readers—of such a story is obvious. The tale transposed the conventions of heterosexual melodrama into the key of passionate friendship and sensitive manhood. The shopkeep world forced the prostitution of the intellect and language rather than the prostitution of the body; the vulnerable woman was replaced by the vulnerable man. The purity of Edmond and Frederic's love for each other and for literature was demonstrated, to the ideal *Port Folio* reader, by its juxtaposition against the world of commerce and the pursuit of interest and advantage. Whatever their own participation in commercial activities, readers could prove their distance from the market's demands by a sympathetic response to Edmond and Frederic's doomed love.

The tale of Edmond and Frederic portrayed literary hackwork as destructive to the soul and to the body of the true man of letters. The periodical portrayed writing for the crowd as ruinous as well to the cause of good literature. Critiquing the ostensibly liberatory potential of the anonymous audience of the print marketplace, Dennie depicted the successful American author as he who wrote in "a manner so fulsome, so stupid, so independent, so free, so truly American as could not fail of delighting 'millions.'" To write in such a way was not to be independent or free at all; the author who

35. "From the Microcosm," *Port Folio*, Mar. 27, 1802, 91–92. The *Microcosm* was a periodical produced at Eton that ran for forty numbers in the mid-1780s; it was read in London, and participants went on to contribute to the *Anti-Jacobin*. See Walter Graham, *English Literary Periodicals* (New York, 1930), 137.

wrote to please a broad and impersonal literary market was as incapable of true judgment and creativity as was the politician who sought to please a broad and impersonal political market.[36]

But the *Port Folio* itself was a commercial object, and Dennie himself a salesman. On one level, Dennie worked to disguise this involvement in commerce. Whereas, in the *Museum,* advertisements were printed among the pages, in the *Port Folio* they appeared only on a removable wrapper. The *Port Folio* would not deign to mingle commerce with its content; "No advertisements," Dennie wrote in the *Prospectus,* were "to be inserted in the body of the work." Dennie's grasp of the necessity of business relationships, however, remained firm: although he disdained advertisements in the text itself, he reassured "Merchants and Booksellers" that "their advertisements shall be conspicuously printed on a separate sheet, which will serve as an useful *envelope* to the *Port Folio.*" Dennie also realized that the content of the *Port Folio* was an object to be sold, and his audience was not only a set of sensibilities to be tutored but also a market. Nowhere did his willingness to cater to that market emerge more clearly than in his treatment of the Irish poet Thomas "Anacreon" Moore.[37]

36. [Joseph Dennie], "Miscellany," *Port Folio,* Aug. 17, 1805, 249. Michael Warner argues that, in the eighteenth century, print created a new kind of public: "an abstract public *never localizable in any relation between persons*"; he follows Jürgen Habermas in finding that print fostered "new opportunities for individuals to make public use of their reason" in ways separate from markers of social status (*Letters of the Republic,* x, 61). Grantland S. Rice argues instead that the era saw a "transformation of author-ship" and that "the lapse of censorship and the explosion of print culture in the last half of the eighteenth century may have freed writers from the threat of persecution from church and state, [but] they did so only by transforming printed texts from a practical means for assertive sociopolitical commentary into the more inert medium of property and commodity" (*Transformation,* 4). The *Port Folio* was a forum for socio-political commentary, but it converted such commentary into a commodity and a form of private expression, thus escaping the bounds of both Warner's and Rice's expecta-tions.

37. [Dennie], *Prospectus,* [5]. Stallybrass and White note of Alexander Pope's writ-ing: "Pope's obsessive negation drew attention inevitably to the arch-negator himself, who was no more able than those whom he attacked to climb outside or above the marketplace" (*Politics and Poetics,* 118). Dennie's involvement in the marketplace is apparent, if we need to be reminded, in the *Port Folio* accounts and subscribers' letters contained in the Meredith Family Papers. They reveal the editor's dealings (with the help of J. E. Hall and Thomas Boylston Adams) with printers, paper suppliers, and subscribers who often failed to pay in advance or who wrote demanding replacement copies of lost issues.

Moore's verse was celebrated in America, and Dennie and the Tuesday Club were delighted to host the young writer during his 1804 visit to America. When, in 1806, Moore published a volume lambasting America as a place of pretension, vulgarity, and blasted promise, he singled out the Tuesday Club as the "sacred few" who possessed "the strength to reason and the warmth to feel, / The manly polish and the illumin'd taste." In a footnote, Moore added that he assumed "Mr. Dennie" and his circle would not object to Moore's condemnation of the rest of the country: "If I did not hate as I ought, the rabble to which they are opposed," he wrote, "I could not value, as I do, the spirit with which they defy it." Dennie most likely was delighted by Moore's notice and by his attacks on American barbarism. But the American community that read, wrote for, and bought the *Port Folio* was more important to Dennie than transatlantic fellowship. Moore's book criticized not only Dennie's foes but also Federalists, whom he claimed imitated the "vulgarity of rancour" evinced by Democrats. Stung, the culturally ambitious Americans who had once applauded Moore savaged him. He was even condemned for his "ingratitude" by one of the Tuesday Club's staunchest members, William Meredith. Criticism of the book reached Gertrude Meredith before the book itself did, and she observed drily, "Has Moore written such a book, I have no doubt in my own mind that Dennie was his instigation." But Dennie mounted no defense of his friend's writing. Moore had offended America's literati, and Dennie needed those literati were his periodical to survive. Dennie would be as critical of the nation as his market would bear, and no more so.[38]

Even as he acted as savvy salesman, however, Dennie longed to escape the demands of the marketplace and to turn his audience into an intimate circle. He looked to his lost world, England, for a model, and he portrayed personal patronage, as he imagined it had once existed in that country, as

38. "Epistle VIII, to the Honorable W. R. Spencer," in *The Poetical Works of Thomas Moore, Including His Melodies, Ballads, etc. Complete in One Volume* (Philadelphia, 1831), 136. After noting Dennie's probable role, Gertrude queried her husband, "In such a case to whom will the sin of ingratitude best apply?" Both William Meredith's and Gertrude Meredith's judgments are found in Gertrude Meredith to William Meredith, Sept. 19, 1805, Meredith Family Papers. Even after the success of the *Farmer's Weekly Museum*, Dennie's effort to sell collections of his own works failed; only a periodical created and marketed by a large network of unpaid participants allowed him to sustain himself as a man of letters. Gertrude Meredith wrote that the "Lay Preacher" and the "Farrago" had been in press, "but . . . for want of a full subscription they were withheld" (Gertrude Meredith to William Meredith, Aug. 26, 1802, Meredith Family Papers).

the system within which an independent American artist could flourish. Like the desired alliance between politicians and men of letters, patronage in the *Port Folio* was a powerful friendship, one somehow unstained by the self-interest and mutual dependence that patently lay at its heart. Lacking such patronage, American men of letters suffered from neglect and, ironically, from a loss of liberty. In a "Note by the Editor," Dennie remarked wistfully on the decline of patronage as a purified financial relationship. "The union between Horace and Maecenas was such as subsisted between my Lord Bolingbroke and Dean Swift," he wrote, "or rather between Lord Grosvenor and William Gifford." "This is the lofty and liberal connexion between Wealth and Power and Genius, where the first extend protection without requiring the suit and service of a vassal, and where the last receives patronage, without acting as a sycophant, or suffering as a slave."[39]

Women, Redux

Women writers and images of women were integral to the *Port Folio's* pathos and its wit, to its criticism of and its participation in politics and the market. Dennie appealed in his *Prospectus* to women subscribers, following the precedent of British periodicals such as the *Tatler.* The subscription files that remain from the *Port Folio,* although incomplete, reveal the names of at least two women, Eliza Smith and Ann Davies. A man wrote on Smith's behalf for a subscription, but Davies not only renewed her own subscription and sent her (late) payment but also rather sternly informed Dennie at the close of the letter that her name was "Davies not Davis." The periodical's women readers, moreover, were not confined to those on the subscription lists. Gertrude Meredith wrote that Baltimore's women praised "the learning and genius of the paper" and added that the only Baltimore woman

39. [Joseph Dennie], "Note by the Editor," in "Life of Horace," *Port Folio,* July 30, 1803, 245. Distraught by his inability to support himself through literature, Dennie begins to refer to "that respectable and *British* family from whom it is my pride to derive my being" and to his "North Briton country[men]." Financial disappointment becomes political anger: "At bottom," Dennie writes: "I am a malcontent, and consider it a serious evil to have been born among the Indians and Yankees of New England. Had it not been for the *selfish* patriotism of that hoary traitor, Adams, and the bellowing of Moliniux 'that Bully in disguise / That noted bite from Yorkshire that magazine of lies' I might now perhaps, in a Literary, Diplomatic, and lucrative situation been in the service of my rightful King" (Dennie to Joseph Dennie, Sr., Apr. 26, 1797, Dennie Papers).

whom she believed "has the least show of mind" was a particular admirer of the editor. Women mattered to the *Port Folio* and to its editor in other ways as well. The periodical approvingly cited the works of Madame de Maintenon and Madame de Sevigne. Of eighty-eight contributors to the *Port Folio* identified by Randolph C. Randall, eight were women. The list includes Gertrude Meredith, Sarah Hall, Harriet Fenno, and Elizabeth Wister. Each, like many of the women involved in Smith's networks, was related by birth or marriage to a man who participated, but each, again like the women of Smith's world, participated in her own right. "Let the women once withdraw their aid," reads a "Lounger" column, "and you will have to put your own shoulder to the wheel; and, if reduced to this necessity, I venture to prophecy a life of incessant labour is so inconsistent with your fondness for ease, that the American Lounger will be no more."[40]

Dennie also turned to married women for emotional and intellectual companionship. Gertrude Meredith named a child for Dennie after his death and during his life had him as a frequent visitor. Meredith's mordant wit must have delighted the dyspeptic editor: she once responded to a man's teasing inquiry about her "scandalous" female conversations by reassuring the man that she and her friends took no notice of him, so he need not worry about what they said. (Meredith greeted his later attempt to apologize for his salvos with word that she didn't even remember them. "You never saw a poor fellow more mortified than he appeared to be at his wit making so little impression," Meredith recalled with satisfaction.) Dennie was also fond of Sarah Hall, and an ornate description of their friendship can be found in the nineteenth-century text *Female Biography:* "At [Mrs. Hall's] hospitable mansion," the author wrote, "the feverish scholar found more charms to cure his misanthropy than could be found elsewhere." "If Dennie had outlived her, he would, in the fullness of his soul, have borne testimony to all this, but heaven decreed that she should survive him many years. When the

40. Gertrude Meredith to William Meredith, May 3, 1804, Ann Davies to Dennie, Aug. 2, 1806, both in Meredith Family Papers; M. G., "The American Lounger, No. LV," *Port Folio*, Apr. 16, 1803, 121; Kathryn Shevelow, *Women and Print Culture: The Construction of Femininity in the Early Periodical* (New York, 1989), 94. J. Wright of "Geo. Town Cross Roads" wrote the letter on Eliza Smith's behalf and sent money for a year's subscription; he also appealed to Dennie to send "Anacreon Moore's last Work"; see Wright to Dennie, Sept. 1, 1806, Meredith Family Papers. Elizabeth Wister was also the sister of Sarah, the Revolutionary diarist. These identifications are taken from Randall, "Authors of the *Port Folio*," *American Literature*, XI (1940), 378–416.

evil spirit came over him . . . he went, to use his own words, to the house of Mrs. Hall, to drive off all his blue devils. Her conversation abounded in classical recollections, in playful remarks, and in delicate satire, and, like the harp of David, gave new soul and life to the gloomy editor."[41]

Despite women's importance both to Dennie and to the *Port Folio,* Dennie created the *Port Folio* as a masculine community. Manliness was its persistent standard of virtue. Senator Uriah Tracy was praised for possessing "all the strength of a manly mind," and the *Port Folio* urged readers to cultivate a "manly and rational vigor." The epithet "manly" was also used to praise authors as disparate as Joseph Addison and Henry Fielding. In the *Port Folio,* the word did not signify possession of a particular aesthetic or political quality. Rather, manliness meant membership in the periodical's community. Femininity, in turn, often represented the bad. In the *Port Folio,* women lacked self-control and destroyed it in men. There were also moments of sheer misogyny; women, reads a translation of a Latin couplet, have the power "twice in your lives to give us bliss," on the "bridal night" and at death. And yet women made other appearances as well. There were love poems in the *Port Folio,* most of them bittersweet odes to women purified by their unattainability. "Yet tho' I hurried from her sight, / *Roam* whereso'er my footsteps will, / That *full blue eye,* that *face so bright,* will HAUNT ME, LIKE A SPECTRE, STILL," concludes one poem. The yearning lines testified to the beautiful souls of the male poet and his male reader as much as to the spectral beauty of their female object. Even this ode to the "face so bright" was introduced, in "An Author's Evenings," with the explanation that one "could pretty accurately estimate the quantum of sensibility in a man's bosom, by knowing with what kind of emotions he rose from the perusal of the following lines, faithful to nature; so descriptive of the heart, and so honourable to the muse of the sensitive author." Women appeared as the unattainable objects toward which the poet and reader might continuously unfurl their own beautiful and self-regarding sensitivity.[42]

41. Gertrude Meredith to Mary Green Dennie, June 13, 1814, Dennie Papers; Gertrude Meredith to William Meredith, 1805, June 7, 1809, Meredith Family Papers; Samuel Knapp, "Female Biography; Containing Notices of Distinguished Women, in Different Nations and Ages," *New-England Magazine,* VI (1834), 505–511.

42. "Miscellaneous Paragraphs," *Port Folio,* Jan. 23, 1802, 24, "Miscellaneous Paragraphs," Feb. 13, 1802, 46, Phosphor, "The American Lounger, No. 132," Aug. 2, 1805, 233; Randall, "Dennie's Literary Attitudes," in Woodress, ed., *Essays,* 84. "A poetic form dedicated to the contemplation of the beloved object," Laura Enterline

Given such pieces and the *Port Folio*'s fascination with women's sexual lures, it is tempting to suggest that women appear in the *Port Folio* in the familiar dichotomy of angel or whore—unattainable beauties or sordid exemplars of degradation and greed. To do so, however, would be to give the *Port Folio* too much credit for consistency. The *Port Folio* also boasted pieces that approached an argument in favor of women's intellectual potential. One such piece regretted that "matrimony has this sad effect of depreciating the fair." The words of the marriage ceremony, the article continued, transform "a perfect divinity" "into a mere housewife, whose sole use is considered, as being that of breeding a family." Women's intellect, suggested other pieces, deserved to be cultivated; women's apparent inferiority was the result of social constraint, not of nature. This argument is reminiscent of some of the assaults on Jefferson's racial essentialism, but women themselves were allowed to make the case for their own capacities as African Americans were not. The correspondent Sarah Hall, writing as "Constantia," slyly responded to the suggestion that American ladies needed to emulate Madame de Sevigne and increase their "stock of ideas": "Alas, Florian, *our* lovers and husbands are no Voltaires!—they have no particular value for a woman who reads 'Geometrical systems.' The former attach themselves to the fair and the fashionable—while the latter find their life and animation best promoted at the coffee-house or the club!" Because American husbands were both more exacting than men of other nations and "confined to the office or the counting-house," "the whole charge of the house, table, servants and children, all, all devolve upon the careful wife." In such pieces, authors argued that women's apparent inferiority—like so many other problems of American society—emerged from American men's foolish devotion to commerce.[43]

Dennie nonetheless also printed pieces directly mocking learned women. The "Adventures of Crita," for example, purported to be a letter from a woman who had read "Locke, Malebranche, Bayle, and Hume" and who had, as a result, taken lovers and borne children out of wedlock with blithely insensible equanimity. And, for all its defenses of women's intellect, the *Port Folio* also defined its own mission, more than once, as being that

---

has written, "consistently generate[s] melancholic self-reflection" (*Tears of Narcissus*, 3).

43. Constantia [Sarah Hall], "The American Lounger, No. 89," *Port Folio*, May 12, 1804, 145, Phosphor, "The American Lounger, No. 132," Aug. 2, 1805, 233.

of defying a foolish, female audience. "We leave it to the loquacity of faded gossips," Dennie wrote in disdainful response to requests for "scandalous anecdotes," "and to the pert malignity of the *murderesses* of reputation."[44]

Ultimately, the *Port Folio* reinforced the associations of femininity and womanhood with fickleness, frivolity, volatility, and greed, even as it sometimes suggested, by its content and its practices, that those associations were suspect. The opposition of man to woman became, along with that of black to white and Federalist to Republican, a polarity that was to remain fixed even when so many others had collapsed. Still, gender was in the *Port Folio* less stable than either race or partisanship, not only because Dennie printed pieces from women whose wit defies the *Port Folio*'s gibes but also because he printed pieces that revealed the mechanics of the *Port Folio*'s own use of gender. Sarah Hall and an equally incisive correspondent, Emily Mifflin Hopkinson—Joseph Hopkinson's wife—each pointed out that femininity became, in the *Port Folio*, an empty category to be filled with all undesirable qualities. "It is by no means necessary," noted one column, "that your satires should be appropriate to this country; a fragment picked up by a friend in the streets of London, or even of Constantinople, would do just as well for a libel on the *American* women, as if it had been fabricated in the metropolis of our own follies." Indeed, Emily Hopkinson noted, America

44. [Joseph Dennie], "To Readers and Correspondents," *Port Folio*, Apr. 25, 1801, 135. The "Adventures of Crita" may be a satire of Mary Wollstonecraft. The piece might also have been influenced by James Fordyce's *Sermons to Young Women* (London, 1765), in which he warned that excessive education in females would mean "the sex should lose in softness what they gained in force; and . . . the pursuit of such elevation should interfere a little with the plain duties and humble virtues of life" (Quoted in Harriet Guest, *Small Change: Women, Learning, Patriotism, 1750–1810* [Chicago, 2000], 156). Letters in the "American Lounger" column also both defend and attack "learned ladies" with equal frivolity. A letter from H includes a swipe at Timothy Plainsense, who "is making memorandums for his next dinner, and is very angry that [his wife] attends to any thing else. . . . He does not know that women have genius enough to read, work, and scribble all at once" ("The American Lounger, No. LVIII," *Port Folio*, May 7, 1803, 145). Priscilla Patience, meanwhile, writes to complain that her sister has been seized by "the writing mania," because of the *Port Folio*, and scribbles "half sentences, such as Dear Lounger—Delighted you are come to life again—Beseech you to say something smart—Tired death of old Cicero—Ladies grown so reasonable. . . . Men now-a-days such mere nobodies," to emulate Constantia and Beatrice. Patience begs Lounger to dissuade her sister from this course ("The American Lounger, No. 110," Mar. 2, 1805, 57). David S. Shields describes the traditional Anglo-American association of gossip with women in *Civil Tongues and Polite Letters*, 99–107.

and women were alike in their infinite ability to represent all that was bad. In its calumnies against women, she wrote, the "Lounger" was "almost as indiscriminate, in your censures, as the *Interesting Dutch traveller* [von Bulow] who asserts that *all* the Americans are *Cannibals; all* drink *sixty* glasses of wine *daily;* and *all* the waters, in America, are unwholesome; that all the people, in Pennsylvania, die of pleurisies." Adopting the sarcastic tone of the *Port Folio* itself, Hall wryly pretended to agree that the central *Port Folio* practice of associating femininity with foolishness would only be misunderstood by women themselves, who, she mourned, "have picked up a foolish notion, that vice is vice, whether it wears petticoats or pantaloons: but here again how sadly are their limited understandings imposed on." "Simple ones!" she scolded, stealing the *Port Folio's* ironic pique, "will ye never learn to discriminate?" Rather less wittily, a male correspondent signing himself "Florian" wrote that he had agreed to a "penance" assigned by infuriated members of "the sex" ("We'll be revenged, he shall know that we have tongues," Florian quotes them as saying): "The subject of my next essay [should be] . . . our complicated injustice and effrontery, in taxing [ladies] with imperfections, which so far from being their exclusive and distinguishing feature, are equally, if not more, distinguishable in ourselves."[45]

Ultimately, the *Port Folio* even mocked the sensitive, manly reader-spectator it sought to create. Emily Hopkinson took direct aim at the ostensibly sincere, audience-disdaining sensibility of the male *Port Folio* persona. Responding to the accusation—put forth, she drily notes, by the "sensitive Leander"—that women were insensible, she wondered whether it was not the case that "in paying so close an attention to discover whether the dear little ladies are *properly affected,* Leander does not forget his own tear of *manly sensibility,* so justly due to the shrine of merit." Sensibility was revealed as solipsism, and the all-male literary club itself came in for mockery; in "Lounger" columns, it was more than once depicted as a forum in which to indulge one's ego and use bad Latin. In 1802, Gertrude Meredith wrote columns in which she posed as a mother worried about the ill effects—foolishness, pretension, a tendency to mock women—that the *Port Folio's* Tuesday Club had on her vulnerable son.[46]

45. Constantia [Sarah Hall], "The American Lounger, No. XVII," *Port Folio*, May 8, 1802, 137, Beatrice [Emily Mifflin Hopkinson], "The American Lounger, No. XL," Jan. 1, 1803, 1, Florian, "The American Lounger, No. LXVII," July 15, 1803, 225.

46. Beatrice [Emily Mifflin Hopkinson], "Levity," *Port Folio*, Apr. 3, 1802, 97. In addition to Gertrude Meredith's columns, others wrote in to "defend" the club, usually

To a startling degree, these "Lounger" columns question the ideas of manhood and manliness. Femininity was used as negative and manliness as positive, but the stability of the associations and the opposition was rendered suspect. In such instances, the *Port Folio* came closest to true subversiveness, because it came closest to acknowledging that its own rules, like those of the America it criticized, were comical inventions. In these playful "Lounger" columns, authors undermined all identities until all roles seemed imperfect fits and all relations seemed artificial. Playful, fluid gender roles were not simply a commentary on gender but also a wry parlor version of the disorder and lack of moorings Dennie's contributors saw in American life. The *Port Folio* offered solace to those worried about America's assaults on tradition not by refusing to discuss them or by finding a way to prevent them. Instead, it turned disorder into something to be laughed at. The civic reform the *Port Folio* counseled was the puncturing of hypocrisy, and the civic stance it proffered was a mixture of gaiety and bitterness. "I applaud a disappointed lover, laughing at the perfidy of his mistress," reads one *Port Folio* extract from the first volume, "or a politician slumbering in his elbow chair, though his labours for the commonwealth are rejected." Dennie praised the "gay philosophy" of the French cavalier who had witnessed the destruction of his position and country but "with inextinguishable vivacity . . . recounts his own and his country's misfortunes, curses nothing but the club of Jacobins, and anticipates better days. Last night I heard him singing under an old elm '*Banissons la melancholie*.'" "Let me be deft and debonnair," concluded an extract from the *London Magazine*, "*I am content, I do not care*." In the "Original Poetry" section's "Ode to Spleen," readers found the assertion: "No tear shall trickle from my eye, / My heart shall

---

in tongue-in-cheek fashion. See M [Gertrude Meredith], "The American Lounger, No. XIV," Apr. 17, 1802, Aristippus, Junior [Thomas Boylston Adams], "The American Lounger, No. XVI," May 1, 1802, 129, M [Gertrude Meredith], "The American Lounger, No. XVIII," May 15, 1802, 145, Quixote, "The American Lounger, No. XIX," May 22, 1802, 153, M [Gertrude Meredith], "The American Lounger, No. XX," May 29, 1802, 161. "'M.' is advised to write for the *Port Folio*," Dennie wrote in the column "To Readers and Correspondents" later that year. "In the absence of her Satire, more *clubs* than one require the wholesomeness of advice, and, perhaps, the discipline of reproof" (Sept. 4, 1802, 279). A satire of an Irish Democratic-Republican club is mixed into this series ("Levity," July 17, 1802, 219). See also more general satires: "The Sleepy Club," Nov. 28, 1801, 376, "The Marble Club," Nov. 28, 1801, 383. In *Civil Tongues and Polite Letters*, David S. Shields describes the way in which Anglo-American clubs "emphasiz[ed] the irrationality of their commonality in club identity" and mocked their own reliance on members' shared appetites (203).

own no swelling sigh; / Thy power I'll scorn, I'll laugh at care, / And brave the haggard fiend despair."[47]

Deep feeling partnered aggressive gaiety. And, in the early Republic, such gaiety, when matched with the passionately critical stance Dennie assumed, qualified as a defiant departure from the earnest nation building taking place. It was a pointed insistence that something other than politics still mattered and that something other than the judgment of the crowd still had meaning. "In this languid season of the natural year, and in this gloomy season of the political one," noted the speaker in one "Author's Evenings," "I am obliged to take more than ordinary pains to ward off the attacks of melancholy, and strive to lose, or at least to mitigate my sense of the tyranny of the American populace, by reading merry books, produced by laughing wit in tranquil times." "While we are restrained in this *'prison-house the world,'*" the piece continued, "it is the most judicious part to look as smilingly as we can from our *grate,* and to ridicule and deride the wayward pranks of the many fools and rascals, who pass by. When my ear has been pained through the day, with the awkward music of *militia* drums, and with the *lying* principles and broken metaphors of a hot holiday declaimer, I sit up all night to read FIELDING and RABELAIS." The *Port Folio*'s dissent consisted, that is, of more than a rejection of the Jefferson administration.

47. At times, the *Port Folio* approached what seems to the modern reader like an almost Lacanian sense of gender as masquerade, in which "the ideal or typical manifestations of behavior in both sexes, up to and including the act of sexual copulation, are entirely propelled into comedy" (Jacques Lacan, *Feminine Sexuality: Jacques Lacan and the école freudienne,* ed. Juliet Mitchell and Jacqueline Rose, trans. Rose [New York, 1985], 84). See [Joseph Dennie], "The Farrago, No. XIII," *Port Folio,* Feb. 28, 1801, 66. See also "Careless Content," Mar. 20, 1802, 88. "An Eulogy on Laughing Written by Mr. Sewall, of New-Hampshire, and Communicated by a Gentleman of This City" expresses similar views: "Let sentimentalist ring in our ears / The tender joy of grief—the luxury of tears—. . . . I like an honest, hearty, ha, hah, hah! . . . Braces the nerves; corroborates the brain; / Shakes ev'ry muscle, and throws off the spleen" (Feb. 14, 1801, 55). "The author was a rational Epicurean," Dennie writes in his introduction to "An Ode to Spleen," "and his system of life nearly resembles that of busy indolence in 'The Spleen.' This ballad is very old, but its independent spirit is 'ever fair and ever young'" (Apr. 2, 1803, 112). A calmer transcendence of life's pleasures and pains was also recommended; a "Morals" column from the magazine's first year recommends a wisdom that will deliver one from "all these quiet anxieties of thought, tumultuous perturbations of passion, and tedious vexations of body"; such a wisdom "maintains our minds in a cheerful calm, quiet, indifference, and comfortable liberty" (Oct. 24, 1801, 341). Dowling discusses what he deems Dennie's "philosophy of merriment" in chapter 3 of *Literary Federalism.*

It was also a rejection of the tyranny of ever present political talk. On a still deeper level, it was a rejection of the tyranny of the American people, of the idea that the majority should rule the mind and heart as well as the land. In a note to subscribers in 1802, Dennie haughtily asserted that "neither a subscription, angrily withdrawn, nor the insolence of democratic dictation, will urge a disciple of the OLD SCHOOL to temporize; to court the populace, or tremble with the pusillanimous; to surrender up the manliness of sentiment." In the *Port Folio*'s ethos, only the man free of the desire for the crowd's love was free to exercise independent judgment. Edmund Burke expressed for *Port Folio* readers the majestic loneliness of this kind of dissent. In 1802, Dennie extracted Burke's lament that those who stood opposed to the "multitudes" are "deprived of all external consolation. They seem deserted by mankind, overpowered by a conspiracy of their whole species." In another issue, Dennie quoted Burke's description of the dissenter's salubrious insanity: "Oppression . . . makes wise men mad; but the distemper is still the madness of the *wise*, which is better than the sobriety of fools." In the *Port Folio*, the dissenter was a lonely, isolated voice—but a voice that was in its unhappiness sane and in its discontent strangely joyous.[48]

What kind of community was the *Port Folio*, and what did that community achieve? The periodical's essays, jokes, and poetry masterfully interpret world and national events according to the *Port Folio*'s own scheme of insiders and outsiders, good behavior and bad. Almost everything shocks the *Port Folio*, but nothing surprises it. All events and all people are fitted into its cosmology without disruption. In this, the *Port Folio* adapted a British literary tradition to American political use. The essays in British club periodicals such as the *Spectator* tutored readers in a way of responding to the world and welcomed them into a fellowship of shared reference points and language. The Federalist Party needed to do something similar. It needed not only to create an agenda and to argue on its behalf but also to teach Americans to see with the party's eyes and to speak with its tongue. When Americans had absorbed the rules and language of the party, they would interpret events in a Federalist way. The *Port Folio* tutored readers to see Republicans as dependent and depraved, and it set forth and established

48. [Joseph Dennie], *Port Folio*, Jan. 16, 1802, 6, [Dennie], "An Author's Evenings," July 10, 1802, 213, "Miscellaneous Paragraphs," Aug. 24, 1805, 263. Dennie, as would the Anthologists, insists that America is particularly hard on the man of letters and that patronage has been destroyed as a direct result of democracy. See "Miscellaneous Paragraphs," July 31, 1802, 239.

rhetorical frameworks into which any politician or election could be placed. Just as Benjamin Franklin had molded himself into a British gentleman by immersing himself in the *Spectator*'s columns, so was it possible to mold oneself into a Federalist by learning the language and rules of the *Port Folio*.[49]

The *Port Folio*, then, served Federalism. But serving Federalism was not the reason for its existence. Dennie used partisanship to gain attention and subscribers, and he used it to provide a civic legitimacy to deeper concerns: Were men hopelessly in the sway of women? Were women doomed to being caricatured and mocked by anxious men? Did the market force authors to mold their writing to the taste of the crowd? Did the age of Revolution mean societies would be held together by cold self-interest and not by tradition and love? The *Port Folio* was a forum for transforming anxiety into wit. Its mixture of personal bitterness and cultural discontent, fiction and political commentary, ribaldry and sentiment gave it an extraordinary vibrancy. Never were the public and the personal separate. The *Port Folio* drew readers' eyes to the relations of dependence, self-interest, and desire that lay beneath Americans' efforts to imagine an independent, rational manhood and citizenship. It urged them to laugh at the idea that autonomy, liberty, or equality could arise from a nation made of real and figurative seductions and enslavement. It encouraged them to nurture independent judgment and to revel in being rejected by the crowd.

Seeking a way to participate in the nation other than through formal politics, the *Port Folio*'s editor and contributors rendered political speech itself personal and cultural. The *Port Folio*'s Federalist rhetoric, moreover, built a walled community whose members took pleasure in their distinction from the world outside. As a result, the periodical's partisanship turned inward, much like the ideals of sensibility and sociability from which it was made. And, although Dennie's urgent, scabrous criticism of politicians and the nation pioneered an extreme form of dissent, the flamboyance and predictable repetition of the *Port Folio*'s criticisms—breathtakingly disdainful commentaries arrived each week just as expected—were a performance, not a call to arms. The *Port Folio* daringly criticized the nation, but it did so in a way that was unlikely to cause true change. It participated in making America safe for dissent, but it did so by making a safe dissent for America.

The *Port Folio*'s criticism of America's gender and racial ideology was, like its political speech, both radically critical and fundamentally conser-

49. Michael G. Ketcham, *Transparent Designs: Reading, Performance, and Form in the "Spectator" Papers* (Athens, Ga., 1985), 8.

vative. The periodical pointed out the foolishness of racial hierarchy when it wished to reveal the hypocrisy of Republicans' claim to respect human equality and liberty. But the periodical asserted the need for permanent distinctions between the races and for a permanent hierarchy of white over black when it wished to evoke Burkean thrills of horror at the prospect of unending disorder. African Americans, moreover, were not welcomed into the Tuesday Club or Dennie's group of national contributors. Thus, the *Port Folio* was not truly a forum for disrupting racism. On the contrary, its use of race demonstrates the limits of irony as a political stance. When it turned its skeptical gaze on race, the *Port Folio* drew attention to the difference between American ideals and American practices, but it offered no competing ideals or practices to take their place.

In its approach to gender, the *Port Folio* was more subversive. Women such as Gertrude Meredith and Sarah Hall participated in the Tuesday Club and in the magazine, and the periodical became a forum in which contributors argued for women's intellectual capacity and poked fun at the idea that women were flighty, dependent creatures and men independent paragons of virtue. But the *Port Folio* itself also used those associations to score political points, praise authors, and assert the worth of its male readers. The periodical mocked gender stereotypes but, in the end, relied on them.

Joseph Dennie created the *Port Folio* at a time when the American and French revolutions had left the artifice of identities and hierarchies exposed. Like Edmund Burke, Dennie argued that artifice did not render those identities and hierarchies meaningless. In his *Reflections on the Revolution in France*, Burke wrote that the aristocratic system of ranks and privileges was "the Corinthian capital of polished society" and that it must be preserved, not because it was a real or essential emanation of human nature, but because it was beautiful and useful. "He feels," scolded Burke, "no ennobling principle in his own heart who wishes to level all the artificial institutions which have been adopted for giving a body to opinion, and permanence to fugitive esteem." If hierarchy was a human invention, humans needed to continue inventing it; social constructions were the necessary theater of civilized life.[50]

The *Port Folio* quoted Burke's "Corinthian capital" passage at least twice in the early years of its existence, and the periodical consistently argued that America's new ordering principles—race and gender—were no less invented, but only less fine-grained and aesthetically pleasing, than England's

50. Burke, *Reflections,* ed. Pocock, 122.

traditional hierarchies. A more elaborate political and social hierarchy would be no more artificial and would produce more harmony and beauty. Still, race and gender were what America had. Although he pointed out the theatricality of America's polity and society, Dennie, like his hero Burke, had no wish to trash the sets. Nor did he have the ability to create new ones. No matter how suspect the privileges of the white American man, they were seized in the *Port Folio* as they were outside it. The *Port Folio* participated in the nation not only through dissent but through assent, and gender and race were the grounds of each.[51]

51. [Joseph Dennie], introduction to "The Character of Edmund Burke," *Port Folio*, Apr. 9, 1803, 117, [Dennie], "The Lay Preacher," Sept. 3, 1803, 281.

6 These Quiet Regions

CHAPTER

The Boston Athenaeum and the
Monthly Anthology, and Boston
Review, *1804–1811*

As Joseph Dennie brought the *Port Folio* to flamboyant life in Philadelphia, Arthur Maynard Walter, William Smith Shaw, and Joseph Stevens Buckminster labored in Boston to revive a bedraggled literary "orphan" who had been brought, one of their collaborators wrote, "naked, hungry, and helpless" to their door. The orphan was a periodical, and its name was the *Monthly Anthology, and Boston Review.* The *Anthology* had been founded in 1803 by a schoolteacher, Phineas Adams, who wished it to be a respectable compilation of original and extracted reviews, scientific articles, essays, and poetry. Adams, not part of the prominent Adams family, lacked connections and networking ability, and, by 1804, the *Anthology* was failing. Buckminster, Walter, and Shaw assembled friends and local elites to revive the periodical. The *Anthology* and a related project, the Boston Athenaeum, were the centerpieces of their effort to claim a civic role for the American man of letters. Belletrism, returned to its roots as a world apart from political engagement, would cultivate the individual judgment that a republic's empowered citizenry sorely needed and that its majoritarian ethos threatened to destroy.[1]

1. [William Emerson], "Preface," *Monthly Anthology, and Boston Review, Containing Sketches and Reports of Philosophy, Religion, History, Arts, and Manners* (hereafter cited as *MA*), I (1804), i. See also M. A. DeWolfe Howe, ed., *Journal of the Proceedings of the Society Which Conducts the "Monthly Anthology and Boston Review," October 3, 1805, to July 2, 1811* (Boston, 1910), 5, 7. Phineas Adams was the son of a Lexington, Massachusetts, farmer. Although he was apprenticed to a papermaker, he attracted the patronage of a Mrs. Foster of Brighton, Massachusetts, and entered Harvard at the age of twenty. He graduated from Harvard in 1801 and edited the *Anthology* from his creation of it in 1803 until April 1804; he later served in the navy as a chaplain and mathematics teacher, and he does not seem to have published again. Adams might have shared something of Dennie's striking persona as well as his Lexington origins and literary ambitions. His "invincible diffidence and an excitable temperament," Josiah Quincy notes, "were the cause of great eccentricity of manners"; see Quincy, *The History of the Boston Athenaeum, with Biographical Notices of Its Deceased Founders*

Creating the Society

The group that saved Phineas Adams's periodical styled itself the Anthology Society, and its participants quickly elected officers and drew up a constitution. Most participants in the *Anthology* were Harvard-educated professionals. There were lawyers: Peter Thacher, Arthur Maynard Walter, William Smith Shaw, and James Savage; doctors: John Warren, Jr., and James Jackson; ministers: William Emerson, Joseph Stevens Buckminster, Thomas Gray, Samuel Cooper Thacher, and Joseph Tuckerman; and a fledgling merchant, William Tudor, Jr. Many were connected to influential Massachusetts families: Shaw was a nephew of Abigail Adams and served as John Adams's private secretary from 1798 to 1800; Samuel Cooper Thacher was the son of a prominent attorney; William Tudor was a scion of a cosmopolitan Boston merchant family; and both Buckminster and Walter were descended from well-known Boston ministers. The society chose as titular heads two prominent men. John Sylvester John Gardiner, who was the reverend of Trinity Church and a longtime correspondent of Joseph Dennie, was named president of the Anthology Society, and William Emerson, who was pastor of the First Church at Boston and served in 1803 as chaplain of the state senate, was named vice president. The society and its projects, however, were inspired and shaped less by Gardiner and Emerson, who were in their late thirties, than by Walter, Buckminster, and Shaw—younger men possessing distinctive tastes and a distinctive vision of how to create meaningful cultural institutions.[2]

(Cambridge, Mass., 1851), 1–2. See also Sue Neuenswander Greene, "The Contribution of the *Monthly Anthology, and Boston Review* to the Development of the Golden Age of American Letters" (Ph.D. diss., Michigan State University, 1964), 15–19.

2. For the life of William Tudor, Jr., see Quincy, *Boston Athenaeum*, 54–63; James Spear Loring, *The Hundred Boston Orators Appointed by the Municipal Authorities and Other Public Bodies, from 1770–1852 . . .* (Boston, 1854), 135–138. For the life of James Savage, see ibid., 353–360. Ronald Story explains that five clans "filled most of the principal administrative offices from 1807 to 1860"; among the families composing the clans were the Quincys, Adamses, Shaws, Lowells, Grays, Appletons, Jacksons, Lees, Higginsons, and Cabots. See "Class and Culture in Boston: The Athenaeum, 1807–1860," *American Quarterly*, XXVII (1975), 178–199 (quotation on 192). Names of members listed in the first volume of the Anthology Society Minutes are "Rev. Mr. Gardiner, Rev. Mr. Emerson, Rev. Mr. Gray, Rev. Mr. Harris [editor notes that this name was crossed out], Rev. Mr. Buckminster, Rev. Mr. Tuckerman, Peter Thacher, Esquire, Wm. S. Shaw Esq., A. M. Walter Esq., Dr. John Warren jr., Dr. James Jackson, Mr. Willm Wells, Mr. Wm Tudor, Mr. S. C. Thacher, Mr. E. T. Dana, Mr. Benjn Welles, Mr. Rt H. Gardiner, Mr. J. Savage, J. Stickney, Dr. Kirkland,

Within weeks of their first official meeting as the Anthology Society in October 1805, members began work on what would become the Athenaeum. Several pledged items from their own collections of American and European periodicals. In May 1806, Anthology Society minutes reveal a discussion, "in which Mr. Shaw was principally active," to develop a formal "Reading-room." Later that same month, Shaw drew up a prospectus, which was approved "after dinner." Soon, plans were afoot to sell memberships, amass collections of periodicals and books, and purchase a building. John Quincy Adams donated a collection of nearly six thousand books for the use of the Athenaeum. The idea drew not only on the burgeoning custom of the public library but also on the practices of circulation and exchange on which young men such as Elihu Hubbard Smith and Joseph Dennie had relied to broaden the number of texts and readers available to them. It drew as well on the symbiotic relationship between printer-booksellers and avid readers. Shaw's instructions to Buckminster regarding the Athenaeum reveal his understanding of the need to bind together the work of willing amateurs and cultural professionals. "You must be very sensible," Shaw wrote to Buckminster, urging him to develop close relationships with booksellers, "that the success of an institution like ours will depend very much on the punctuality and despatch with which we receive our foreign newspapers, pamphlets, new books, and periodical publications."[3]

The society, in creating a periodical, cooperating with booksellers, and mingling friendship and literary ambition, resembled Philadelphia's Tuesday Club. And the *Anthology* gained the attention of Joseph Dennie, who in

---

Rev. S. C. Thacher, Mr. A. H. Everett, Mr. G. Ticknor, Dr. J. Bigelow." See Howe, ed., *Proceedings*, 35. For the life of John Sylvester John Gardiner, see Quincy, *Boston Athenaeum*, 3–10. For the life of William Emerson, see Samuel Cooper Thacher, "Memoir of the Life and Character of the Late Rev. William Emerson," Massachusetts Historical Society, *Collections*, 2d Ser., I (1838), 254–258; Quincy, *Boston Athenaeum*, 11–12; Loring, *Hundred Boston Orators*, 311–312.

3. Anthology Society Minutes, Oct. 23, 1805, in Howe, ed., *Proceedings*, 41; Quincy, *Boston Athenaeum*, 5–6, 32, 39. The Anthologists had one additional model in mind: "In drawing up the regulations," William Smith Shaw wrote to Joseph Stevens Buckminster, then traveling in England, "we have followed very closely the laws of the Athenaeum of Liverpool, for which I am greatly indebted to your kindness in transmitting immediately on your arrival at Liverpool. It is an admirable institution, and we intend to make ours as much like that as the different circumstances of the two countries will admit" (Shaw to Buckminster, Dec. 1, 1806, William Smith Shaw Papers, Boston Athenaeum). Shaw's plan was to elevate American culture by re-creating a British institution.

FIGURE 5. Reverend Joseph Stevens Buckminster (1784–1812).
By Gilbert Stuart. Circa 1810. By permission, Boston Athenaeum

1805 greeted it as a fellow participant in a broad project to refine American culture. "The Editor would be culpably insensible to the progress of Polite Literature in America," Dennie wrote in the *Port Folio*, "if he omitted to notice, with applause, a Literary Journal of a most respectable character, published at Boston, entitled 'The MONTHLY ANTHOLOGY,' combining the characters of a Magazine and a Review." The Anthologists were no doubt pleased by the notice of one of America's best-known men of letters, but they had little sympathy with the lament (or with the implicit goal) that Dennie appended to that praise. "So unfrequent in America is the intercourse between men of letters, so sullen is the genius of republicanism, so wide is our *waste* of territory, so narrow our prejudices, so local our interests, so humble our means either of receiving or imparting knowledge," Dennie complained, "that we have but little of that *esprit du corps,* which characterizes the Literati of Europe. Our men of letters scarcely ever act in concert." Dennie had fostered an *"esprit du corps"* grounded in a shared performance of loneliness, and he likely expected the Anthologists to try to piece together a similar network of literati across America's *"waste* of territory." But, although the society chose a set of "contributing members" and received submissions from individuals in northern New England and New York, the periodical relied heavily and intentionally on the efforts of the small band of stalwarts who attended the society's weekly meetings in Cambridge.[4]

Both the *Anthology* and the reading room reflected their creators' faith in the ability of Boston and Cambridge to support local cultural institutions. "The Judges of the Supreme Court, the Judges of the Athenaeum within the network of local Circuit and District Court, the President and Professors of Harvard College, the President of the Academy of Arts and Sciences, and of the Historical Society, shall be considered as honorary members of this institution," read No. 14 of the Athenaeum's governing rules. Such appeals linked generations within a locality rather than linked members of a single generation or sensibility who were spread across a wide geographic expanse. Indeed, the Anthologists sought almost to coerce local participation: although members could invite what the rules pointedly called "strangers" to the Athenaeum, they specified that "no inhabitant of Boston, who is not a subscriber to the institution, shall be allowed to have access to the library and reading-room," and they added that no admitted stranger could reside

4. Joseph Dennie, "Literary Intelligence: The Monthly Anthology," *Port Folio,* Aug. 2, 1805, 238.

"within five miles of the library." Even Shaw's diligent efforts to gather materials from abroad relied on a kind of Bostonian, rather than a cosmopolitan, network. "I think," he wrote to Buckminster, "you might also advance the interests of our establishment by conversing with the Americans, particularly the Bostonians, in England, on the utility and the pleasure which will probably be afforded by an institution on our plan."[5]

As a result of being comfortably ensconced in Massachusetts, the society developed a more parochial vision of cultural community than had Dennie or Smith. A lack of necessity was the mother of a lack of networking invention: society members turned to well-connected local elites to support their reading room and periodical rather than pieced together the far-flung audiences of Smith and Dennie, and the *Anthology* survived for eight years despite having fewer than five hundred subscribers. This form of cultural production tied the man of letters who thrived within it to the money and evaluations of his city rather than offered an alternative source of funding, readership, and critical judgment. But the Anthologists' localism coexisted with their ambitious vision of what the periodical could mean to the wider world. Although Walter, Shaw, Buckminster, and other society members evinced little desire to create a widespread, practical association of individuals, they were motivated by a sense of themselves as intellectual and emotional participants in an imagined transatlantic and transtemporal republic of letters. They sought to use the resources of their metropolis to create an institution that would, by its sheer existence, indirectly refine the nation and even the world. Thus, although the world outside Massachusetts was not necessary to the conduct of their enterprises, it was essential to their purpose. The Anthology Society wished to create a visible but removed and tightly knit fellowship, one that would be observed, admired, but untouched by the rest of the world.[6]

5. Shaw to Buckminster, Dec. 13, 1806, in Quincy, *Boston Athenaeum*, 33–34.

6. The *Anthology*'s first printer, the firm of Munroe and Francis, expressed concern over the society's small circulation. A second firm, Snelling and Simons, withdrew from a proposed agreement. The next printer, Hastings, Etheridge, and Bliss, became insolvent. The final printer, Thomas B. Wait and Company, printed the magazine for less than two years before the society agreed it was impractical to continue. The succession of printers willing to take on the pallid journal suggests they might have hoped such well-connected editors and contributors could reach a wider audience—or they might have hoped the *Anthology* would become another *Port Folio* with a national audience. Neither occurred, and the society used assessments on its members during trying times. See Munroe and Francis to Shaw, July 16, 1806, Shaw Papers. Printers' relationships can be traced—although the exact terms are not recorded—in Howe,

That fellowship was in its way a city on a hill, not surprising given that the society was largely peopled by New England ministers and their descendants. But, despite the importance of ministers among its ranks, the society argued that secular high culture could create a virtuous, harmonious community. When the Anthologists did intervene in theological controversy, they did so to argue that individual judgment, such as that cultivated through literature, was also valuable in the realm of religion. When orthodox Christians founded Andover Theological Seminary in 1808, the Anthologists, led by Buckminster, strenuously opposed the institution's Confession of Faith. The Confession, or creed, required that Andover's professors declare themselves in opposition "not only to Atheists and Infidels, but to Jews, [Papists,] Mahomatans, Arians, Pelagians, Antinomians, Arminians, Socinians, [Sabellians,] Unitarians, and Universalists." The creed offended Anthologists as a restraint on thought and as a false guarantor of Christian virtue. Buckminster, who admired Joseph Priestley and studied German scholarship that historicized the Gospels, attacked the "ridiculous controversy" among Christians. "We abhor bigotry whether in an Episcopalian, or a dissenter, in a Trinitarian or an Unitarian," he wrote. Samuel Cooper Thacher and another, unidentified *Anthology* author deplored the creed's demand for uniformity of opinion at the cost of intellectual and spiritual liberty. The Anthologists thus objected to the Andover Confession of Faith for much the same reason they objected to the power of the mass market and the democratic majority: it suggested that virtue and merit could be achieved through conformity, rather than through the exercise of reason and the cultivation of sensibility. In their genteel way, the Anthologists were modern antinomians, advocating a faith in individual judgment the extremity of which departed from both Protestant and republican orthodoxy.[7]

———

ed., *Proceedings*, 81–217. See also Lewis P. Simpson, ed., "Introduction," *The Federalist Literary Mind: Selections from the "Monthly Anthology and Boston Review," 1803–1811, Including Documents Related to the Boston Athenaeum* (Baton Rouge, La., 1962), 19–22. Simpson describes the appeal of the "republic of letters" to Federalist men of letters in "Federalism and the Crisis of Literary Order," *American Literature*, XXXII (1960), 255–259.

7. [Joseph Stevens Buckminster], review of *Lectures on the Catechism, on Confirmations and the Liturgy of the Protestant Episcopal Church*, by James Abercrombie, MA, V (June 1808), 340, [Samuel Cooper Thacher], review of *The Constitution and Associate Statutes of the Theological Seminary in Andover; with a Sketch of Its Rise and Progress*, V (November 1808), 606. The Anthologists' secularism inspired the creation

For the Anthologists, the belief that an individual mind should remain unfettered coexisted with a passionate desire for harmony. Buckminster's vision of Christ's disciples, presented in an 1805 sermon, paints a portrait of a divinely inspired circle in which minds roamed free and converged on truth. "While the recollection of [Christ's] person remained among his disciples," Buckminster told his congregation, "we are told that the multitude of them that believed were of one heart and one mind. All was arduous enquiry, unanimity, exertion, and love." The quest for a fellowship free of coercion and of conflict had inspired Elihu Hubbard Smith's utopia, and it inspired the creation of the Anthology Society as well. When Buckminster, Walter, and Shaw drew up the society's constitution, their document reflected an almost obsessive desire for unity. Article 10 established the difficult procedure by which new members were to be accepted. "No new member shall be admitted except by a unanimous vote of the members present," it read, adding, "after he shall have stood on nomination during four successive meetings of the Society." Article 12 described the elaborate consensus building necessary before a book review could be published: "Books shall be assigned by a vote of the majority of members present, and every review shall be read to the Society before its publication. If any objections which require further discussion shall be made to any part of a review, a committee of three shall be then appointed to examine said review, to confer with the writer and to report at the next meeting."[8]

But even this constitution could not meet the men's wish to speak with one mind and one heart. One of its articles established the position of an "Editor." Although broadly charged with "superintending the publication of this work," his actual duties were almost exclusively administrative, such

---

of a competing periodical, the *Panoplist*, which assertively yoked culture to orthodox Christianity (Peter S. Field, *The Crisis of the Standing Order: Clerical Intellectuals and Cultural Authority in Massachusetts, 1780-1833* [Amherst, Mass., 1998], 151-153; see also 167-171, on the controversy over the creed). Buckminster's interest in Joseph Priestley is evident in his journal, "which shall contain a brief record of the progress of my studies, and of the distribution of my time" (Eliza Buckminster Lee, *Memoirs of Rev. Joseph Buckminster, D.D., and of His Son, Joseph Stevens Buckminster*, 2d ed. [Boston, 1851], Dec. 18, 1803–Oct. 1, 1804, 243-255 [quotation on 243]). Lewis P. Simpson discusses Buckminster's studies in "Joseph Stevens Buckminster: The Rise of the New England Clerisy," *The Brazen Face of History: Studies in the Literary Consciousness in America* (Baton Rouge, La., 1980), 11.

8. Buckminster, Sermon draft, April 1805, Matt. 28:20, Joseph Stevens Buckminster Papers, Boston Athenaeum; Howe, ed., *Proceedings*, art. 10 and 12, 31.

as attending to correspondence "by direction of the Society" and keeping track of writing assignments. Thacher, however, was unhappy that "some persons unconnected with the S. had considered him as the Editor of the A"—which, of course, Thacher was, but not in the sense that the outsiders understood. After threatening to resign, Thacher succeeded in having the constitution altered. His duties do not seem to have been changed at all, but "the word 'Editor'" was "expunged from the constitution" to be replaced with the phrase "Superintending Committee." The switch was unanimously approved, and first Thacher and later William Smith Shaw acted, alone, as a committee.[9]

This desire to avoid becoming known as the individual responsible for the *Anthology*'s content could not be more different from Joseph Dennie's gleeful courting of both approbation and infamy. The difference reflects the constraining nature of a local cultural community: Thacher might have wanted to shield himself from disapproving local elites. The creation of an editorial committee, like the intense scrutiny of book reviews and the vetting of potential members, also arose from the Anthologists' understanding of the nature and purpose of their activities. Although they rejected Jeffersonians' hope that republican politics might create a unified people, they, too, hoped to escape the constant clash of interests and opinions. They would do so through culture, not politics. In their harmonious society, they would demonstrate to other Americans that individual judgments could converge, if not on a vision of polity or society, then on an understanding of beauty.

The Anthology Society published texts that would represent and foster the harmony they sought in their gatherings. As a result, friendship was a beloved subject. Twice in its first year, the *Anthology* published extracts from John Barclay's seventeenth-century political romance *Argenis*. Barclay's tale had attracted attention both as a complex political allegory in which characters represented European monarchs and states and as a morality play designed to incite self-recognition and reformation in its readers. What fascinated the Anthologists was, neither its political nor its moral goals, but rather its description of a passionate friendship between individuals of strikingly similar appearance and worth. In one extract, two men "contemplated each other's appearance with eagerness and delight, each admiring in the other some grace, which the other saw in him. They resembled each other in age, in symmetry, in attire, in the animated glance

9. Howe, ed., *Proceedings*, 31 (art. 11), 54 (Anthology Society Minutes, Jan. 9, 1806).

of the eye, and, though with different features, there appeared the same nobleness of countenance." The other extract presented a similar union. "They heartily embraced," it reads; "The form of the one now met the eyes of the other; they both stood fixed in contemplation, and each gazed, in his turn, with wonder and delight. Each, indeed, had the same appearance with the other in age, in form, in dress, in the vivid light of his eyes, and in the majesty of his whole countenance." This was a concord that perfectly suited the Anthologists' hope for an utterly harmonious male community. That wish echoed Elihu Hubbard Smith's utopian vision of a society free of conflict, but the Anthologists felt no need to project their vision onto a polity real or imagined.[10]

The society's desire for unity led it explicitly to banish wit from its pages. "In wit," reads a piece from the *Anthology*'s first year, "there is something so subtle and insinuating, that we are apt to feel ourselves secure, when we are in imminent danger; for if the imagination can be diverted, poison is imperceptibly conveyed to the heart." Wit had long been essential to Anglo-American club life because it was valued as a means of competition and as a way to speak truths others might not want to hear. The Anthologists, however, could not countenance the competition and potential disunion wit created within a fellowship. Wit threatened to undo the Anthologists' dream of creating a publicly useful model of harmony and beauty and so, in a dramatic departure from belletristic tradition, they forbade its exercise.[11]

References to sex were also forbidden in the *Anthology*, and the *Port Folio* was condemned for delighting in them. When Dennie's old contributor John Sylvester John Gardiner inserted a ribald story, Arthur Walter indignantly removed it before publication. "The filthy story of Pope's going with Cibber to a Brothel," Walter fumed in a letter to Buckminster, was "worse than *Port Folio* shamelessness." The sensual Thomas Moore, favorite poet and personal friend of the *Port Folio* circle, earned the Boston periodical's mistrust. "Unhappily[,] the genius that could have taught every breath of the

10. [D. P. Adams], "Argenis: A Moral and Political Romance, Book 1," *MA*, I (April 1804), 269–273 (quotation on 272), "Argenis: A Romance, from the Latin of Barclay," II (January 1805), 26; Edward Bensly, "Robert Burton, John Barclay, and John Owen," in A. W. Ward and A. R. Waller, eds., *Prose and Poetry: Sir Thomas North to Michael Drayton*, vol. IV of Ward and William Peterfield Trent et al., eds., *The Cambridge History of English and American Literature* (1907–1921) (New York, 2000), http://www.bartleby.com/cambridge (accessed July 18, 2006).

11. [Phineas Adams], "Evening Entertainments, No. 2," *MA*, I (February 1804), 179.

zephyr to whisper morality," intoned a review of Moore, "was the slave of his own passions and disciplined to the tyranny of lust. In this," the piece continued, "lurks the danger of his page; nature animate and inanimate is made to administer to gross and criminal enjoyment. A delicate refinement silvers over the surface, and all the noxious qualities are hidden." No such author was welcome in the society's pages or at its table.[12]

Joseph Dennie filled the *Port Folio* with sexual references and loved to portray the relations whose avoidance he counseled. Throughout the *Port Folio*, he insisted on the inevitability of conflict and competition and slyly conceded that it was impossible to escape all undignified associations and dependencies. The Anthology Society, by contrast, refused to acknowledge that purity, absolute truth, and total consensus were impossible to achieve. Members posited in their magazine a realm of letters—and provided in the Athenaeum a physical space—where merit, beauty, and authentic expression might appear to emerge free of conflict, compromise, seduction, or irony. Sexual imagery and jokes had no place in such a world.

The Anthologists also mistrusted and avoided direct political expression; thus, the dominant trio of the *Port Folio*, wit, sex, and politics, were the dominant absence of the *Anthology*. Jefferson was not the target he was in the *Port Folio*, nor do the Federalist secession crises appear, in recognizable fashion, in the *Anthology*'s quiet pages. "We claim also this merit," the editors wrote in their final address, "that we have never lent ourselves to the service of any party, political or theological."[13]

---

12. Arthur Maynard Walter to Buckminster, Sept. 29, 1806, Buckminster Papers; [Paul Allen], "Silva, No. 64," *MA*, VIII (June 1810), 379. See also [Arthur Maynard Walter], "The Boston Review for April, 1806: Notice of Poems from the Portuguese of Lues de Camoens," *MA*, III (April 1806), 217. Walter, noting that "ladies," among others, enjoy Camoëns's poems, writes: "We know not what remedy to offer; for when impropriety is decorated by the charms of delightful poetry; when indelicacy of allusion is almost evanescent in the refinement of elegant phraseology; and, when the criminality of passion is superficially concealed by the fashionable embroidery or delicate needle work of fancy or sentiment, who will regard any interdiction of perusal; who will receive any counsel for discrimination?" The best he can offer, Walter concludes, is that readers "neutralize" the "contagion" of licentious poetry with the "moral poetry" of authors such as James Thomson and William Cowper.

13. [Samuel Cooper Thacher], "Address of the Editors," *MA*, X (June 1811), 363. The *Anthology* has in fact inspired two quite contradictory assessments of its political content. "In contrast to the politicians of their generation," James M. Banner, Jr., argues, "who organized to fight democracy with democratic techniques, the Anthologists organized for refuge from politics itself. By cleansing the literary republic of

Yet Anthologists and contributors, including Walter, Buckminster, and Shaw, were deeply interested in politics. Shaw angrily wrote to his friend Thomas Boylston Adams shortly after John Adams's electoral defeat: "Last night a mob of about fifty collected about the houses near to the capitol and compelled the inhabitants to illuminate them in honor to Mr. J[efferson]," he fumed. "This passive submission of the federalists to the will of a rascally mob is in my opinion degrading in the lowest degree. I never would have submitted. I would have died first." The contributor Josiah Quincy wrote overt political satire for the *Port Folio* during the same years that he participated in the avowedly suprapolitical *Anthology*. In a sermon, Joseph Buckminster even set forth a critique of political neutrality that reads as a companion piece to Dennie's contemporaneous assaults on the Republican—and Godwinian—pretense of universal brotherhood. "We sometimes," Buckminster declared in a November 1804 sermon, "observe a certain neutrality of character which holds out a modicum of goodwill for all causes, parties, and persons." Of such a character, he continued, "it is proper to say not that to it all men are equally dear, but that all are equally indifferent and so far from being the result of universal love this disposition is the insipid deceitful froth of the most despotic selfishness." Buckminster feared for the soul of any man who claimed to feel affection and sympathy for all mankind. Mingling his theology with a Federalist-inflected disdain for the abstractions of "French philosophers," Buckminster warned that he who affected "universal disinterested benevolence" would fail to realize that the "charity of the gospel" was not intended to be "a cold speculation" or a "glittering palace of ice." Samuel Cooper Thacher had a harder-headed concern: reviewing John Quincy Adams's writings, he wrote, "In a country like ours, where politicks possess an interest so overwhelming, that he who will not talk of them must be content to pass his days in silence."[14]

Society members were known to discuss politics at their meetings, and occasionally Federalism did burst forth in the *Anthology*. John Quincy Adams

---

extra-literary influence, they hoped to escape the corruptions of the world" (*To the Hartford Convention: The Federalists and the Origins of Party Politics in Massachusetts, 1789–1815* [New York, 1970], 150–152). Daniel Walker Howe, by contrast, deems the *Anthology* a "Federalist political manifesto" (*The Unitarian Conscience: Harvard Moral Philosophy, 1805–1861*, Wesleyan ed. [Middletown, Conn., 1988], 176).

14. Shaw to Thomas Boylston Adams, Feb. 19, 1801, Shaw Papers; Buckminster, Sermon draft, Nov. 11, 1804, Mar. 20, 1806, Buckminster Papers; [Samuel Cooper Thacher], "The Boston Review for April, 1810: Article 10," *MA*, VIII (April 1810), 250.

published a satire of Joel Barlow's ode to the Lewis and Clark expedition. The poem mocks Jefferson's scientific ambitions and—in the *Anthology*'s lone foray into this field—his alleged relationship with the enslaved Sally. Demonstrable partisan sentiment is reflected in essays such as the condemnation of embargoes, which the magazine printed in the middle of its run. Federalism was evident as well in the magazine's endless mistrust of France and its Revolution, which the Anthologists equated with an embrace of radical deism and uncontrollable change. In France, read one extract, "human nature, insolent and presuming in its own strength, spurning the aids of divine revelation, and even of ancient learning, may relapse after convulsions into lethargy." Both Edmund Burke and Jean François de La Harpe, noted another author, aptly compared Jacobins to "obscene harpies." A review of Federalist and "democratick" Fourth of July orations, meanwhile, brings to mind not only the *Port Folio*'s overtly Federalist content but also its tone. The gloomy Federalist orations, the author writes, were heard "with a melancholy pleasure by those who love their country." What Elihu Hubbard Smith once acerbically deemed "the pleasures of despair" still held its partisan delights, as Federalist orators deplored the national ascendance of the Republican Party.[15]

Such pieces expressed identification with the Federalist Party, but they eschewed analysis of political issues. They were the exceptions, moreover, to the periodical's rule against overtly Federalist content. What explains such a rule? The Anthologists did not share Elihu Smith's hope that the spread of information would eventually render politics obsolete. Instead, they accepted the importance of political speech and action in America. But they wanted to create a realm of culture that did not revolve around such speech and action. Such a realm, they believed, would promote harmonious fellowship and the cultivation of individual judgment. By creating a forum largely free of partisan conflict, the Anthologists believed they served the nation.

15. The society "talked much upon politics and literature" (Howe, ed., *Proceedings*, 70). See "Whether the World Will Ever Relapse into Barbarism [from Dr. Arthur Browne's Miscellaneous Sketches]," *MA*, III (January 1806), 5, "Law of Blockade," IV (March 1807), 118-121, [John Quincy Adams], "On the Discoveries of Captain Lewis," IV (March 1807), 143-144, [Joseph Stevens Buckminster], "Silva, No. 35," V (January 1808), 31, "Boston Review for June, 1808: Article 18," V (June 1808), 334-336, [John Stickney], "Boston Review for August, 1808: Article 28," V (August 1808), 450; Elihu Hubbard Smith to Charles Brockden Brown, May 27, 1796, in James E. Cronin, ed., *The Diary of Elihu Hubbard Smith (1771-1798)* (Philadelphia, 1973), 171.

Even as they suppressed Federalism, the Anthologists believed that their civic duty lay in deploring the judgments of the crowd. The combination resulted in a nationalism built of criticism rather than of celebration. The *Anthology* avidly recorded America's current deficiencies as a civilization; such criticism was not traitorous, in the Anthologists' view, but rather the best fulfillment of their national duty. Often, the Anthologists deplored America's lack of cultural achievement. The "want of taste, which is evident in all our productions," noted a "Remarker," "may be observed in the senate, at the bar, and in the pulpit; so that a man of refined ear will seldom hear a speech, a plea, or a sermon, in which there will not be something harsh or grating." "There has been little to excite emulation, nothing to generate an *esprit du corps*," wrote Buckminster in the 1808 "Retrospective Notices of American Literature," "and the hope of posthumous fame has, from our remote situation, always been too faint to stimulate to solitary exertions." At other times, the *Anthology* mourned America's failure to become an affectionate community; even George Washington, one piece argued, was insufficiently loved: "The Mausoleum of Washington," published in 1804, bemoaned the "cold calculations" of those in Congress who wished to spend as little as possible in order to "shelter the remains" of the first president. "Will he not blush and hang his head," the author asked, "him, who has a sense of moral excellence . . . who feels gratitude, and burns to express it"?[16]

Such pieces were intended, not to alienate readers from the country, but to prompt in them an emotional connection, albeit one made of shame rather than of pride. An 1808 *Anthology* piece expressed indignation over America's effect on Indians, whom it deemed "the unhappy descendants of those warlike ancestors, who once exercised the just rights of sovereignty over the soil we inhabit." "We invaded the quietude of their forests," read the piece, "corrupted the simplicity of their manners, and left to their posterity all the curses of civilization, without one of its benefits." The virtuous American citizen should be wounded by such injustices. But was he required to rectify them? Sentimental literature could provoke true anger, and in the later nineteenth century Harriet Beecher Stowe harnessed that anger to the abolitionist cause, using sentimental literature to affect a polity from which she as a woman was formally excluded. The Anthologists, by

16. Censor, "The Mausoleum of Washington," *MA*, I (April 1804), 243, [Joseph Stevens Buckminster], "Retrospective Notices of American Literature," V (January 1808), 56, [John Sylvester John Gardiner], "Remarker, No. 38," V (November 1808), 599.

contrast, turned to literature to escape politics, not to enter it; pieces such as the condemnation of America's mistreatment of the indigenous population divorced criticism from any obligation to act, since none among the Anthologists contemplated returning the forests to the Indians from whom they had been unjustly taken. The extension of sympathy was its own end. The Anthologists' effusions, moreover, tended to create distance between them and the objects of their pity rather than to lessen it. There was the same tone in the critique of unjust treatment of Indians as there was in the essay "On Cruelty," in which a young lady stops two men from torturing an animal because "every insect of the field and the air, has a circle of connections, to whom its welfare is naturally dear; and a set of relations, with whom it is engaged in the confidence of a reciprocated friendship." Indians and insects received the same pitying and self-congratulatory gaze. The result was sympathy exerted from a height.[17]

Distressed at the sorrows of the world but dissatisfied with the ability of politics to alleviate them, Anthologists turned to benevolent organizations. Like members of the Friendly Club, they wanted to act rather than simply to think and to feel. Even in such activities, however, the sensibility the *Anthology* advocated and modeled seemed often to contemplate its own worth as much as it contemplated the sufferings of others. In this, its ties to Dennie's overtly Federalist persona are clear. The sensibility Joseph Dennie portrayed in the *Port Folio* could inspire political analysis but could also swoon into a kind of pained and paralyzing self-witnessing; the distressed sensibility the Anthology proffered, for its part, could become so self-regarding as to be unintentionally comic. "From the catalogue of human calamities," read a review of an address before the Massachusetts Charitable Fire Society, "he [the speaker] has selected '*External war, internal commotion, famine, pestilence, despotick rule, national decline*, and *fire*.'" "His reflections on each of these are few, but appropriate and interesting. The style is suited to the sub-

---

17. [Samuel L. Knapp], "Appeal to Puerile Humanity," *MA*, I (March 1804), 201–203, "On Cruelty," I (June 1804), 356, [Paul Allen], "Aboriginal Indians," V (February 1808), 65. See also Shaw's letter to Walter, describing five Indians who had come to see the president: "Had Buffon and the Abbe Raynal been present, they would have blushed for their assertion, that man was belittled in America. Some of their sentences forcibly struck me. They were these, 'Brother, although we are in your house, and sheltered from the cold winds, still we are in the eye of God. From his sight we never can hide ourselves. . . . Although we are not of the same color with you, brothers, still our hearts are as white as yours'" (July 22, 1798, quoted in Joseph B. Felt, *Memorials of William Smith Shaw* [Boston, 1852], 38).

ject; and though it do not, in any instance, rise to the sublime, it is through-out perspicuous."[18] An excerpt from William Emerson's speech to the Boston Female Asylum praised Emerson as much as the asylum. "To a person conscious of merit, whose actions are guided by wisdom, and terminate in private happiness, publick utility, and the honour of religion," it reads, "how grateful the commendation of a discerning friend! It is like the precious ointment, which was wont to moisten the head of the Hebrew priest." Such passages converted benevolence into self-congratulatory performance. The *Anthology*'s sentimental critique of America's failings curled in on itself just as did the *Port Folio*'s showier melancholy and irony. At times, the *Anthology* published pieces that portrayed thought as a way of escaping the world, rather than of engaging it. "Let him then, whose soul is pure and holy with the love of nature," read an 1804 piece by Benjamin Welles, "take his position in the midst of creation, and commence the mighty work of the eternal perfection of thought." "Over the souls of most persons," read another piece,

> evanescent honours and dispraise hold a cruel dominion; and the spirits are depressed or elevated as the popular neglect or patronage fails. By fastening ourselves on the pinions of an excursive fancy, we quickly get beyond the atmosphere of these terrestrial littlenesses, and, after soaring a while in tracts of thought, return to the realities of ordinary life, with our social feelings more dignified and lovely than before, with a greater readiness to discharge our duties, and with a keener susceptibility of simple pleasures.

Such pieces posited individuals rendered capable of feeling and action by their ability to ride the imagination to a place removed from earthly concerns. They were then to "return" to the world ready for action. The American man of letters was not effete and alienated; rather, he was useful because of his ability to ignore popular opinion as manifested in markets or in politics. But an air of impermeable self-satisfaction hangs around Welles's thinker poised "in the midst of creation." And the world around him threatens to become only a dim backdrop to his celebration of himself.[19]

18. "Boston Review for September, 1804: Review of an Address, Delivered before the Massachusetts Charitable Fire Society," *MA*, I (September 1804), 512. "The distancing pleasures the proponents of a cultivated sensibility derived from 'pain,'" G. J. Barker-Benfield observes, "depended in part on the misery of others" (*The Culture of Sensibility: Sex and Society in Eighteenth-Century Britain* [Chicago, 1992], 228).

19. [Mary Moody Emerson], "To Cornelia," *MA*, I (August 1804), 45, [Thomas

The Anthologists offered a vision of an elite literature and man of sensibility freed—except for the tricky satisfactions of pained defiance—from the political and social circumstances that had taken center stage in the projects of Elihu Hubbard Smith and Joseph Dennie. Smith tried to marshal observations to understand and eventually to eliminate the social and physical conditions that produced vice and illness. In his utopia, he imagined a world in which institutions and environment produced a morally and physically healthy society, and he tried to believe that imagining such a place could improve the real world. In the *Port Folio*, Dennie outlined himself and his ideal reader against improper relationships and the chaos they produced; the pull between the volatile, responsive man of sensibility and that which he disdained or feared both lent intensity to the opposition and produced the moments of empathy and self-critique that gave the texts their charm and insight. In the *Anthology*, however, improper relations and chaos are gestured toward but only vaguely depicted. What remained was often simply the self, protesting its independence from a vaguely hostile but largely unfeatured world.

America

Intrinsic to the *Anthology*'s distinctive nationalism was its skepticism about the existence of a unique American identity. Such skepticism did not prevent Anthologists from admiring the literary efforts of individual Americans; guided by Buckminster, the society undertook a "review of books in American literature which have either been forgotten or have not hitherto received the attention they deserve." But compiling a list of literature produced in America was not the same thing as proclaiming the existence of an "American literature." The *Anthology* largely rejected the idea of "Americanness" as a meaningful trait of either an individual or a work of art. "In all the more liberal and noble branches of science and literature," read one piece from 1810, "it would certainly be difficult, perhaps mischievous, to

---

Gray], "Boston Review for February, 1806: Article 9," III (February 1806), 102, [Benjamin Welles], "The Remarker, No. 10," III (June 1806), 288. Sue Neueswander Greene, who finds the Anthologists to be among America's first romantics, argues that this passage by Welles is "an example not only of romanticism but of transcendentalism as well" ("Contribution of *The Monthly Anthology*," 133). Gardiner, Greene notes, was dismayed by this passage, deeming it, according to Walter, "the most contemptible thing that has ever appeared in the *Anthology*" (Walter to Buckminster, Aug. 7, 1806, quoted ibid., 135).

attempt very accurate limits of our *nationality.*" There was no distinctively American perspective; a review of *Letters from Europe, during a Tour through Switzerland and Italy, in the Years 1801 and 1802* (1805), by Joseph Sansom, mocked its author for suggesting that "his reason for publishing" was that "'he is the first American, who ever wrote his travels.'" Nor was there an American tongue, except for indigenous ones. "We know of no American language, that is not Indian," read a typically arch declaration, "and feel no inclination to resort to the Choctaws, the Chickesaws, the Cherokees, and the Tuscaroras for literary instruction." Shaw mocked the idea of an American language by suggesting that it "must be composed of five parts, viz. one part Indian, another Irish, and three fifths Negro tongue." What would differentiate American from British English, that is, was, not edenic purity, but rather barbarism.[20]

Such assertions reveal more than the expected Federalist claim of America's connection to England. The *Anthology* was also denying "Americanness" a controlling or transforming meaning. Its writers declared independence from the grasp of an unchosen identity, Americanness, while simultaneously claiming a role for themselves within the American community. The Anthologists' nationalism was not a romantic one that envisioned America as a brave new world and themselves as its Adamic citizens. Instead, it was a neoclassical patriotism that sought to bring America into

20. [John Sylvester John Gardiner], "To 'Harvardiensis,'" *MA*, II (January 1805), 44–45, "Boston Review for February, 1806: Article 4," III (February 1806), 86, [William Smith Shaw], "Remarker, No. 12," III (August 1806), 399–400, [Joseph Stevens Buckminster], "Retrospective Notices of American Literature," V (January 1808), 54–57 (in this piece, Buckminster describes his hopes for the review series and for the Athenaeum), [William Tudor], "Address of the Editors," VIII (January 1810), 4. The Anthologists' skepticism of claims for a unique American identity is part of but is not confined to their defense of a Federalist love of England. See, for example, [Josiah Quincy], "The Boston Review for January, 1810: Article 1," *MA*, VIII (January 1810), 45. In this review of Fisher Ames's *Works*, Quincy writes: "The only inquiries concerning every principle ought to be its nature and consequences. On which side of the Atlantick it originated, or is maintained, ought to have no weight in the discussion." "If such privilege be denied," Quincy continued, expanding on his theme, "or if intelligent men by artful clamour be prevented from exercising it, though nominally free, we are in fact subjects of a despotism; the worse, because it is of the mind." For discussions of Americans' concerns about the Americanization of English, see Linda K. Kerber, *Federalists in Dissent: Imagery and Ideology in Jeffersonian America* (New York, 1970), 96–102; David Simpson, *The Politics of American English, 1776–1850* (New York, 1986), 42–47, 78–81. Simpson notes that the *Anthology* casts Noah Webster as, in his words, "one of the destroyers of civilization" (78).

an existing, Western circle of sensibility. This vision, which participated in the tradition of the *translatio studii* (or imagined movement of learning from east to west), was a central element of the *Anthology*'s patriotism. The *Anthology* offered readers a way to participate in the nation without being transformed, or seduced, or overwhelmed by it. They intended to exert influence over America from within their own charmed and bounded circle. The more uncouth the nation was, the more they felt their own usefulness to it, and the more they felt the sweetness of their own community's separation from the nation. The imagined spiritual distance between the Anthologists and their compatriots, and not that between America and the world, lent emotional and intellectual urgency to their national sentiment.

Women and Gender

The opposition that nurtured and haunted the cultural networks examined in this study is that between male and female. The Anthologists had as intricate a relationship to women and to images of women as did Smith, Dennie, and the networks they marshaled. In letters, Walter and Buckminster each expressed belief in women's intellectual capacity. "Woman," wrote Walter to his friend Shaw in 1798, "was never made solely to toil in the kitchen and sooth in the night, but was intended for the partner of our joys and sorrows and the partaker of intellectual pleasures." "The world," Buckminster mused to his sisters, "has talked too long about books for ladies; you ought to read fundamentally the same books with the other sex." Buckminster was also a friend and supporter of the writer Hannah Adams. "From Mr. Buckminster," reads a memoir of Adams, "she received the most judicious, and extensive assistance. She was in the habit of visiting him in his study, and had his permission to come when she pleased, to sit and read there as long as she pleased, or take any book home and use it like her own." Two other women of formidable intellect, Mary Wilder White and Mary Moody Emerson, contributed a series of letters to the *Anthology*; their contributions, like those of women involved in Smith's and Dennie's projects, were the result both of their family connections and of their own ambition and talents.[21]

21. Walter to Shaw, Jan. 8, 1798, Shaw Papers; Buckminster to sisters, Mar. 11, 1807, [Hannah Farnham Sawyer Lee], *A Memoir of Miss Hannah Adams . . .* (Boston, 1832), both quoted in Lee, *Memoirs*, 216–217, 299. Mary Kelley describes the prevalence, among early Republic commentators, of defenses of women's intellect in

Despite these many relationships, women were banned from membership in the Anthology Society and from entrance to the Athenaeum (although their "indirect interest" in the prospect of a city filled with more enlightened men was duly noted in the institution's prospectus). And, despite Buckminster's kindness to Hannah Adams, the secretary's notes for an 1809 meeting of the Anthology Society record that "Mr. Buckminster read an acrostick on Miss Hannah Adams, which I believe, was rejected, for we were in such a roar of laughter, that no vote could easily be taken, or remembered." Whatever her personal merits, Hannah Adams could be reduced to a vehicle to bolster masculine fellowship. Women as a class, furthermore, served, as they did in the *Port Folio,* as a kind of shorthand for those possessed of poor judgment. While traveling in Europe, Arthur Walter commented on the inappropriate reaction of two acquaintances to what he perceived to be a treacly story: "The first," he wrote, in a model of ideological compression, "is a very foolish woman and the second is a Frenchman."[22]

The Anthologists' vexing relationship to the feminine helps to explain their exclusion of "woman" from their institutions and self-conceptions, despite their enjoyment of and faith in the intellects of individual women. The magazine's vision of letters as a realm of purity led to a tension that played out in explicitly and implicitly gendered terms. The Anthologists' withdrawal of belles lettres from partisanship was intended to stake a claim of manly independence and to create a way to serve the nation without being drawn into insoluble, all-consuming disputes. This withdrawal separated literary pursuits from what one *Anthology* author described as "the tumults and contentions of active life." "We should feel the same sort of repugnance at introducing the passions of party into these quiet regions," the piece continued, "as at bringing a band of ruffians into the abodes of rural innocence and happiness, to mar their beauty, and violate their peace."

"'Vindicating the Equality of Female Intellect': Women and Authority in the Early Republic," *Prospects,* XVII (1992), 1–28.

22. Arthur Maynard Walter, Paris journal, July 20, 1804, Arthur Maynard Walter Journals, Boston Athenaeum; Anthology Society Minutes, Oct. 24, 1809, in Howe, ed., *Proceedings,* 209. The *Memoir of the Boston Athenaeum; with the Act of Incorporation, and Organization of the Institution* (Boston, 1807), noted: "The ladies have at least an indirect interest in this design. Whatever raises the character of men has a favorable influence upon that of the other sex. Undoubtedly when the citizens are sensible and well-informed, the intercourse of the sexes is proportionably more rational and agreeable" (13).

A literature that served as such a refuge was not far from a literature that was utterly removed from public life, one in need of protection rather than capable of serving. Such a literature was domesticized and effeminized. "If it were possible to draw a distinctive line where the colours so imperceptibly fade into each other," noted a line from 1810, "we should say that science is the province of man, literature of woman." The Anthologists usually did not want to draw that line but rather argued that literature, like science, was a fit subject of men's attention. Yet even their claims to public relevance threatened to draw them toward women's conventional role. The preface to the magazine's first volume spelled out a vision of the role of the man of letters in the new nation that gave to him the tasks of educating individuals and beautifying the culture:

> If unable at present to rear oaks for our navy, and repair breaches in the walls of national defence, he can yet cherish a new plant for the botanist, and occasionally tender a bouquet of indigenous flowers to the bosom of love. If he should be unable to mend the constitution of our country, or save it from ruin, he may yet mend the morals of a private citizen, and can at least engage in the more
>
> Delightful task! to rear the tender thought,
> To teach the young idea how to shoot,
> To pour the fresh instruction o'er the mind,
> And fix the generous purpose in the glowing breast.

Americans agreed that a republican government required an educated and virtuous citizenry. But the responsibility for educating citizens and rendering them virtuous was more often assigned to women and expected to take place within the home. The Anthologists' model man of letters was perhaps no man at all.[23]

The lurking threat of cultural emasculation left the Anthologists determined to demonstrate that their gentle communion and retiring sensibility truly did fulfill the public duties of manhood.[24] Throughout the *Anthology*'s

23. [Emerson], "Preface," *MA*, I (1804), ii, [Thacher], "Boston Review for April, 1810: Article 10," VIII (April 1810), 249, "Boston Review for September, 1810: Article 9," IX (September 1810), 195. This unusually direct description of the attempted purity of their literature is prompted by the unusually direct political commentary that their displeasure over Adams's apostasy had prompted and perhaps as well by an internal debate over Thacher's draft.

24. See, similarly, the early national Masons' emphasis on the public usefulness of

run, the society tried to sever aesthetics from politics only to then justify its potentially unmanly and uncivic-minded pursuit of beauty by reference to the needs of the polity and the dictates of manly citizenship. The most extended exploration of the gender tension implicit in the *Anthology*'s vision of letters appears in Joseph Stevens Buckminster's address to Harvard's Phi Beta Kappa Society, which was reprinted in the *Anthology*. The piece dwelled at length on the temptation to retreat from active involvement in the nation, and it cast that temptation in doubly feminized terms. "The young man, early enamoured of literature," Buckminster cautioned, "sometimes casts a disdainful glance at the world, and then sinks to repose in the lap of his mistress." "His learning," he continued, "becomes effeminate." America's clamor, Buckminster argued, fostered this desire for sanctuary; the "temptation" was "felt by many studious minds," he noted, "in the actual state of the politicks of our country." Yet it was the nation's very disorder and degradation that rendered participation so essential and alienation so deplorable; Buckminster insisted that graduates resist the impulse to retreat and instead do their duty "to that country, which gave us birth, to that society, which protects and encourages us, to those parents and friends, who have aided our progress, and to that religion, which is the strength of our excellence." Active men of letters, he wrote, "are of more value to the community, than a whole cabinet of dilettanti." Just as Elihu Smith had insisted that cultural work was real and manly labor, so did Buckminster insist that the Anthologists' vision of letters was real and manly civic participation. "There is hardly to be found a consummate statesman or warrior in a literary age," he declared, "who was not himself a man of letters."[25]

For all his belief in the need for men of letters to serve the state rather than some private vision, however, Buckminster, in accord with the *Anthology*'s ethos, was convinced that such service should not take place through direct partisan engagement. Buckminster did make an exception for the beloved Edmund Burke, writing that *"what he gave up to party, he gave to mankind."* In general, however, Buckminster argued that, "from the moment that [the man of letters] is found yielding himself up" to "the people, or rather to

---

their lodges even as they increasingly portrayed those lodges as a refuge from public life in Steven C. Bullock, *Revolutionary Brotherhood: Freemasonry and the Transformation of the American Social Order, 1730-1840* (Chapel Hill, N.C., 1996), 256-261.

25. J. S. Buckminster, "On the Dangers and Duties of Men of Letters; an Address, Pronounced before the Society of Phi Beta Kapa, on Thursday, August 31st, 1809," *MA*, VII (September 1809), 146-155.

some of their factions," "his studies, and his powers yet in their bloom, are all lost to learning." On one level, Buckminster and his Anthology collaborators placed literature in the role of the republican mother; they idealized literature as a source of virtue to a polity it was not permitted to enter. But the Anthologists themselves, who resisted feminization, did not see it this way; withstanding the temptation to "yield" to the people was not a betrayal of the duties of manly republican citizenship but rather a fulfillment. Of the society, Buckminster wrote:

> They are gentle knights, who wish to guard the seats of taste and morals at home, from the incursions of the 'paynim host;' happy, if they should now and then rescue a fair captive from the giants of romance, or dissolve the spell, in which many a youthful genius is held, by the enchantments of corrupt literature. If with these objects, they can retain the pleasures of lettered society . . . they will try to be as insensible to the neglect or contumely of the great vulgar and the small, as they are to the pelting of the pitiless storm without, when taste and good humour sit round the fire within.

These noble knights created a virtuous population by breaking the spell of vulgar literature and by creating social bonds grounded neither in fear nor in craven desire for admiration but in mutual respect, affection, and appreciation for beauty. The perils such knights faced were real; Buckminster titled his address to the Phi Beta Kappa Society "On the Dangers and Duties of Men of Letters" because to defy public opinion in the new nation was to risk scorn and irrelevance. But the cold neglect of the world made the fire of their fellowship burn brighter, and they hoped its flame would be visible to those outside the circle as well as within.[26]

The Athenaeum

The interactions between the Anthologists' wish for peaceful refuge and their claims of manly civic relevance shaped their rhetoric and self-conception. They also led to the establishment of what would become their most conspicuous legacy, the Boston Athenaeum. Institutions of high culture in Boston served to legitimate the wealth of their benefactors. "A nation that increases in wealth, without any corresponding increase in knowledge and refinement, in letters and arts," Anthology Society members wrote

26. Ibid., 149; "Address of the Editors," MA, VI (January 1809), 4.

in their 1807 *Memoir*, "neglects the proper and respectable uses of prosperity." But the Anthologists' vision of culture needed the support of money even as Bostonian money sought the laundering effects of culture: because the Anthologists wanted to create a bricks-and-mortar sanctuary for literature, and because they refused to cultivate a geographically broad readership for their periodical, they relied on wealthy patrons to keep alive their projects and thus their belief in the value of cultural activities.[27]

The cultural elitism of the *Monthly Anthology* and of the Athenaeum might suggest that their creators were possessed of great wealth. In fact, the financial circumstances of some of the contributors suggest that education and refinement offered a public and private respectability that had to compensate for a lack of cash. Shaw, whose father had died during Shaw's youth, was not wealthy and had to rely on the assistance of his mother's family to finish his schooling. The Tudors lost their fortune during the middle of the *Anthology*'s run. Plans for the Athenaeum reveal a real interest in making the flow of transatlantic texts and ideas accessible to those of limited means. Even were the Athenaeum designed to benefit only "those who wish to perfect themselves in sciences and literature," the founders wrote in their 1807 *Memoir*, "it would be worthy of the munificent spirit of our opulent citizens to give effect to a plan for affording to persons, ambitious of superior acquisitions, the means of extensive knowledge, and the gratification of an adequate supply of books." Some of the members of the Anthology Society, moreover, would not have been able to afford the life subscriptions to the Athenaeum that they awarded themselves as recompense for their cultural labors.[28]

27. *Memoir of the Boston Athenaeum*, 9. Ronald Story explores the relationship between the Anthology Society and Boston's men of business in "Class and Culture in Boston," *American Quarterly*, XXVII (1975), 178–199. "Patronage of the arts," Peter S. Field writes, "helped to assuage the merchants' uneasiness about their extraordinary acquisition of personal fortunes" ("The Birth of Secular High Culture: *The Monthly Anthology and Boston Review* and Its Critics," *Journal of the Early Republic*, VII [1997], 579). See also Howe, *Unitarian Conscience*: "The implicit bargain that the Harvard moral philosophers were trying to drive with the merchants came down to this: the moralists would provide a rationale for capitalism and the protection of property, if the merchants would grant them the positions of cultural and moral leadership" (140).

28. *Memoir of the Boston Athenaeum*, 12; Lewis P. Simpson, "The Era of Joseph Stevens Buckminster: Life and Letters in the Boston-Cambridge Community, 1800–1815" (Ph.D. diss., University of Texas at Austin, 1948), 79–80, 98–99; and Simpson, "The Tudor Brothers: Boston Ice and Boston Letters," in *The Man of Letters in New*

To obtain funds for the creation of the Athenaeum, the Anthologists offered different membership levels, each of which conveyed different privileges and degrees of public recognition. In addition to annual memberships, they offered expensive life subscriptions and proprietorships, whose possessors would be "furnished with certificates of their property, under the seal of the corporation, signed by the President." The Anthologists were offering for sale not only access to texts but also a cultural seal of approval. Society members had no qualms about pursuing their own cultural ambitions by rendering support of the Athenaeum a marker of elite status, nor did they hesitate to cater to the taste of those they believed had less exalted aims but more ready cash. Shaw and Buckminster, who together did much of the labor involved in amassing the Athenaeum's first collections, attended not only to what they thought meritorious but also to what would please supporters and so allow the Athenaeum to continue. "We must," Buckminster wrote to Shaw in 1807, "at least for some time, think of popularity; and I know of no method so likely to procure it as to keep our rooms furnished with abundance of magazines, pamphlets, and new books. This, I am satisfied, should be our primary object; and our second, to lay slowly and secretly the foundation of a permanent library of works difficult to be procured in America." Cultural ambition lurked inside the Trojan horse of genteel fluff. And the society's appeals to the wealthy and culturally ambitious of Boston and Cambridge were, indeed, successful. Shaw wrote to Buckminster in December 1806 that work on the Athenaeum progressed satisfactorily and that the *Monthly Anthology* was gaining subscribers and "rising in reputation."[29]

For all its reliance on the monies and institutions of a wealthy and self-satisfied city, however—indeed, perhaps, because of it—the Anthology Society evinced in its periodical a palpable unease with its own relation to wealth and privilege. In his introductory note to an "Account of Paintings in the Louvre," Arthur Maynard Walter declared art's independence from commerce. Defending poetry and painting, he argued: "It is not the contemplation of Nature or her resemblances that weakens the sinews of a nation.

England and the South: Essays on the History of the Literary Vocation in America (Baton Rouge, La., 1973), 39.

29. Shaw to Buckminster, Dec. 3, 1806, Shaw Papers; "Terms of Subscription to the Boston Athenaeum," Trustees' rules adopted Apr. 7, 1808, and adopted by the proprietors on Aug. 11, 1808, and "Biographical Notices of the Founders," all in Quincy, *Boston Athenaeum*, 43, 48–49, 52. Terms, rights, and privileges of subscribers and proprietors are also explained in *Memoir of the Boston Athenaeum*, 28–30.

. . . Luxury is born of the body, and rebel to the soul; and we may say with Fuseli, that towards the aggrandizement of character and the cultivation of Genius, gold, gold has done nothing!" But gold, Walter and his collaborators well knew, had in fact done quite a bit. To shield their dependence on money from their own eyes, contributors to the *Anthology*, like those to the *Port Folio*, consistently associated the degradations of commerce and the pursuit of gain only with the demands of a broad, popular marketplace. The *Anthology* portrayed literature that was designed both to sell widely and to be politically palatable as a degrading intersection of art, crowd, and commerce—and as the opposite of its own ethos. Reviewing Mason Weems's hagiographic biography of George Washington (a book that sanctified America on its way to canonizing Washington, and so could not suit the *Anthology*'s taste), the society noted dryly that, rather than biography, the volume was "an epick poem . . . with a suitable quantity of preternatural machinery." The reviewer criticized the book as a kind of self-conscious and unconvincing mythologizing, in which Washington "is born on angel's wings to the skies" after his death, and the piece concluded on a distinctly acerbic note: "The sale of nine editions of this work, is a pledge of its popularity. This run it can have obtained, we think, only as a school book, in which sphere it is best calculated to move." A book that catered to Americans' unthinking and uncritical patriotism would be a popular success, but such literature degraded American taste and thought, and it was the civic duty of the man of letters to combat it. "The office of a reviewer is, in the republick of letters, as beneficial and necessary, though as odious and unpleasant," read one strident assertion, "as that of an executioner in the civil state."[30]

In deploring the effect of the popular marketplace on literature, the *Anthology* was participating in an English Augustan tradition. The satiric advice, "*Write what will sell*," that the *Anthology* printed was in fact excerpted from the London *Monthly Magazine*. Yet, as did the *Port Folio*, the *Anthology* insistently cast the problem as one caused by circumstances unique to America: democratic politics and a nationwide obsession with commerce. Obligingly, scholars have portrayed these American men of letters as intellectuals alienated against their will from the nation. Yet ambitious

30. [Arthur Maynard Walter], introduction to "Account of Paintings in the Louvre," *MA*, II (August 1805), 400 (ellipses in original), [Dr. J. Bigelow], "Silva, No. 24: Reviewers," IV (February 1807), 85, "Boston Review for December, 1810: Article 16," IX (December 1810), 419.

letters and intellectual pursuits were not, in these years of the early Republic, in quite the dire straits that the *Anthology* portrayed. The election of
1800 had pitted a president of the American Academy of Arts and Sciences
against a president of the American Philosophical Society. The Federalist
Port Folio enjoyed circulation and esteem, as did the *Medical Repository*.
The Anthologists themselves gained the patronage and money they needed
to begin their longed-for Athenaeum, and, although the *Anthology* itself was
less successful, it outlasted the average life of an early national periodical.
The *Anthology* sought the role of outsider because to do so was to claim the
independence society members believed was essential to their cultural citizenship. Distance and discontent were not alienation; they were the key to
their civic role.[31]

The Market

The Anthologists assiduously associated the indignities of audience seeking with popular, Republican-tinged literature. What, however, of their dependence, to ensure publication of the *Anthology* and the existence of the
Athenaeum, on the monies of wealthy, Federalist merchants? The society
solved this problem, at least on the surface, by carefully parsing commerce
into good and bad in a way that allowed participants to feel themselves, and
their literature, to be possessed of a manly independence. In these efforts,
Anthology writers pursued a path traveled by Joseph Dennie. Their advantage over Dennie was that they were less often plagued by the irritating
self-awareness that periodically made a mess of Dennie's self-justifying con-
structs.

31. "Advice to a Young Reviewer, with a Specimen of the Art, from the *London Monthly Magazine*," MA, IX (August 1810), 74. "Broadly speaking," Pat Rogers
writes of England in *The Augustan Vision* (London, 1974), "eighteenth-century writers
felt that they had suffered some loss of social identity as a result of the disappearance
of noble patrons. They were now dependent on a race of middle-class tradesmen, in
other words a commercial interest" (77). Literary Federalists such as Dennie and the
Anthologists were, Laurence Buell writes, "self-appointed . . . arbiters of virtue and
taste." The evident failure of this mission to civilize America, Buell argues, converted
Federalist writers into "the first group of alienated American intellectuals" (*New
England Literary Culture: From Revolution through Renaissance* [New York, 1986],
93–94). Buell notes that so inauspicious had Boston been for periodicals before the
Monthly Anthology that, "by 1800, Bostonians were wondering whether it was true, as
Philadelphia alleged, that no literary magazine could survive in Boston" (31).

The *Anthology* claimed virtue for the two forms of commerce on which the society and its projects relied. One was the kind of large-scale, transatlantic merchant activity that sustained New England elites and so sustained the Athenaeum. Such commerce was portrayed as different in kind from the petty transactions that John Sylvester John Gardiner deemed "the shop"; it elevated individuals and society rather than debased them. A piece defending "foreign trade" found James Savage arguing: "If all are constrained to daily labour with their hands, there can be no cultivation of mind: and without intelligence there will be few delights of society and little interchange of benevolence. Man in such a state ceases to be sociable, and becomes only gregarious. So that from gradual degeneration to barbarism we shall best be preserved by commerce." Just as commerce in its broadest terms could be cast as a social and a socially elevating impulse, so, too, could commerce in one of its smallest guises: the bond between artist and patron. As in the *Port Folio*, personal friendship, not the marketplace, was the Anthology Society's model of the ideal union between literature and wealth; personal friendship was also a practical foundation of the society's projects. And so one writer praised poet William Gifford's patron, William Cookesley: "Blessed with such a friend, the subject of these memoirs is safely sheltered from the storms of life, in an harbour which affords him competence, tranquility and respect." In these sentimentalized and aestheticized visions of commerce large and small, monetary relationships produced art, virtue, and independence, the exact opposite of that which unsanctified commerce created. Meanwhile, the young men of the Anthology Society praised their patrons while imagining themselves possessed of a radical sensibility: they portrayed their beloved literary pursuits and cultivation of good taste, in short, as bold and daring activities constituting a defiance of power, not its service.[32]

Just as the Anthologists sought to mask their periodical's relation to commerce, so did they often turn their eyes away from the ways that wealth and privilege shaped individuals. Shaw insisted on the disjuncture between authentic self and external attributes in an 1803 letter to Walter. "According to my ideas," he wrote, "there is a certain abhorrence of associating with men, of the same standing with yourself, whom you are in constant habit of seeing, unless there is some congeniality of feeling—some assimilation of

32. "Biographical Sketch of William Gifford, Esq.," *MA*, I (February 1804), 170, [John Sylvester John Gardiner], "Silva, No. 11," III (January 1806), 18, [James Savage], "The Remarker, No. 27," IV (November 1807), 577.

minds, which shall mutually interest and delight, and the happiness of the one, in some measure, be interwoven in that of the other." Following Shaw's lead, the *Anthology* never claimed literary skill, sensitivity, and refinement as the prerogative of the rich. On the contrary, pieces often expressed sympathy and admiration for those "geniuses" who transcended their lowly beginnings. The poet Gifford, one contributor wrote, confronted difficult circumstances; "To the properties of GENIUS alone," the *Anthology* declared, "can such a preservation of mind be attributed." "It seems to me vain and idle to speculate upon education and outward circumstances, as the causes or promoters of poetical genius," reads a discussion of William Cowper and Robert Burns. "It is the inspiring breath of Nature alone, which gives the powers of the genuine bard." "That gift has regard neither to rank, station, nor riches," the piece continues, and can arise in a "thatched hovel" or a "palace."[33]

The Anthologists refused to concede that the sensibility in which their identities and community resided was simply the result of the privileges that their gender, race, and lack of poverty, if not actual wealth, had provided them. Such a concession would have robbed them of a sense of self and community that was more than the sum of its advantages. In their view, taste was refined by education but also reflected an innate capacity. This conception of taste allowed the Anthologists to take pride in a shared sensibility without acknowledging its dependence on birth, education, and leisure time—and, more important, without acknowledging its dependence on circumstance and on other people's money. The Anthologists insisted they were self-made men of letters. In the 1790s, Elihu Hubbard Smith had attempted, however unrealistically and tentatively, to confront this issue in his arguments that society should redistribute wealth to enable the education of all citizens. A decade later, the Anthologists shied away from analysis of inequities and their potential resolution and argued instead that true sensibility and genius did not depend on privilege—and therefore that cultural flowering required no social transformation.[34]

33. Shaw to Walter, Feb. 4, 1803, Shaw Papers; "Biographical Sketch of William Gifford, Esq.," *MA*, I (February 1804), 170, "Parallel between Cowper and Burns, from the Censura Literaria for November, 1805," III (February 1806), 68. The piece also prefers Burns to Cowper because of, among other things, "his want of education, while the other enjoyed all the discipline and all the advantages of a great publick school" (67).

34. Richard L. Bushman notes in *The Refinement of America: Persons, Houses, Cities* (New York, 1992), that, among the colonial gentry, gentility had not been understood

The Anthologists portrayed sensibility as creating a hierarchy, not result-ing from one. They also portrayed it as making possible distinctive fellow-ships: "Probably the height at which [friendship] arrives in one, who cul-tivates it," read one *Anthology* selection, "is proportional to the strength of his mind." "You are not to upbraid your friend with want of sincerity, because he does not love you with the same warmth of affection, which was reciprocal between Jonathan and David, and between Damon and Pythias. His soul perhaps is incapable of feeling what they felt." The sensibility that allowed for passionate connection to those who shared it created an un-bridgeable distance from others. Like the *Port Folio,* the *Anthology* reassured its readers that they were not part of the crowd and that their distinction was a sign of superiority. In its reverence for idiosyncratic vision and its insistence on maintaining a critical distance from American society, the *An-thology* presaged later-nineteenth-century American Romanticism.[35]

The *Anthology* rejected creedalism in poetry as it rejected it in religion. The argument that beauty should be judged, not by adherence to rules, but by an individual's communion with a text received its most direct as-sertion in a series of articles that Joseph Buckminster wrote in defense of the poet Thomas Gray. John Sylvester John Gardiner—again at odds with the society's ethos—had written a satire of the poet, who did not appeal to Gardiner's neoclassical taste. Buckminster responded promptly and ag-gressively. Gray's was not the easily accessible poetry of public events or codifiable rules, Buckminster explained, but rather a vessel of subjective experience. Adapting Burke's *Origin of Our Ideas of the Sublime and Beau-tiful* to his own purposes, Buckminster argued that Gray's was a poetry "chiefly employed about ideas generated within the mind . . . and conse-quently always in some degree obscure to those, whose intellects have not

---

to be entirely congruent with wealth; this differentiation, he explains, only "deep-ened the division between rich and poor, adding a moral dimension to differences in wealth" (182–183). Julie Ellison describes a similar rhetorical move later in the nine-teenth century. Discussing Ralph Waldo Emerson's prose in the context of republican "conduct-of-life" books, Ellison explains: "Defining masculine subjectivity through its visible evidences binds differences in wealth and reputation to 'inherent' qualities. These qualitative distinctions in the domain of character function like rankings de-rived from 'artificial' grounds in the neighboring domain of society" ("The Gender of Transparency: Masculinity and the Conduct of Life," *American Literary History,* IV [1992], 589).

35. Benevolus, "On Friendship," *MA,* I (June 1804), 354. Lawrence Buell illumi-nates the relationship between New England's "Federalist literary culture" and later romanticism in *New England Literary Culture,* 91–102.

been exercised in similar contemplations." Rather than simply indicating a difference in taste, Buckminster insisted, a dislike of Gray marked a failure of the self; in just one of these articles, the term "insensible" appeared seven times. "He who can endure to dwell upon . . . petty blemishes," Buckminster scoffed, "must be as insensible to the pomp and grandeur of poetick phrase, as that traveller would be to the sentiment of the sublime in nature, who could sit coolly by the cataract of Niagara, speculating upon the chips and straws that were carried over the fall."[36]

The disagreement between Buckminster and Gardiner was intense. James Savage later recalled its dramatic end. "A fourth attempt at the ludicrous, by our president [Gardiner], contained something unguardedly personal from the satirist to his antagonist," he wrote, "which produced strong though silent emotions of sympathy in many of the party. In an instant, the writer threw the inconsiderate effusion into the fire." "From that moment," Savage concluded, "no allusion was made in the club to Gray's merits." This literary dispute had joined political ones as unspeakable and unwritable. Esoteric as it might have been, the dispute was nonetheless deeply felt, arising as it did from Buckminster's conception of the proper nature of taste, independence, and the fellowship of readerly sympathy to which he passionately believed he belonged. Through these pieces, Buckminster asserted the existence of a mysterious, inexpressible self and of an organic, highly selective fellowship. The fellowship and sensibility were publicly expressed—and in fact conceived only with the help of an opposing, insensible public—but they also offered privacy. Ultimately, taste functioned for Buckminster as did wit in the *Port Folio*—or as did narrow rivers in Smith's "Institutions of the Republic of Utopia"—to create a community inaccessible but visible, admirable to those who did not share its inhabitants' sensibility.[37]

Shaftesburian fellowship had always been bounded, but, whereas Elihu Smith had imagined widening the circle through the spread of education and enlightenment and Dennie had cast the circle in aggressively public terms by pretending it was coterminous with a partisan community, the Anthologists embraced the exclusivity of their communion and its roots in the private self. A similar privatization of literature was already occurring in England, where authors such as Samuel Taylor Coleridge and William Wordsworth

36. [Joseph Stevens Buckminster], "Remarker, No. 34," *MA*, V (July 1808), 370, [Buckminster], "To the Author of the 35th Remarker," V (September 1808), 485.

37. [Buckminster], "The Remarker, No. 34," *MA*, V (September 1808), 369; James Savage, quoted in Lee, *Memoirs,* 236–238. See also Anthology Society Minutes, Oct. 25, 1808, in Howe, ed., *Proceedings,* 158–159.

had begun to portray the pleasure of literature as emerging from its appeal to an irreducible, inexpressible self; sharing such literature produced intimate, intense friendship rather than a potentially broad and socially transformative circle. This transformation in Great Britain coincided with the government's willingness to exile troublesome, politically engaged authors. The Anthologists' vision of literature responded, not to the oppressions of monarchy, but to the temptations of a developing republic; they faced, not the threat of exile, but the threat of co-optation. Resisting others' tendency to bend their judgment to the demands of the people and to write politicized literature was their way to express true selves and to exert a salutary influence on the Republic. Such a view effectively republicanized Edmund Burke's understanding of the ideological purpose of art and beauty. Burke argued that art could strengthen monarchical governments by rendering them more awesome and more beautiful to their people; art bolstered order by binding the ruled to the ruler. In a republic, the people were both rulers and ruled; the Anthologists conceived of the civic purpose of art, not as conveying political ideology, but as offering an escape from it.[38]

The Anthology Society grounded patriotism in a critique of American philistinism and a skepticism about the possibility of a distinctively American culture. It launched an assault on the market from within pages and walls bought and paid for by commerce. It shielded literature from engagement in the polity while justifying the existence of literature by its usefulness to the polity. The *Port Folio,* in the years after 1805, would begin to follow suit.

38. Jon Mee, "'Reciprocal Expressions of Kindness': Robert Merry, Della Cruscanism, and the Limits of Sociability," in Gillian Russell and Clara Tuite, eds., *Romantic Sociability: Social Networks and Literary Culture in Britain, 1770–1840* (New York, 2002), 116–118; Kelvin Everest, *Coleridge's Secret Ministry: The Context of the Conversation Poems, 1795–1798* (Brighton, England, 1979), 90, 91. For a discussion of Burke's view of the political use of art, see Tim Fulford, *Romanticism and Masculinity: Gender, Politics, and Poetics in the Writings of Burke, Coleridge, Cobbett, Wordsworth, De Quincey, and Hazlitt* (London, 1999), 12, 31–65.

CHAPTER 7

The Port Folio Remade, 1806–1812

From 1806 until 1812, Joseph Dennie continued as editor of the *Port Folio*. During those years, what he referred to as "three potent adversaries, Sickness, Sorrow, and Adversity," more than once forced him temporarily to step aside. After 1808, he remained as editor at a salary but no longer had a direct financial stake in the *Port Folio*. In January 1812, he was dead. By then, the Dennie of the *Farmer's Weekly Museum* and the *Port Folio*'s early years had faded from view. In the last six years of Dennie's life, he reshaped his editorial persona and reconceived his audience: presenting himself as a man of letters who disdained direct political engagement, Dennie appealed to a cross-partisan American elite seeking community and harmony through support of arts and letters.[1]

The *Port Folio*'s transformation was thorough but gradual. As readers turned the pages of issues from 1806 through 1808, the *Port Folio* remained a weekly publication, and they might have imagined themselves still in their familiar Dennie-created landscape. Authors such as that of "The Day," a series devoted to political analysis, worried over Thomas Jefferson's response to the wars between England and France, and Dennie elicited Federalist commentary from politically connected contributors. "On the highly interesting topick of THE PRESENT STATE OF WARFARE, between the United States and Great Britain," he wrote pointedly in 1807, "we invite men of political wisdom to express their sentiments in the most distinct, frank, liberal, and SPIRITED manner." Dennie also continued occasionally to print satiric assaults on America's race-based slavery: "I will allow," read one passage, "that their hair is short, and ours long, that their nose is flat and ours raised, that their skin is black and ours white; yet after all these concessions, I still have my doubts respecting our rights to make them slaves."

---

1. [Joseph Dennie], "To the Public," *Port Folio*, n.s., VII (January 1812), 92; Harold Milton Ellis, *Joseph Dennie and His Circle: A Study in American Literature from 1792 to 1812*, Bulletin of the University of Texas, no. 40 (Austin, Tex., 1915), 201.

The *Port Folio* had not abandoned its delight in drawing readers' eyes to the central hypocrisy of their nation.[2]

Readers could also find, if they sought them, less earnest critiques of America's politics and culture, just as they had from 1801 through 1805. Jefferson—described in one 1806 piece as "a *Lilliputian hero*, a collector of spiders and a gazer at *wooden mammoths*, a master of slaves and a bawler for the inestimable rights of liberty and equality"—did not escape mockery, nor did America itself. "We are all Indians, we are all republicans, as it is beautifully expressed by the First Magistrate of a free people," read a familiar-sounding article from 1806. Pretending to celebrate the arrival of a delegation of Indians to Washington, D.C., this piece offered a vision of boundarylessness and decline. "Behold, ye sickly sons of refinement, ye absurd worshippers of the genius of Greece, and of Rome, and of England," it drawled sarcastically, "behold the triumph of Barbarism." And, in 1807, doggerel that would have been at home in the *Port Folio*'s very first volume ridiculed the carnivalesque triumphs of democracy. "And hey! then up go we . . . / We'll *cry both arts and learning down*," reads this "old ballad from uncertain author." Lest readers somehow miss the point of the extract, Dennie, as he so often had before, appended a helpful note: "This, as a modern philosopher might say, is the very germe of the French Revolution. The same principle is fully laid down and vigorously enforced in that admirable production, the American Bill of Rights."[3]

If readers continued looking for familiar landmarks, they could find discussions of sex and gender that bore the marks of the *Port Folio*'s old mischief. A "bachelor" writing in 1806 poked fun at the way women were praised and maligned by turns, musing: "The [female] sex have been generally, either superlatively exalted, or infinitely debased; represented either as the ornaments of the universe and the first of the creator's works, or as beings, in disposition and understanding, almost beneath the level of human nature." Trying to determine the truth that lay beneath the rhetoric, the "bachelor" concluded, as had authors from earlier *Port Folio* volumes, that environment rather than nature must partially account for women's differ-

2. *Port Folio*, n.s., Feb. 14, 1807, 110, [Joseph Dennie], "To Readers and Correspondents," July 11, 1807, 31. See also, for example, a poem, "taken from an English publication . . . supposed to have been written by an AFRICAN PRINCE," who sold a child for a watch and bitterly regrets it (May 23, 1807, 336).

3. "The American Lounger, No. 154," *Port Folio*, n.s., Jan. 25, 1806, 33–35, [J. E. Hall], "The American Lounger, No. 177," Oct. 4, 1806, 193–194, "Song of Anarchus," Aug. 15, 1807, 103.

ences from men. The *Port Folio* presented gender in an even less essentialist fashion in 1809, when Dennie printed Benjamin Rush's "Account of the Life and Character of Mrs. Elizabeth Ferguson." Describing the colonial belletrist as the intellectual center of her heterosocial conversation circles, Rush noted: "Upon these occasions her body seemed to evanish [sic], and she appeared to be all mind." Gender might be a limitation, but it was one a woman such as Ferguson could, at least in sociable settings, escape.[4]

Sex and politics also made facetious joint appearances in these years of the *Port Folio*, as they so often had before. The periodical, for example, continued to associate Jefferson's enthusiastically patriotic supporters with femininity rather than with civic manhood. "The 'Communication' from the young ladies of Augusta, we may not refuse to insert, without violating the *sweet courtesies of life,* and forfeiting all character for gallantry," read the notice in an 1807 "To Readers and Correspondents" column. "If, in the opinion of certain grumblers, the President and his administration are too lavishly commended, let it be remembered, that the Fancy and Invention of the Fair are naturally warm and romantick" and that women have "an *unalienable right* to decorate the Fourth of July." Democratic politics was the province, not of independent men, but of easily seduced women.[5]

And yet, readers might have wondered, did not that swipe seem a bit mild in contrast to the *Port Folio*'s earlier attacks on Jefferson's supporters? And did not readers have to search for the references to sex and politics that were so abundant in the magazine's first years? As 1807 turned into 1808, moreover, such pieces became fewer and farther between, until there was no denying that the *Port Folio* had changed. In 1809, Dennie converted the magazine from a weekly to a monthly, abandoned the pseudonym Oliver Oldschool, and disavowed partisanship. The transformation was complete. The strident exposé of state, society, and self that constituted the *Port Folio*'s first years had become a smoothly elegant literary potpourri. The *Port Folio* now resembled the *Anthology,* a magazine Dennie read and admired. "No periodi-

4. Orlando, "The American Lounger, No. 176," *Port Folio,* n.s., Sept. 27, 1806, 177, Analyticus, "The American Lounger, No. 178," Oct. 11, 1806, 209–210, Analyticus, "The American Lounger, No. 180," Oct. 25, 1806, 241–242, Clara, "The American Lounger, No. 183," Dec. 13, 1806, 353–354, [Benjamin Rush], "An Account of the Life and Character of Mrs. Elizabeth Ferguson," n.s., I (June 1809), 526, "Supplement: Female Education," IV (July 1810), 85.

5. [Joseph Dennie], "To Readers and Correspondents," *Port Folio,* n.s., Aug. 15, 1807, 110. This is more or less repeated in [Dennie], "To Readers and Correspondents," Feb. 13, 1808, 110.

cal work, that has ever appeared in the Capital of New England," he wrote in 1808, "is comparable to The Monthly Anthology." The quiet Cambridge periodical led the way toward a new, nineteenth-century vision of letters in America, and the wicked, daring *Port Folio* had in the end fallen in line.[6]

Writing a prospectus for the new, monthly series of the periodical, Dennie made explicit and complete the change that had been quietly occurring for years. "On the first vernal month, a Phoenix *Port Folio* rises from the ashes of its predecessor," read his announcement. "Rigidly excluding party politics and the intractable topics of Theology," Dennie wrote, "all the Gentlemen, who are interested in the work, are resolved that it shall vindicate the literary reputation of America." "If ably conducted," Dennie continued, with a startling nod to local and national boundaries rather than to the far-flung community of sensibility he had long cultivated, "the *Port Folio* may contribute to the interest of individuals, to the power of Philadelphia, and the aggrandizement of our empire." Dennie did not abandon his flamboyant woes; even in this optimistic document, he issued a litany of grievances whose tone brings to mind the theatrically miserable heroics of his college days. "Hitherto the success of The *Port Folio* has been of no brilliant complexion," he noted. "Commenced at a sinister epoch, and pushed through all the thorns of perplexity, exposed to the cavils of party, though pure of any but honest purposes, and neglected, in consequence of the bad health and misfortunes of the editor, ill supported, and worse paid, still he made it a point of honour never to abandon it ingloriously." Having weathered these trials, however, Dennie claimed now to look forward to triumph—and to triumph of a kind he had not, in the beginning of his efforts as editor, sought. "As it is resolved that no papers shall be admitted into The Port Folio, but those of a scientific, a literary, an amusing, or a fashionable character," he wrote, "it follows, that, without offence, it may be perused by the most clashing parties." What Dennie now cultivated, in a remarkable, *Anthology*-like transposition of civic terms to apolitical ends, was "a party of gentlemen, studious to please according to the laws of urbanity."[7]

6. [Joseph Dennie], "To Readers and Correspondents," *Port Folio*, n.s., Nov. 5, 1808, 304. See also introduction to "Literature of North-Carolina," Dec. 13, 1806, 359, which refers to the *Anthology* as "a literary work of the highest merit" that "claims our attention as much for the taste which is discovered in the selections, as for the judgment and erudition which are displayed in the original compositions which grace its pages."

7. [Joseph Dennie], "Prospectus of the Port Folio . . . ," *Port Folio*, n.s., I (January 1809), 1–11.

As had the *Anthology* from its inception, the *Port Folio*'s new, monthly series claimed to ban political discussion entirely. One of the *Port Folio*'s disavowals of partisanship in fact came appended to an extract reprinted from the *Anthology* itself. "A Constant Reader," sending in the "dignified introduction to a criticism upon Adams's Lectures on Eloquence, which I met with in the Monthly Anthology for last April," approved of the *Port Folio*'s new, nonpartisan stance, explaining: "In a free country, like ours, where party passions too frequently reign uncontrolled, and sometimes extend their baneful influence into the very pulpit, in which, to preach 'peace and good will to all men,' even 'those that hate and persecute us,' is the paramount duty of the sacred functionary, any effort to circumscribe their sway—to screen from it the retreats of literature as a sanctum sanctorum— must call forth the warmest plaudits of every liberal man, whatever may be his political feelings and opinions." Limiting the reach of political conflict served the Republic. Creating a nonpartisan literature was, not fleeing from civic duty, but fulfilling it.[8]

In the new *Port Folio*, no incident or rumor arose to take the place of Jefferson's alleged relationship with Sally Hemings as the focus of antic rage. That event had mixed sexual anxiety with political. In the *Port Folio* of 1809 and later, ribaldry no longer merged with political and social commentary. Instead, when sexualized rhetoric did appear, the jokes stood alone and read as Falstaffian echoes in the *Port Folio*'s increasingly respectable present. Not only were savage portrayals of political and personal dependence and degradation in decline, so, too, were the kind of "Lounger" columns that upended the *Port Folio*'s gender conventions. Instead, the *Port Folio* told its own straight-faced tales of women's sex-bound virtue. It participated in the shift, begun in the last decades of the eighteenth century, toward portraying motherhood as the essence of femininity: an 1810 lithograph of a mother and child accompanied a long poem insisting that women must breastfeed, lest their children suffer and they themselves die. Later that year, a paean to "The Ladies of Philadelphia" proclaimed: "The beauty of women is as much a subject of national pride and exultation as the wisdom and valour of men. These being qualities which each sex the most highly prizes in themselves and the most warmly admires in each other, it is perfectly natural that in a community such should equally be objects of general concern." Five years earlier, the *Port Folio* would have reveled in pointing out the vulgarity of a nation vesting its worth in the appearance of its women, and a joke

8. "The Beehive, No. I," *Port Folio*, n.s., IV (July 1810), 65.

about patriotic prostitutes probably would not have been far behind. In 1810, however, the *Port Folio* was content to portray women as it portrayed polite literature: as a source of beauty on which Americans could concur and in which they could take pride.[9]

Despite all these changes, the later *Port Folio* was not entirely a land of peace and good manners. Dennie retained a sense of discomfiture at American society, culture, and politics throughout his editorship, and he continued to publish writings from correspondents who shared his unease. The ornithologist Alexander Wilson's depictions of the West, for example, offered *Port Folio* readers a satisfyingly grim view of American barbarism. Even here, however, there was a difference from the periodical's earlier essays. East Coast readers could shudder at the vulgar, rag-wearing Kentuckians as they had at Republicans, yet now they could feel themselves removed by geographic distance rather than simply by sensibility and a capacity for irony. Wilson's letters, moreover, at times expressed admiration for westerners and hope for the future. Lexington, Wilson noted, was recently the site of "only two log huts." "Now," however, "numerous excellent institutions for the education of youth, a public library, and a well endowed university under the superintendence of men of learning and piety, are in successful operation." The *Port Folio* had set aside Federalist depictions of permanent, carnivalesque barbarity and the meditations on human frailty that came in their wake. Kentucky was proof, not of the endless depravity of the Republic, but of an alliance of educated men who could eventually civilize America.[10]

9. "Maternal Affection," *Port Folio*, n.s., IV (July 1810), 158–162, [Thomas Franklin Pleasants], "The Ladies of Philadelphia," IV (December 1810), 604. By 1810, the occasional jokes are usually quite mild, such as the gentleman's "meteorological journal of his wife's temper," which has the listings of "Rather cloudy," "changeable, gloomy, squally," and so forth ("Variety," III [February 1810], 175). We still occasionally find rather startling moments, however, such as two poems in the August 1810 issue, one of which concludes, "Say yes, and be kiss'd—or say no, and be d——d," and the second of which, "On One Who Wedded a Thin Consumptive Lady," reads: "With a warm skeleton so near / And wedded to thy arms for life, / When Death arrives it will appear / Less dreadful—'tis so like thy wife" ("Levity," IV [August 1810], 194). Dror Wahrman argues that it was in the last decades of the eighteenth century that maternity began to be portrayed, in English culture, "as inextricably intertwined with the essence of femininity for each and every woman" (*The Making of the Modern Self: Identity and Culture in Eighteenth-Century England* [New Haven, Conn., 2004], 13).

10. [Alexander Wilson], "Extract of a Letter from Lexington," *Port Folio*, n.s., III (June 1810), 506, "Correspondence," IV (October 1810), 318.

During these last years of Dennie's editorship, there was one long series of letters that, by returning to the *Port Folio*'s old themes of Revolution and sexualized disorder, revealed precisely how much had changed. The series was about postrevolutionary Haiti, written by the young Philadelphia merchant Condy Raguet. Raguet had spent several months in Haiti in 1804 and 1805, acting as supercargo for a countinghouse, and on his return he wrote of what he had seen. Raguet depicted a postrevolutionary society that was a part comic, part tragic world of inversion, interest, and sexual depravity. Its benighted leader proclaimed: "I have wives in all parts of my dominions, of every shade, black, yellow, and white, and to me they are all alike; I love them equally well." Raguet used the same language and imagery to criticize black residents of Haiti that the *Port Folio* had in earlier years used to criticize Republicans. The Republicans' unsuccessful assumption of gentlemanly airs and prerogatives became the freed blacks' ostensibly inappropriate demeanor. The commandant of Port-de-Paix, read a representative passage, "is a negro black and hugely ugly, and like many of his countrymen furnished with a pair of delicate lips." "His manners were rough and awkward, though he attempted the gentleman, and his conversation coarse. He wore a sort of military dress with a cocked hat, and strutted about with a degree of consequence." In a letter describing Jean-Jacques Dessalines's coronation as emperor, Raguet also mocked the pretensions of the enslaved who had turned the world upside down: "A friend of mine, an American, who marched in the procession as one of the deputation of foreign commerce, has diverted me exceedingly by contrasting the real appearance of it, with the idea one would conceive from a view of the *programme*. Thus what are called 'the troops of the garrison' who were to assemble on the Camp de Mars to receive the procession, was composed of about two or three hundred negroes with arms, 'some without coats hats and shirts, and others even destitute of *culottes*.'" The racial politics of the series were, given the author's condemnation of slavery and of Haiti's complex society of blacks, whites, and "mulattoes," less than neat. Yet the cumulative effect of the author's depiction of clownish black leaders, "diverting" black armies, and ferocious acts of black revenge against white Haitians was to create a division between blacks and whites. Both author and editor, moreover, declined to link unease over Haiti's transformational revolution with partisan animosity, as had occurred in Philadelphia publications, including the *Port Folio*, in the preceding decade. Here, by contrast, the picture of those Haitian rulers of African descent implicitly united white readers. The frightening Haitian scenes presented a Federalist vision of a revolution from below destroying social order, personal liberties, and lives; they also presented Jefferson's own horrified vision of the end of racial slavery leading to murder, torture, and white exile. Federalists and Jeffersonian Republicans could, in the *Port Folio*'s Haiti, finally share a nightmare. And they could share a hope as well: Haiti restored as a trading partner would be a boon to Philadelphia's merchants, regardless of their party. Haiti, in short, presented itself to Dennie as a subject likely to unite elites in worries over revolution, laughter at the vulgar, and longing for profitable trade.[11]

In the last years of Dennie's editorship, the *Port Folio* also presented to readers of both parties an arch, mildly reformist patriotism. This patriotism

11. [Condy Raguet], "Memoirs of Hayti, Letter XII," *Port Folio*, n.s., III (May 1810), 426, [Raguet], "Memoir of Hayti, Letter XIII," IV (July 1810), 2–3 ("This harangue was delivered in the very coarsest Creole dialect, which is the species of language always used by his majesty: not because it is supporting the appearance of republicanism by affecting the manners of the plebeians—but because his majesty can speak no other"), [Raguet], "Memoir of Hayti, Letter XVII," V (February 1811), 127. See also [Raguet], "Memoir of Hayti, Letter V," *Port Folio*, II (July 1809), 188–192. Both the mockery of Republican airs and that of black Haitians' conduct fit within the Grub Street tradition described by David S. Shields in *Civil Tongues and Polite Letters in British America* (Chapel Hill, N.C., 1997), 46–50, in which writers offered "ironic comment on the attempts of would-be beaux and belles to ape genteel discourse" (47). Language of extraordinarily racist content coexists with remarks acknowledging the formative influence of slavery on both backs and whites. The author, for example, describes his disgust at the way in which black and mixed-race Haitian soldiers go "hunting and, as it were, smelling after the blood of their fellow-creatures, like a pack of hounds after game, or the wild beasts of the forest in search of their prey. I have seen it so repeatedly, that I always associate in my mind, with the idea of a Haytian soldier, that of a bloodhound." The author immediately adds, however: "The former feels no more compunction in killing a Frenchman than the latter does in tearing to pieces a negro. Both delight in that species of employment. It is a recreation and a feast to them" ([Raguet], "Memoir of Hayti, Letter IX," *Port Folio*, n.s., III [January 1810], 45). See also [Raguet], "Memoir of Hayti, Letter III," II (July 1809), 39, and [Raguet], "Memoir of Hayti, Letter XVI," IV (October 1810), 323. Winthrop D. Jordan explains Jefferson's belief that "Negroes could never be incorporated into white society on equal terms" in *White over Black: American Attitudes toward the Negro* (Chapel Hill, N.C., 1968), 436. John Saillant describes the similar worries of Jefferson and James Madison in "Lemuel Haynes's Black Republicanism and the American Republican Tradition, 1775–1820," *Journal of the Early Republic*, XIV (1994), 320–324. See also Donald R. Hickey, "America's Response to the Slave Revolt in Haiti, 1791–1806," *JER*, II (1982), 364–378; Everett Somerville Brown, ed., *William Plumer's Memorandum of Proceedings in the United States Senate, 1803–1807* (New York, 1923), 435; Timothy Pickering to Thomas Jefferson, Feb. 24, 1806, Thomas Jefferson Papers, reel 35, Library of Congress, Washington, D.C.

should not be confused with an optimistic vision of a unique, American community in which the *Port Folio* reader could participate unreservedly. On the contrary, the *Port Folio* continued its Anglophilia unabated; rarely did readers lack for scenes of happy peasants or for English instructions on how to treat one's betters. Dennie continued, moreover, to proclaim his refusal to praise American literature simply because it was American. "Let us not be afflicted with insipid elegies upon milliners' and seamstresses' apprentices, and dead girls in general," read a "To Readers and Correspondents" column. "Against that *tumid* style, so much in vogue in this country," Dennie continued, "we enter our most solemn and decided protest. While, from the literary loom, we can manufacture, or furnish rich brocade, and stuff, *which will wear well,* we wish not to *expose* for sale a single sample of American *fustian.*" In such paragraphs, Dennie juxtaposed his manly and cosmopolitan independence against the silly effeminacy he had long associated with uncritical participation in an ostensibly American project. Moreover, the *Port Folio,* like the *Anthology,* continued to express doubts about the existence of an American identity that consisted of more than shared bad taste. "A *national character* cannot, for a long time, be looked for in the United States," read one piece, "settled by people from various countries, of various persuasions, various habits—where few men are stationary, where the local circumstances are so different in different parts, where every thing is constantly changing and shifting; where a butcher today finds himself a statesman tomorrow, and in a short time after returns to his stall."[12]

Such emotional and intellectual distancing continued the *Port Folio's* Burkean insistence that men's first loyalties were to their "little platoon," not to a largely abstract nation. It also emphasized that the United States was not a true community in the way that the *Port Folio* readership was. Nonetheless, the *Port Folio* proffered an increasingly untortured relationship to the American nation. As had the *Anthology,* the *Port Folio* proposed a way to participate in the nation from within the confines of a bounded circle of sensibility—a circle not congruent with partisanship. In the early years of the *Port Folio,* the opposition between Federalism and Republicanism had been vigilantly maintained. Now it moderated into the more comfortable distance between the man of letters and the nation he wished to reform.

In other ways, as well, the distance between community of sensibility

12. E. B. [Justus Erich Bollman], "Man Constitutionally Moral," *Port Folio,* n.s., II (October 1809), 303–304, [Joseph Dennie], "To Readers and Correspondents," VII (January 1812), 100.

and the world outside created a peevish patriotism. Like the *Anthology*, the *Port Folio* praised Revolutionary figures while criticizing the ungrateful Republic they had created. After a brief description of Revolutionary War General Anthony Wayne, for example, came this reproach: "With blended sorrow, shame, and indignation we add that the remains of this warrior, of whom his ungrateful country ought to be justly proud, repose ingloriously, not to say ignominiously, on a distant frontier, amid the savage rudeness of the forest." Such passages bring to mind the *Anthology*'s advocacy of a mausoleum for George Washington; they expressed a wish to transform America's shameful emotional and literal landscape while deriving immediate fellowship from the refusal to read triumph into America as it existed. "But though the state may be negligent of [General Wayne's] fame, and leave his ashes to be dissipated by the night winds," the piece continued, "there are [those?] who feel for his renown, and who erect for him as fair an obelisk, as Sensibility can conceive, or ardent Enthusiasm rear." The *Port Folio*'s circle of superior sensibility proclaimed distance from and devotion to the Republic at once, preserving some of the pleasures of Federalism while moving away—in this newly protected realm of literature—from direct partisan speech.[13]

Goodbye, Oliver Oldschool

The less exposed, less exposing *Port Folio* arose for several reasons. Dennie had faced a libel charge in 1805 over a paragraph critical of democracy; his attorney friends Charles Jared Ingersoll, Joseph Hopkinson, and William Meredith had extricated him, but, having faced one libel suit, Dennie was likely not eager to face another. The change in the *Port Folio*, however, did not occur until a few years after the suit, and it reflects more than an effort at self-protection. It had become apparent that Jefferson's administration would not draw America along the path of the French

13. [Joseph Dennie], "To Readers and Correspondents," *Port Folio*, n.s., I (May 1809), 455–456. Lawyers also began to occupy, in Dennie's addresses, the role of educated and unappreciated virtue that Federalists previously had; this substitution, too, served to preserve the role of the alienated prophet while depoliticizing it. Amid praise for lawyers, for example, Dennie notes that they are "perpetually assailed by the American vulgar." "Genius and Virtue are always hated by every Vandal and every villain. The flame of persecution, which these execrable wretches have long been kindling, we hope soon to see extinguished in their own blood." See introduction to "Integrity of the American Bar," *Port Folio*, n.s., May 16, 1807, 317.

Revolution. The *Port Folio*'s portrayal of a world in which all hierarchies and distinctions disintegrated in the same revolutionary solvent had proved misguided; categories of race and gender turned out to be as durable as the *Port Folio*'s own reliance on them demonstrated. It had also become apparent that the role of the man of letters had not disappeared in the new nation. Dennie was a respected figure, and Philadelphia, like Boston, saw an increasing number of cultural institutions that united wealth, learning, and status in a way that Dennie had argued was impossible in America. Finally, although Federalism's influence continued in the *Anthology*'s New England, it was in eclipse as a national political force. When speaking in a Federalist voice no longer conveyed, to a national audience, a beleaguered but viable authority, Dennie turned instead to the voice of the suprapolitical cultural arbiter.[14]

The years of the *Port Folio*'s disengagement from politics also coincided with a budding rapprochement between Republicans and Federalists in Philadelphia and on the national scene. In Washington, D.C., partisan disagreements continued over domestic and international policy, but Republicans and Federalists created an integrated social life; meaningful nationalist sentiment emerged as men and women found common ground and good company in parlors and ballrooms. Closer to the *Port Folio*'s home, a split developed within Philadelphia's Jeffersonian Republicans, and an alliance arose between the moderate branch of Philadelphia Republicans, or "Quids," and the area's Federalists. Both were eager to contain the era's volatile political debates over private property, labor, and capital accumulation. The Quids had come to believe, as Federalists long had, that America's liberties would inevitably result in differing economic, social, and political interests among its people. A republican government did not produce a unitary people who would speak with one voice; instead, it ensured that there would be conflict and competition. Federalists had been defeated politically, but their underlying understanding of the world as composed of competing interests and limited sympathies had prevailed, and it formed an area of common ground between Federalists and moderate Republicans. Quids and Federalists agreed that such conflict and competition should be contained within politics and that politics itself should be constrained. Unlike France,

14. Ellis, *Joseph Dennie and His Circle*, 184. Ellis notes that, during the libel case, William Meredith and William Lewis advised Dennie, although Charles Jared Ingersoll and Joseph Hopkinson alone represented him at trial.

America would not seek absolute consensus and so would not risk unending revolution.[15]

The *Port Folio*'s abandonment of politics, that is, began, not in despair, at the point of greatest distance between Federalism and Republicanism, but rather at a moment when a détente seemed possible. Dennie had been adroit throughout his career as an editor at harnessing cultural, social, and political resources. From Walpole, New Hampshire, he had pieced together a national network of correspondents and readers; in Philadelphia during Jefferson's first administration, he had drawn heavily on the practical, rhetorical, and emotional uses of partisan anxiety. Now, in the final years of his editorship of the *Port Folio,* he perceived the existence of a stratum of society through which he could find personal status and financial and cultural support. He needed to offer them a nonpartisan cultural product that steered clear of remaining divisive issues and rhetorics. And so he did.

Like the Anthologists before him, Dennie had declared independence from politics rather than through it. His disavowal of partisanship was repeated, moreover, as the new monthly series progressed. "The work is munificently patronized, not by **Politicians,* not by faction, not by the vulgar," he declared, with an exuberant abundance of starred footnotes, "but by the most illustrious descriptions of American society, by the Liberal, the Ladies, the Lawyers, the Clergy, and all the Gentlemen and CAVALIERS of Columbia." Dennie, that is, no longer deemed Republicans "the vulgar" but rather all unreconstructed partisan politicians. "*The pernicious influence, or interference of a certain description of this class of American *animals,"* he wrote as his note to the word *"Politicians,"* "has frequently jeopardized the interest of the Editor, and driven him repeatedly to the very verge of ruin. He has felt their ingratitude; he abhors their meanness; and, contemptuously assures them, in the language of an indignant writer, that they do not RISE TO THE DIGNITY of being hated, and are only despised with moderation." This utter rejection of partisanship would have been startling

15. Catherine Allgor, *Parlor Politics: In Which the Ladies of Washington Help Build a City and a Government* (Charlottesville, Va., 2000), 77; Fredrika J. Teute, "Roman Matron on the Banks of Tiber Creek: Margaret Bayard Smith and the Politicization of Spheres in the Nation's Capital," in Donald Kennon, ed., *A Republic for the Ages: The United States Capitol and the Political Culture of the Early Republic* (Charlottesville, Va., 1999), 111–112; Andrew Shankman, *Crucible of American Democracy: The Struggle to Fuse Egalitarianism and Capitalism in Jeffersonian Pennsylvania* (Lawrence, Kans., 2004), 96–125.

to *Port Folio* readers, and Dennie seemed to believe that some elaboration was needed in order "to obtain the cooperation of the learned *of all parties.*" As the last in this cascade of footnotes, he explained: "*A note, appended to a preceding paragraph, pertinent to politicians, the Editor avers, upon the faith of a Cavalier, has no sort of allusion to the reigning administration, its admirers, or adherents. What are called, in the language of party, democrats, or republicans, often contribute liberally to this journal, which is nothing like the journals of faction, and is wholly vacant of political and theological discussion."[16]

In the *Port Folio*'s early years, Dennie had used partisan rhetoric and allegiance to mock the centrality of electoral politics and the dependent relationships electoral politics created. The *Port Folio* had also deplored the way political liberty drew men so close to the polity that they could not perceive the warts and malformations of the process that had seduced them. By heightening the antidemocratic tendencies of Federalist thought and expressing that thought through a racialized and sexualized rhetoric of visceral power, Dennie turned his periodical of those years into a celebration of idiosyncratic judgment and critical distance from polity and society. By 1809, however, Dennie found that partisanship no longer summoned the cadre of educated, critical readers and writers he needed as audience and as collaborators. From now on, he would depoliticize both the critical distance and the fellowship his periodical community proffered.

As Dennie reconceived his audience politically, he also recalibrated the periodical's portrayal of commerce and the marketplace of print. The *Port Folio*'s loathing of an obsessive concern with money-getting had originally adapted a staple of English Augustan writing into an attack on American Republicans. In later years, this critique lost much of its anti-Republican specificity and became a critique of America as a whole. The insistence that America's highly commerce-oriented society was particularly ill suited to creating works of artistic merit was not a stance of alienation. On the contrary, it provided a civic purpose for both men of letters and men of commerce. "It was a favourite opinion of Pope, Swift, and Arbuthnot," wrote Dennie in his 1809 prospectus, that "an alliance among a few men of acknowledged ability, would be potent enough not only to form the taste, but to chastise all the knavery and folly of a nation. We believe implicitly in the truth of this sentiment." To accomplish this chastisement, the "alliance" would have to be presented to the larger community through print, and,

16. [Joseph Dennie], "To the Public," *Port Folio*, n.s., VII (January 1812), 93, 96.

because a publication required financial support as well as "ability," wealth was granted civic value at the same time literature was. In his prospectus to the new series, Dennie expressed gratitude to "Our Merchants and Manufacturers, the adventurous heroes of enterprise" who upheld a periodical that upheld the nation. The bonds of commerce were aestheticized and sentimentalized into the bonds of taste and friendship, and the mass audience of print was reconceived as an intimate patronage that allowed for authentic, independent, manly expression.[17]

The later *Port Folio* offered not only a changed view of the world but also a changed view of the relationship between politics and literature. The Revolution had pried open a space in which all fears were speakable, and Dennie and his contributors had filled that space with anxious prophecy. In these last years of the *Port Folio,* as Americans succeeded in imagining spheres of depoliticized, organic identity and harmony such as the home, literature, and voluntary organizations, the time for discussing all relations and identities as built of interest and dependence—as, that is, political— had begun to pass. In the later *Port Folio,* moreover, Dennie swore off the alchemy that once converted personal anxieties into Federalist rhetoric. There emerged a *Port Folio* that delved less deeply into human intimacies and American practices; having uncoupled public from private, it no longer had secrets of either state or self to tell. Where once question had begot question, silence now led to silence. Denied civic meaning, worries over the porous boundaries of the self were no longer expressed so freely—in either political or sexual language. Discussions of partisan issues, in turn, were no longer transformed into meditations on human interdependence or into battles over identity and relationships. Instead, they were portrayed as vulgar, easily avoided struggles for a narrowly political power and influence.

A final look at these later years of the *Port Folio* reveals, finally, two striking disappearances. One is the disappearance of Oliver Oldschool. The pseudonym was, Dennie explained, no longer required. "In the winter of 1801," he wrote, "the editor of the *Port Folio* commenced the publication of a politico literary paper. He then deemed it expedient to adopt a fictitious name, after the manner of my lord Bolingbroke, sir Richard Steele, Addison, and others." Now that he is no longer publishing a journal "devoted to party politics," Dennie continued, "the appellation of Oliver Oldschool, in the opinion of its foster-father, is no longer expedient or necessary." "As the liberal conductor of a liberal work, dedicated to the Muses, the Sciences

17. [Dennie], "Prospectus," n.s., I (January 1809), 5.

and the Graces, all mystery and artifice should be disdained. Hence the editor chooses to appear before the bar of the public in his proper person; and the high and anxious responsibility, which he now assumes, will, it is hoped, have this salutary effect, to make him, still more studiously than ever, solicitous for the reputation of his literary labours."[18]

In fact, the pseudonym had not, during the *Port Folio*'s "politico literary" days, defended Dennie from criticism or even from a libel suit; there had never been any doubt who the *Port Folio*'s "foster-father" was. The pseudonym had, however, served the magazine's invention of two separate audiences. It was not simply that the reader could pretend that hostile outsiders did not know who Dennie was but also that there was irony inherent in a patently ineffectual pseudonym, and irony was the only protection the *Port Folio* offered or sought from the uncomprehending crowd. In these later years, the crowd disappeared from the audience. The *Port Folio* had always been addressed to "Men of Liberality," but now they were the only imagined audience—and the *Port Folio*, in fact, now only wished to address the man of letters within the man. The later *Port Folio* offered, to that newly isolatable and isolated creature, what the magazine had once despairingly sought for the whole individual: escape from the competitions, transformations, and dependencies of the Republic and of life.

Disappearing from the audience, the larger public disappeared as well from the text. The early years of the *Port Folio* boasted a raucous parade of Americans brawling with, yelling at, adoring, seducing, and being seduced by one another and by politicians. This public was the locus of Dennie's fears; it embodied those dangerous, almost irresistible bonds between individuals that would transform men into women, whites into blacks, leaders into the led. By the final years of the *Port Folio*, that public was almost entirely gone. The lithographs that adorned the last years of the magazine made the change visible: in them, there are no groups of Americans, no political rallies or market scenes. Instead, there is only land and portraits— usually heads only—of eminent individuals. The troubling relations—between men and women, between emotion and reason, between buyer and seller, ruler and ruled, public and private—had been exiled, and Dennie had found a way home to America.

18. [Joseph Dennie], "To Readers and Correspondents," *Port Folio*, n.s., V (January 1811), 87.

CONCLUSION

The ambitious men of letters of the early Republic created lasting forums and institutions devoted to the pursuit of enlightenment and fellowship. Elihu Hubbard Smith's *Medical Repository* thrived even after his death, making it possible for Americans to collect and contemplate scientific observations and theories. Joseph Dennie's *Port Folio* lived on into the nineteenth century, offering a genteel setting for original and extracted literature. William Smith Shaw oversaw the Athenaeum's collections after the deaths of Joseph Stevens Buckminster and Arthur Maynard Walter, and to this day the institution amasses books and periodicals for the education and pleasure of its members.

The cultural circles and networks these men marshaled also left legacies. Charles Brockden Brown's novels and William Dunlap's plays are testaments to the power of intellectual companionship, and the network in which they and Elihu Smith participated brought to press texts that might otherwise have languished and helped printers venture into publishing. Dennie's consortia of readers and writers enhanced the Federalist Party's ability to spread its arguments and rhetoric throughout the United States, and the Anthologists created forums in which elite, educated Bostonians set aside partisan rhetoric in the cause of civic refinement and enlightenment.

Years after their days and nights of eager conversation, participants in these networks and circles continued to "throw in their mite" to the cause of civic enlightenment. William Dunlap wrote *A History of the American Theatre*, in which he reminded readers of the salutary effects of theater on a republic and—as his old friend Elihu Smith had done—told Americans of their history of cultural creativity and ambition in order to inspire further achievements. Former Anthology Society members helped found in 1815 the *North-American Review and Miscellaneous Journal,* which published literature and advocated the improvement of secondary and graduate education in America. Friendly Club member James Kent ascended to the position of chief justice of New York's highest court in 1804, and he pressed fellow lawyers to record and collect their written decisions to develop a body of shared legal knowledge and precedent. Owing in part to Kent's influence, William Johnson—former roommate of Elihu Hubbard Smith and Friendly Club member—was appointed official recorder of New York's high court and later of the decisions of the Court of Chancery. Johnson's reports were notable for thoroughness and accuracy, and in 1815 he published a digest of court decisions that first rendered accessible the collected opinions of the American judiciary. In 1826, Kent began to publish his *Commentaries on American Law,* in which he surveyed all the major fields of American jurisprudence. The *Commentaries* went through fourteen American editions, and lawyers and judges used the volumes throughout the nineteenth century. Kent and Johnson were continuing the quest to collect and diffuse information and create a community of intellect. Kent, Johnson, and Dunlap, moreover, continued to be driven by the fellowship they had enjoyed as young men. Dunlap's *History* memorialized friends from his past, and Kent and Johnson dedicated their legal works to each other.[1]

These men of letters created. They contributed. But did they find a way usefully to criticize their new nation? Did they make a case for the importance of speech that was not political? Did they project the communities of inquiry and fellowship they loved onto the nation as a whole? Did they prove to themselves and others that America needed them and needed their different kind of citizenship? The historical record does not favor them. Americans continued to rely on politics and commerce to build a nation, conduct disagreements, and judge the value of ideas. Each of the three models of intellectual citizenship explored here was a poignant, productive failure.

Elihu Hubbard Smith found in science and in the *Medical Repository* a way to pool observations so that they might converge on useful facts. In the *Repository,* he institutionalized the collaborative, questioning ethos that inspired him throughout his brief life. But Smith had also hoped to remake America as a whole along the lines of a Shaftesburian community, and he had longed to replace political practices of debate and compromise with unfettered inquiry and the communal pursuit of objective truth. He found it impossible to do so. The processes and relationships he longed for could coexist with America's devotion to politics and commerce, but they could not replace them.

Unlike Smith, Joseph Dennie had never hoped to remake the world—he too much enjoyed mocking its foibles. And rather than wishing to render politics irrelevant, he converted Federalism's mistrust of the masses into a civically respectable vehicle for his own sense of difference. Years before

1. David W. Raack, "'To Preserve the Best Fruits': The Legal Thought of Chancellor James Kent," *American Journal of Legal History,* XXXIII (1989), 321–322.

Alexis de Tocqueville lamented the "tyranny of the majority," Dennie used Federalist rhetoric to lambaste the tendency of democratic and commercial relationships to create dependence and constrict thought. Dennie also succeeded in using Federalism to summon a network of readers, collaborators, and marketers that made it possible for him to devote all his time to life as a man of letters. He was a pioneer of radical, unrepentant dissent in a nation in which others still dreamed of a united public. But Federalism became Dennie's master as well as his servant. Dennie's effort to use Federalist-inflected rhetoric to critique the dominance of political speech in America proved an impossible task: the prevalence of political expression in the *Port Folio* implicitly conceded that it was the lingua franca of the new nation. Moreover, Dennie's ability truly to investigate the hypocrisies of democracy and racial slavery was blunted by his willingness to cast all such meditations as assaults on Thomas Jefferson and his supporters: critique became caricature.

What of the Anthologists? Quietly ensconced in Boston and Cambridge, they created a periodical that largely lacked critical bite, scientific usefulness, and circulation. But they linked culture and wealth in a way that shaped Boston for generations. And they developed a distinctive conception of American literature. They argued that literature should not intervene directly in civic concerns, and they conceived of culture as a realm—perhaps the only realm—in which idiosyncratic self-expression could flourish. Although their periodical disappeared, their understanding of literature did not. Ralph Waldo Emerson disdained the Anthologists as part of a stodgy, blinkered generation, but Emerson's belief in the purity, power, and independence of "Man Thinking" is a recognizable descendant of the Anthologists' quest for a suprapolitical, autonomous, useful man of letters.[2]

Not all of the new nation's men of letters were men. Women circulated texts, wrote essays for publication, challenged men's opinions, and tended the homes in which cultural conversations occurred. Men such as Smith, Dennie, and the Anthologists fully understood that women were indispensable to the activities and joys of their cultural circles and networks. They respected their intellects, published their works, and sought their company. But Smith, Dennie, the Anthologists, and their many male collaborators

2. Martin Green, *The Problem of Boston: Some Readings in Cultural History* (New York, 1966); John Carlos Rowe, *At Emerson's Tomb: The Politics of Classic American Literature* (New York, 1997). "Too often and for too long," Rowe writes, "the Emersonian tradition of 'aesthetic dissent' has defined itself as distinct from those political movements through which historical progress has been achieved in America" (ix).

wanted to redefine manliness as they redefined citizenship; they did not want to give up claim to manliness. Their insistence that their cultural labors were manly led them to ban women from the Friendly Club and the Anthology Society and persuaded Joseph Dennie to portray the *Port Folio* as a community of men even though he printed essays by women pointing out that it was not. Thus, they did not make common cause with culturally ambitious women but rather too often defined themselves against them. Their effort did not persuade other Americans of the manliness of literary life. Instead, it truncated their social criticism and weakened their argument that merit alone mattered in their milieu. Neither the men nor the women of these networks, moreover, evinced a desire to disrupt domestic life. The limits of their critique of gender conventions marked the limits of their critique of society as a whole. They desired intellectual liberation but mistrusted the disorder of social transformation. They dissented, but they did not disrupt.

Dennie, Smith, and the Anthologists wanted to be acknowledged as valuable citizens of their nation. In the end, their names and projects have largely faded from view, but the questions that they raise still matter. Does the dominance of political expression in America inevitably drown out critiques and questions not reconcilable with partisan agendas? Does the majoritarian ethos of democratic politics and the marketplace suppress the expression of idiosyncratic views? Does the rejection of that ethos by artists and authors leave them forever vulnerable to accusations of elitism, irrelevance, even un-Americanness? Does that vulnerability encourage American cultural strivers toward morose elitism and alienation? What place and what use is there in America for the life of the mind, and for those who would live it?

INDEX

Gifford, William, 156, 172
Godwin, William, 19, 27–31, 42, 46, 50, 61–62, 68, 76; *Enquiry concerning Political Justice*, 27, 153; and *Alcuin*, 85–86; and Smith's utopia, 104–105; and perfectibility, 110; in *Port Folio*, 153–155; and *Monthly Anthology*, 195
Graeme, Elizabeth, 20–21

Haiti, 165; in *Port Folio*, 222–223
Hall, Sarah, 39, 173–177, 182
Hamilton, Alexander, 36–37, 49, 72; and Kent, 49–50; and Dennie, 134
Harper, Robert Goodloe, 135
Harvard, 31–32
Holcroft, Thomas, 48, 59, 62, 68–69
Hopkinson, Emily Mifflin, 176–177
Hopkinson, Joseph, 143, 156, 176, 225

Jefferson, Thomas, 97, 105, 110, 136; treatment of, in *Port Folio*, 152–154, 166–168; and Sally Hemings, 166–168, 196; treatment of, in *Monthly Anthology*, 196, 217–218, 220

Kent, Elizabeth Bailey, 62, 84
Kent, James, 6, 49–50, 55–56, 72, 107, 231–232; and Manumission Society, 57
Kollock, Lemuel, 146

Manliness, 40–41, 154–156, 159, 161, 169, 174, 178, 203–204; and *Alcuin*, 83
Manumission Society, 57–59, 103
Mason, Margaretta, 62
Medical Repository, 6, 55, 57, 64, 76–77, 89, 91–96, 113, 231
Melancholy, 147–149, 178–180
Meredith, Gertrude Gouverneur Ogden, 39, 143, 146, 171–173, 177, 182
Meredith, William, 137, 143, 171, 225
Miller, Edward, 57, 76, 89, 92–93
Mitchill, Samuel Latham, 6, 55–57, 89–93; *Nomenclature of the New Chemistry*, 93
Monthly Anthology, and Boston Review, 4, 10–11, 33, 218–220; contributors to, 188;

and friendship, 192; editorial policy of, 193–194; and politics, 194; and sexual mores, 194; and wit, 194; and Federalism, 195–196; and American identity, 200–202; and women, 202–203
Monthly Magazine (England), 42, 69, 108, 153, 209
Monthly Review (England), 76–77
Moore, Thomas "Anacreon," 9, 170–171, 193
Moral sense, 15
Morris, Lewis Richard, 135, 138
Morse, Jedediah, 72, 93

Nancrede, Joseph, 129–131, 134
Networks, cultural, 24, 43–44, 54, 56, 60–73, 103, 125, 202, 231; origins of, 31–33; and students, 32–35; and the Anthologists, 36; and Smith, 43–46, 53, 103; and Friendly Club, 44, 63; and Brown, 51; and slavery, 57; and women, 61–62, 202; and print technology, 69; and *Alcuin*, 80, 85; and *Medical Repository*, 93; and Dennie, 122, 125; and *Farmer's Weekly Museum*, 122, 127; and *Port Folio*, 144–145; and *Monthly Anthology*, 186, 189. *See also* Conversation circles
New-York Hospital, 5
New York Manumission Society. *See* Manumission Society

Periodical culture: in England, 21; in colonies, 22; and students, 33, 69; and development of political parties, 135–136, 180–181
Philadelphia: as home of *Port Folio*, 143–145; relationship of, with Haiti, 165, 223
Pickering, Timothy, 109, 138
Pierce, Sarah (Sally), 61
Port Folio, 4, 8, 41, 193–194, 231; subscribers to, 140–141; and Federalism, 141, 150, 216, 221–228; content of, 141–143; and Tuesday Club, 143–144; readers of, 146–147; Augustan roots of, 147–148, 157; and melancholia, 147–149; and views